D0375138

For Kags,

**The Man in the
Gray Flannel Skirt**

From the Goul!

RANDOM HOUSE 🏠 NEW YORK

JON-JON GOULIAN

THE
MAN
IN THE
GRAY FLANNEL
SKIRT

Published in the United States by Random House,
an imprint of The Random House Publishing Group,
a division of Random House, Inc., New York.

RANDOM HOUSE and colophon are
registered trademarks of Random House, Inc.

Grateful acknowledgment is made to Christopher Buckley for
permission to reprint excerpts from the syndicated obituary of
Sidney Hook written by William F. Buckley and published, among
other places, in the September 1, 1989, issue of the *National Review.*
Reprinted by permission.

LIBRARY OF CONGRESS CATALOGING-IN-PUBLICATION DATA
Goulian, Jon-Jon.
The man in the gray flannel skirt / Jon-Jon Goulian.
p.   cm.
ISBN 978-1-4000-6811-1
eBook ISBN 978-0-679-60448-8
1. Goulian, Jon-Jon.   2. Goulian, Jon-Jon—Psychology.
3. Goulian, Jon-Jon—Family.   4. Young men—United States—
Biography.   5. Jews—United States—Biography.   6. Armenian
Americans—Biography.   7. Masculinity—United States—Case
studies.   8. Androgyny (Psychology)—Case studies.   9. Fear—
Case studies.   10. Fathers and sons—United States—Case studies.
I. Title.
CT275.G6184A3 2011
920.009'04—dc22   2010026780

Printed in the United States of America
on acid-free paper

www.atrandom.com

2 4 6 8 9 7 5 3 1

FIRST EDITION

Book design by Casey Hampton

*This book—with the exception of the dirty parts—
is for my mother and father, with love.*

Author's Note

To protect the privacy of people who might be embarrassed by their association with me, or by my description of their naked bodies, many of the names in this book, along with a few identifying details, have been changed. Otherwise, everything here is true as I remember it.

Contents

Introduction

For the great bulk of my adult life, beginning roughly when I was sixteen and continuing, off and on, until now, at the age of forty, I have fallen short, sometimes dangerously short, of the conventional ideal of masculinity. From my taste in clothing (skirts and high heels and women's underwear), to my taste in cosmetics (pink lip gloss and eyeliner), to my taste in sex (I can't get aroused unless I'm submissive, and it helps if the woman looks like a boy), to my *dis*taste for body fat and body hair and competition of any kind, to the two hours it still takes me to get ready to go out at night, I have behaved, in many respects—and I have gotten no end of shit for it—like a vain, prissy, neurotic, body-obsessed "woman." Or, in the words of a powerful Italian mobster named Jackie the Toad, with whom I worked very closely for a year after college, I have behaved, revoltingly, like "half-a-fag."

By "half-a-fag," Jackie the Toad was not suggesting that

I occasionally sleep with men. Of my heterosexuality he was fairly well convinced, since he believed, erroneously as it happens, that I was sleeping wholeheartedly with a "plump and yummy" Italian hairdresser we knew in common. (And as it happens, I do not sleep with men. On the few occasions in my adult life when I have been in the near company of another man's erect penis, my impulse was to flee.) What Jackie meant by "half-a-fag" was that, though I seemed to be attracted to women, and ostensibly occasionally slept with them, the way I held myself—the way I walked, the way I ate, the way I dressed, the way I obsessively studied my reflection in the mirror, the way I gabbed away "like a little girl" on the phone with my friends, the way I did not salivate at the sight of *every* woman's bouncing tits—was not in keeping with what one expects of a *real man*.

Jackie was not alone, among the important men in my early life, in thinking that my masculinity left something to be desired. My maternal grandfather, a rather prominent political philosopher named Sidney Hook, who wrote, in book after book and for every serious journal imaginable, on subjects ranging from Marxism to existentialism, and from psychoanalysis to euthanasia, and who spent most of his life, in the face of Communist aggression around the world, fighting, with his voice and his pen but never his fists, for the causes of freedom and democracy—a man, therefore, who could not have been further removed, both culturally and intellectually, from Jackie the Toad—also, in so many words, called me "half-a-fag." The word he used was *faygeleh*, a mild Yiddish pejorative for homosexual. *Queer* and *fairy* are close approximations. When he used the word, in a conversation with my grandmother over breakfast at their summerhouse in Vermont, with me, visiting for a week during college, sitting daintily between them, he assumed I didn't know what it meant, forgetting that Leo Rosten's *The Joys of Yiddish,* which I had thumbed through many times, was sitting in a bookcase just ten feet away. I ended up cutting my visit short. The straw that broke the *faygeleh*'s back was my grandfather's more direct confrontation, a few days later, of the issue of my sexual orientation, in which he minced no words, in either Yiddish or English, in expressing his disgust for my appearance. My grandfather later apologized to me for his meanness and intolerance during this visit, his letter including the following: "I hope you will one day forgive your Grandpa. It's not your fault, it's mine. I'm an antediluvian fuddy-duddy, an old stick-in-the-mud, and it's not always easy for me to keep up with the behavior of young people." A year and a half later he died, his apology unacknowledged. This is one of the two or three moments in the book that I had difficulty writing about without choking up.

The one or two other moments that brought me to the brink of tears have to do with my dad. The poor man, to his hurt and disappointment, has never known quite what to make of me. And who can blame him? I've never looked like the children of his friends, or even like the children of strangers, and I certainly haven't looked like the two children (my older brothers) who preceded me. Nor have I acted like any of them. My behavior, in his eyes—the eyes of a hematologist and biochemist for whom there is always either a rational or irrational course of action—has been consistently irrational and bizarre. And I don't know of a single father who would disagree with him. Consider: I rarely have a job, generally living hand to mouth on mung beans and millet and canned herring; I've lived most of my life in a succession of cramped, skimpily furnished rooms on other people's terms, including a five-year stretch in a curtained-off portion of a woman's living room; I don't own a suit or tie or even a single pair of respectable trousers; the heels of my shoes, bordering on stilts, run from four to seven inches; I own very few shirts that fall below my belly button; my tattoos, like that terrible ivy growing up the side of our house that my father was always hacking away at with shears when I was a child, seem to climb another foot every time he turns his back, and now, at the base of my neck, are encroaching on my face; I move from coast to coast seemingly at whim, doing the same "nothing" in Los Angeles that I was doing just as easily in New York; my love life is baffling, my romantic entanglements lasting, on average, about forty-five minutes; I sometimes go for weeks, even months, not speaking to anyone, in a state of willful solitary confinement, and, far from unsettling me, this seems to bring me nothing but peace and fulfillment; despite my having a law degree, and having clerked for a federal judge, which should have earned me a salary by now of at least $250,000 a year, my most recent bout of employment, for $12 an hour, was babysitting a seven-year-old girl named Ruth; I own nothing, and save nothing, and accomplish nothing tangible, and have no permanent hold on life whatsoever. If an alien spacecraft, mistaking me for a representative human being, zoomed down from the heavens and grabbed me for the zoo back home, my absence would be noticed by about ten people, and missed, at most, by five. Ruth would be one of them.

And, yes, I dress like a girl. How many dads out there do we know of who could put up with *that*? About my shiftlessness, my lack of drive, my father has continually expressed frustration, but about my androgyny, to his great credit, he's only directly pressed me once, when I was eighteen, about to head off to Columbia College (his alma mater), my androgyny having just come into full bloom. I was in the kitchen at the time, making a quesadilla with fat-free mozzarella. He snuck up behind me, taking me by surprise just as I was about to open the toaster oven:

"Jonathan? Can you please explain something to me? What is this ensemble all about? The sarong, the earrings, the lipstick, your mother's perfume. My curiosity has finally gotten the better of me, and I can't help but try to satisfy it."

There's an especially obnoxious drawl that every Southern California teenager, when under attack, can adopt in half a second if he wants to tell his parents to "fuck off and leave me alone," and I put on that drawl and said: "I don't know, man. I wear what I wear."

"Don't call me 'man,' and just try to explain. I'm your dad. I think I have a right to know. I don't think I'm asking too much."

He did have a right to know. He was not asking too much. His curiosity had a right to be satisfied. I will give him *all* of that. Unfortunately, I wasn't in a position to enlighten him, because I didn't know myself. I was just doing what came naturally to me. Being called to account for it, as I have been again and again throughout my life, was like being called to account for my need to breathe.

It was not until the writing of this book, a deep and painful stab at self-analysis (the only kind of analysis I can afford), that I was able to come up with a plausible answer to my father's question. It is an answer, I hope, that will satisfy him—his curiosity, if nothing else—and will explain to him why his youngest son, despite having been clearly shown the way to success and happiness, veered so drastically off the path.

But it is not an answer that will satisfy everyone. A book can only be appreciated if you have the courage to crack the cover. And I have no reason to believe that my mother, for example, who, upon learning that I was writing a memoir, begged me, repeatedly, to "please publish it under a pseudonym," will, if she does manage to crack the cover, have the wherewithal to make it past the first paragraph of this introduction.

It also helps, to fully appreciate the contents of a book, if you can read. My five-year-old nephew, Ariel, when he heard the title of this book, called me up and said, with a note of intense worry in his voice: "Uncle Jon-Jon, can I ask you a question?"

"Of course," I told him. "Anything."

"Do you, um, wear bras?" The poor kid was terrified. He lives in North Carolina. The craziest thing he's ever seen is a guy with a long goatee and tattoos who works at the Whole Foods in Raleigh. Ariel heard the words *Uncle Jon-Jon* and *man in skirt,* and his wheels started spinning. He had visions of an angry mob outside his bedroom window, carrying pitchforks and torches, screaming for the head of the nephew of the man in New York City who wears bras.

No, Ariel. I don't wear bras. Unlike cross-dressers (those deviants!), I have a sense of proportion. Five-inch wedges from Steve Madden—I own ten pairs—are respectable. My Tommy Girl tank top, falling just below my hairless nipples, is respectable. My gray flannel skirt, with a rhinestone belt buckle saying JON-JON attached to it, is respectable.

Stockings, wigs, pancake makeup, and whatever else cross-dressers do that I don't do—keep it away from me.

Ariel's confusion was understandable. He was hardly alone—anyone who has ever set eyes on me also comes to mind—in wondering what goes on behind the scenes. One thing I've learned over the course of twenty-four years of behaving and dressing androgynously is that people hate to be confronted with indeterminacy. The uncategorizable is unsettling. If I were a man in drag, people would know exactly what I am, or at least they would *believe* they know exactly what I am, and have fewer problems with me: "Oh, yes yes yes, that man is definitely gay, and he has a very strong identification with women, he probably thinks he *is* a woman, and that's why he dresses like one, and a sex change is probably in the offing, in fact it wouldn't surprise me if his own special vagina is being made to order as we speak." But that's not what I was, that's not what I am. I have a penis, and I am attached to it. My androgyny was, and is, more subtle and confusing, less womanly, say, than *boyishly girly,* or perhaps *girlishly boyish* better captures it, or perhaps *epicene* is the word we're looking for here, but *epicene*'s not very helpful because what the hell does *epicene* really mean? And this difficulty in summing me up drives people crazy. They won't have it. Whether I like it or not, they'll find just the right label for me—homosexual, bisexual, transsexual, polysexual, metrosexual, metasexual, autosexual, cryptosexual, cryp*tic*sexual, protosexual, extraterrasexual, gender-bender, glam-boy, player, poseur, flaneur, slut, aesthete, dandy, Lebenskünstler, lotus-eater, bohemian nymph, bourgeois nymph, bourgeois nymph masquerading as a bohemian nymph!—and, whether they like it or not, they're determined to make it stick.

Well, with this book, the labels are once and for all removed, and I reveal myself for the frigid neurasthenic, plagued by a thousand and one anxieties, that I really am. I reveal myself, with that great sense of relief that comes from unburdening oneself of a painfully held secret, and with instructions to my parents, and to Jackie the Toad, to please not read the dozen or so pages in which I discuss my sadly distorted sex life, as the Man in the Gray Flannel Skirt.

Greetings from La Jolla

F WE IMAGINE MY LIFE as a series of waves, with the crests representing periods of friskiness and vigor, and the troughs representing periods of anxiety, fear, guilt, and despair, then the summer of 2004, when I was thirty-six years old, newly unemployed, with no plans for the future, and hiding out in shame at my family's country house in southern Vermont, was a trough. It was a trough so deep that not even by throwing back my head, and looking straight up into the clear blue sky, could I see the light. My state of mind at this time was not all that different from my state of mind at the age of fourteen, not long after my two older brothers had gone off to college and left me home alone to fend for myself against the overwhelming love and scrutiny of my parents, when I wrote in a journal, while sitting at my brother's desk and looking out his bedroom window toward the sea: "The sun has vanished . . . all is black."

The country house in question had been bought in 1935

by my grandfather, a professor of philosophy at NYU, as a summer refuge from the grime and bustle of New York City, a place to write his books while his wife, my grandmother Ann, gardened and cooked and hunted for mushrooms. The house, along with a few acres of grassy land, cost a total of $1,600, for which an initial deposit of $10 was considered sufficient. A year later, clearly in need of more distance between himself and the outside world, Sidney bought an additional 125 acres of adjoining land, most of it densely wooded, at a cost of less than three dollars an acre, and, proud of his purchase but a little embarrassed at the size of it, he wrote to a friend, half in jest, that he would keep the land in "trust" until the arrival of socialism. The day before he died, in July 1989, shortly before my last year at Columbia College, he yelled out to me, from his hospital bed, after I said goodbye for what I knew would be the last time, "Continue your studies, Jonathan! Your studies first; everything else can come later!" Perhaps he hoped that one day, after continuing with my studies and becoming a scholar, I might use the house in Vermont, the land adjoining which would presumably still be

The house in Vermont, August 1936.

in trust until the arrival of socialism, just as he did, as a summer refuge, a place to write my books while my wife gardened and cooked and hunted for mushrooms.

Instead, fifteen years later, with no wife or job to my name, and a law degree I was letting go to waste, I was using my grandparents' house as a summer hideout, a place to do nothing, free of charge, while trying to avoid my parents' phone calls. The last time I had tried to do this my mom tracked me down in fourteen hours flat. It was late August 1997. I had just finished working as a law clerk to a federal judge, a job that is normally considered a feather in one's professional cap, just so long as one does not take off that cap and toss it in the trash can. Having decided, shortly after the clerkship ended, that I would not be taking the bar exam, and would not be practicing law, and, instead, that I would try to get a job as a personal trainer in a health club on the island of St. Bart's, I had tossed my professional cap in the trash can, causing my mother's hackles, from three thousand miles away, to nearly break through the ceiling of her new kitchen. When I arrived in Vermont late at night, having driven all day from North Carolina (where I had clerked), I immediately pulled the phone out of the wall. And then I got into bed and pulled the covers over my head. Fourteen hours later, after eating a light lunch on the front stoop, as I was preparing to go back upstairs and get back into bed and pull the covers back over my head, Ralph Ayers, our neighbor up the road, drove up onto our front lawn and yelled out to me:

"Your mother's trying to reach you! She says the phone just rings and rings! She says she's at home if you want to call!"

When I called my mother to complain, asking why she

had sent Mr. Ayers to smoke me out of my hiding place, she told me a parable:

"I have a friend named Yael," she said. "Her son was at a very good law school. He had one paper to finish to get the law degree, but he refused to do it. One single paper to get the degree and he wouldn't do it. He left law school and never went back. All that work, all that training, all that expense, was for nothing. Yael, the mother, was of course very upset by this. And, if you ask my opinion, it's very difficult to blame her."

"Tell me, Mom: What is the son doing now?"

"He's a personal trainer."

Seven years later, in that trough of a summer of 2004, I was back on the front stoop. Having recently quit my job at *The New York Review of Books,* and having conceded to my father that, as he put it concisely, "it doesn't seem to make sense to quit a job without having another one lined up," I had driven up to Vermont and pulled the phone out of the wall. After a light lunch, I would go back upstairs, get back into bed, pull the covers back over my head, and wait for something magical to happen. At some point in my thirty-six years on this planet, at around the age of thirteen or so, the magic had disappeared from my life, and I needed, desperately, to bring it back.

It was at this very low point in my life, with the sun invisible and everything black, as I was sitting on the front stoop and preparing to go back upstairs, that Pete Young, our neighbor down the other side of the road, drove up onto our front lawn in his red pickup truck, a big smile on his face. He said he had a surprise for me. Someone, as we might have guessed, was trying to reach me. But it wasn't my mother. And it wasn't my father. It was . . . me.

"Blast from the past!" yelled Pete. "Little Jon-Jon says helloooooo!"

In Pete's outstretched hand was a postcard. It had just arrived, with a brand-new twenty-three-cent stamp affixed to it, at the local post office. On the front of the postcard, against a backdrop of some very old pictures of La Jolla, California, where I grew up, were the words "Greetings from La Jolla," and on the back, in a child's scrawl, was a short note that I had written, when I was a little boy, to my future self. I had absolutely no memory of writing this note. But it was definitely my childhood scrawl. Apparently, in February 1976, when I was seven and a half years old, I decided, in a fit of playfulness, to drop a few words of greeting to my future self, and, with the help of a mailman named Hal, who promised to keep the postcard in his possession for thirty years before putting a stamp on it and mailing it, to send this greeting to one of my favorite places in the world—my grandparents' country house in South Wardsboro, Vermont. The postcard was addressed as follows:

Jonathan Goulian (Me)
The Future
c/o Sidney Hook
S. Wardsboro, VT 05355

Dated 2/21/76 (someone mysteriously later wrote a 4 over the 6), the postcard reads:

Dear Me,
* I just was hanging out with my buddy Rick (you re-*
member him, right?) and we thouht [sic] it would be fun

to write postcards to ourselves in the future. Hal, the mailman said he would send it in about 30 years! Well, I'm just hanging out, playing soccer (did I become a pro-soccer player?) + going to the beach a lot. Mom + Dad are cool. They sometimes give me a hard time though. La Jolla is pretty cool to [sic]. Do you still live there/go surfing? See you soon!

Jon-Jon (me)

It is amazing to me, as I think back to that moment, standing on the front lawn in Vermont and confronting this ghostly visitation from my past, that I didn't scream, drop the postcard, and run into the woods. In *Star Wars,* there's a scene in which Luke Skywalker, while doing some mechanical work on R2-D2, accidentally triggers the appearance of a tiny hologram, which shoots out of a portal in the side of R2-D2's body. The hologram is of Princess Leia. She's holding out her hands in a plea for help. She's in trouble. "Help me, Obi-Wan Kenobi," she says. "You're my only hope." Luke, who is not Obi-Wan Kenobi, is understandably startled. This image of Luke confronting the hologram, a rather creepy image to me when I first saw it, at the age of nine, and still creepy to me as I recall it now, is what comes to mind as I think back to the sudden arrival of that postcard. I was obviously not expecting this little note to suddenly fall out of the past. Nor was I its intended recipient. The postcard was addressed to a man named Jonathan Goulian, a mature, grown-up man who, Little Jon-Jon assumed, would have long since cast off his childhood nickname, and who would be respectable enough by now to possibly be living in La Jolla. I was not that person. That postcard was for somebody else. And, just as the hologram of Princess Leia made its way into Luke's line of vision only through a series of accidents, so did this postcard, which had been idling for thirty years in the possession of a man named Hal, have no business ever finding its way into my hands.

Consider for a moment the mind-boggling literalness with which Hal the Mailman followed either his own idea of waiting "about 30 years" to send the postcard or mine. It's unclear from the note. Regardless of whose idea it was, even if I had commanded him to do it, nothing prevented Hal from waiting only five years—it still would have been a good gag—or ten years, or, though even this would have been pushing it, fifteen years. What kind of lunatic, knowing full well that any one of a number of occurrences, including my premature death (or Hal's, for that matter!), would have ruined the joke, just bides his time? And where did he keep the postcard all this time? In his briefcase? With a Post-it note—"Send in 30 years"—on his forehead? Wherever you are, Hal, thank you for sending it, and now you'll be so good as to stay away from me.

Also, I just happened—just happened!—to be staying, on the day this postcard arrived, over twenty-eight years later, at the very same summer home to which it was sent. We could have easily sold the home by now. Summer homes don't always stay in the family, especially after the original owners have died (my grandfather in 1989, my grandmother in 1995). And even though we hadn't sold it, I could have been anywhere on the planet at the time of the postcard's arrival. I had lived all over. In New York, Los Angeles, North Carolina, Spain, Italy, Israel. Any one of those places could have been captivating enough to claim me for good. Little Jon-Jon, who loved, more than anything, spending his summers at Grandma and Grandpa's house in South Wardsboro, Vermont, of course assumed he'd be spending his summers there for the rest of his life. And, well, he was right.

There's a further reason why that postcard shouldn't

have reached me. We don't have a mailbox in Vermont anymore. Since the house is only sporadically used during the summer, there's no need for one, so we got rid of it fifteen years ago. The woman working at the Wardsboro post office on the day the postcard arrived, Cheryl, was relatively new on the job, and had never heard of either Jonathan Goulian or Sidney Hook, and no one by either of those names had a registered mailbox in Wardsboro. Since there is no return address on the postcard, if Cheryl had sent it back, to the post office in San Francisco from which it had arrived, it would never have been retrieved. It would have been thrown away or languished, in limbo, forever.

But she didn't send it back. She pasted it to the wall near the counter, with a note above it: "Does anyone know these people?" And, lo and behold, in walked, a few minutes later, our friend Pete Young, who has lived on our little dirt road for over fifty years. When, ten minutes later, he drove up onto our front lawn, in his little red pickup truck, and, leaving the engine still idling, hopped out, his dog, Twister, on his heels, I had never seen him look so excited. "Blast from the past! Little Jon-Jon says helloooooo!"

When the initial shock wore off, I was a little disappointed. The note could have been spicier: "Dear Me: I just saw Daddy bury a body in the backyard. I think it was that woman in the fishnet stockings who comes over sometimes to play with Daddy when Mommy's at work." Or, even better, and more to the point of this book: "Dear Me: I don't feel like a *real boy*. I want to play with dolls, and wear skirts, but they won't let me. One day, when I'm bigger, *I will have my way.*"

No such luck. Though as it is, it's still pretty good. "Did I become a pro-soccer player?" is priceless. No, little man, you didn't. You continued to play soccer for nine more years, but then, despite being pretty good at it, you abruptly quit at the age of sixteen and became, instead, the village freak.

And "Mom + Dad are cool. They sometimes give me a hard time though" is also damn good. Yes, my little man, Mom + Dad are still cool and, unlike most of your friends' parents, *still together*. And, yes, they still sometimes give me a hard time. In fact, though I don't want to scare you, take a look at this rather curt letter Dad will send you when you're thirty years old:

> *Jon: I need you to help me understand what it is you are doing, and what you plan to do with your life. On a number of occasions I thought that I saw meaning and direction in what you are saying and doing, but that is not the way it has turned out. I remain confused and concerned. Can you help?*

And, while we're on the subject, take a look at this other, slightly warmer one he'll send you eight years later:

> *Dear Jon-Jon: For many years I've wondered what direction your life would take. But for some time now there has been, to me, very little change. You seem to be in a chronic state of indecision. How else to view the multiple relocations and short-term living arrangements, a state of existence I long assumed (or hoped) was temporary, but is seemingly permanent? You've provided clues. My interpretation: That you aspire to some creative pursuit and continue to search and wait*

for the right path or opportunity. Is this at least partly correct? Can you help me to understand? —da

Don't worry, little man! The reason I'm writing this book is not only to help Mom + Dad understand what's going on inside my head, and to convince them that I'm a good kid, appearances to the contrary, but also to make *you* understand. Though I no longer live in La Jolla (I can't afford it), and though I no longer surf and go to the beach (I'm terrified of getting skin cancer), and though I'm not a "pro" anything, much less a pro soccer player, I'm still, deep in my heart, my bald head full of worries notwithstanding, the same little boy, ready for adventure, that you are. So, if you think you can handle it, hop on board, buckle up, and get ready to travel with me through the world of my life. It won't be quite as fun as a magic carpet ride, and will definitely be more harrowing, but, for now, it's all we've got. And at least Grandpa Sidney will finally be proud of me. After years of doing nothing in this house, I'm finally putting it to good use.

Oh, and one more thing, kid, before I move on with this book: Who the hell is Rick?

The Man in the
Gray Flannel Skirt

CHAPTER 1

An Unwilling Host

T IS THE SPRING OF 1985. I am sixteen years old, naked, lying on a hospital bed. I am staring fixedly at the ceiling, trying to calm myself down by thinking of my warm bed back home, and trying not to worry too much about whether those two young women in the green scrubs—medical students? residents? The one with the freckles, the skinny redhead, blushed when she caught me staring at her—can see the outline of my penis, not erect but still possibly visible, beneath the cold white sheet that I have pulled up to my nipples. This will be my second surgery in eleven months, so I know the drill. At least part of the drill, the part that deals with waiting anxiously for it to begin, and knowing that it will eventually end. The trick to dealing with surgery, I had learned the previous May, when I got the first of my two nose jobs (the second one coming nine years later, when I was twenty-four, and I'm thinking of getting a third one sometime soon, because my nose is out of shape again and I just can't stand it!), is to focus all of your attention on that moment eight hours later, when you are back home in your own bed, in your own room, surrounded by your own stuffed animals—the walrus, the dolphin, the seal, the starfish, and my favorite, Mr. Marvel, the koala bear hand puppet that my mother gave to me for either Hanukkah or Christmas (we celebrated both, the presents for one running seamlessly into the presents for the other) when I was seven. By focusing on that moment of pure tranquillity, you are able to avoid hyperventilating, or crying, or pulling the covers over your head. When your furry friends are on the scene, nothing is too much to handle.

So here I am, staring at the ceiling, thinking of Mr. Marvel, and of the sound of the waves crashing gently against the shore far down the hill below our house, when the two young women, who have been fussing about my bed, unwrapping syringes, and making those awful clinking noises when they put the glass lids back on jars full of cotton balls and gauze, suddenly make a big production of flipping a coin. The redhead calls "heads." It's tails. She snaps her fingers and clucks her tongue against her teeth, as if to say: "Why do I *always* lose this game?" Following this production with one eye, I am curious as to where this game is headed. The redhead, a little nervously maybe, grabs some sort of implement, quickly smiles at me, says, "This will take just a second," and then pulls the bedsheet down below my waist, just below my penis. Using no cream at all, and what seems to be a dull razor blade, she begins roughly shaving off my pubic hair. I am sixteen, and she could easily be no older than twenty-one, a disparity in age not quite pronounced enough to remove all possibility that her pretty freckled arm grazing my penis might lead to the arousal of one or both of us. Perhaps this explains why she shaves my pubes much too quickly and awkwardly, causing painful chafing and ingrown hairs that will continue to plague me weeks after the surgery is over. It certainly explains why I quickly look away from that pretty arm and back up at the ceiling, and focus hard on that moment, eight hours later, when, for the first time in three years, I will be able to go to sleep without wondering if my phantom third testicle, the source of so much painful confusion for me, and the sudden appearance of which marked the beginning of the end of my sanity and happiness, will be waiting for me when I wake up in the morning.

———

Sometime in 1982, when I was thirteen years old, and very close to bucking up the courage to ask either Amy McKnight or Wendy Brazier out on a movie date, a two-inch piece of flesh, in shape and density not unlike a small hard-boiled egg, poked its way out of nowhere and into my scrotum.

My first thought, when the egg appeared, was *cryptorchidism* (or, as it is more commonly known, *undescended testicle*). When you grow up in a family of physicians—my father was a hematologist; his brother was a plastic surgeon; my mother's brother was a geneticist whose area of special interest was birth defects—terms like *cryptorchidism* are thrown around casually at the dinner table at family gatherings. What I didn't manage to catch at the dinner table, I more than made up for by flipping through the pages of the two dozen scientific journals to which my father regularly subscribed, and which were strewn around the house. By the age of thirteen, I had a huge store of these terms at my disposal, a store on which to draw in case I felt, or looked, a little out of sorts. Fatigue, the great all-purpose symptom, was never just fatigue. It was a sure sign of Crohn's disease, or rheumatoid arthritis, or any one of a thousand anemias. Sickle-cell anemia always came immediately to mind, but, for the sake of variety, there was also Fanconi's anemia, or myelophthisic anemia. Tingling in the hands and feet was obviously megaloblastic anemia. Joint pain could be lupus, or it could be hemochromatosis. Depending on how I chose to suffer for the rest of my life, I chose one or the other. Blue lips and fingernails, fairly common when you swim in the ocean in winter, as we often did in La Jolla, were, in my case, either pericardial tamponade or Waterhouse-Friderichsen syndrome. A fever or headache or unexplained bruising was probably thromobotic thrombocytopenic purpura (more commonly known, to amateur hypochondriacs, as Moschcowitz's syndrome), or it might also be Upshaw-Schulman syndrome and, in either case, my sure death within ten years.

And of course a mole was never just a mole. Every single mole that ever existed, if you look closely enough at it through a magnifying glass, as I always did, has *irregular borders,* and *uneven coloring,* the sure signs of cancerous tissue:

"Dad! Look! What is that little splotch?"

"It's a splotch. You're fine."

"Is it a squamous cell carcinoma?"

"No."

"Basal cell carcinoma?"

"No."

"Acral lentiginous melanoma?"

"No."

"You're not even looking!"

"I looked yesterday."

"But that was a different splotch!"

"Different splotch, same prognosis. You're fine!"

Thank God I had a doctor for a father. Always putting those fears, which he had put into my head to begin with, to rest.

But this potential undescended testicle—pending, of course, my father's diagnosis—presented a new problem. In order to get a diagnosis from my father, I would have to pull down my pants and let my father look at, and squeeze, my scrotum. His hairy arm would likely graze my penis in the process. To allow these things to happen would call everything I stood for as a proper La Jolla teenager into question. In La Jolla, just as one did not wear a skimpy Speedo bathing suit to the beach but, instead, wore the longer and more fashionable Birdwell Beach Britches (which, made out of nylon, had the added advantage of drying out very quickly), so did one not let one's father grope one's balls. To let your father grope your balls meant that you were, at a minimum, three-fourths gay.

What was required, in this case, to preserve my manhood, was a *self*-diagnosis. Not an easy thing to do in the early 1980s. Those of you under the age of twenty-five, you have to remember: this was before the Internet. Getting to the bottom of this lump in my sac was not simply a matter of Googling "scrotum" and "bulge." I would have to rely on my own wits. The *World Book Encyclopedia,* a com-

plete set of which we had in our playroom upstairs, was
no help. I looked up "reproductive system," and saw a
normal-looking man with two balls. I then considered
going to one of the local libraries and looking up "testicles,
disorders of," in the card catalogue. But this seemed un-
promising. The small and friendly La Jolla Public Library
had a limited selection of books, and would definitely be no
help. The central library on the nearby campus of the University of California at San Diego (UCSD), where my father
was a professor at the medical school, was another obvious
option, but where the La Jolla Public Library was too limited in scope, the UCSD library seemed too vast and impos-
ing. I would need the assistance of a librarian. She would
assume she hadn't heard me correctly—"You're looking for
a book on disorders of the *what*?"—and, when I repeated
myself, she would instinctively look at my crotch. With a
shudder of horror, she would tell me that my search was
hopeless. "I'm sorry, young man. We have many books on
deformities in this library, but not the specific kind of *sexual deformity* you're looking for. You'll have to go to the
medical school library for that, on the other side of campus." Where, of course, I could easily run into my father.

A final option was asking my parents to make a doctor's
appointment for me. But then my dad, naturally, would say:

"Why? What's wrong?"

"Nothing much. I just have a mysterious, egg-shaped
bulge in my scrotum."

"Well, let me take a look. You haven't shied away from
showing me every other bulge on your body, so why start
now?"

Which, as we know, was out of the question.

So, with no other recourse open to me, all I could do was think back to that discussion around the dinner table many years earlier in which *cryptorchidism* had casually popped up. As I recalled, the condition generally occurred only when a boy had either zero or one descended testicle. If a boy already had two descended testicles, as I did, then the descent of a third testicle, according to the scientific literature, would be unnecessary, and would suggest that the boy at issue was not a boy at all but some other species entirely.

My self-diagnosis, only just begun, had reached a standstill. Relying on my wits had gotten me no further than the hopeful diagnosis that I had a *quasi* third testicle, and not a real one. So I decided to put the diagnosis off until later and, in the interim, take action. Instead of diagnosing the precise nature of this mysterious egg, I would try to get rid of it.

As far as I could tell, the egg had descended into my scrotum through a secret, internal doorway, and, assuming that the door was still ajar, my plan was to force the egg to go back the way it came. Initially, the plan worked beautifully. Lying flat on my back, I squeezed the egg tightly between my fingers and immediately sent it shooting back up into my body. Nothing to it. It couldn't have been easier. Out of scrotum, out of mind. When I stood up, gravity immediately pulled the egg back into the sac.

Both of my attempts to deal with the intruder had failed. The intellectual approach—tame the bastard into submission by coming up with a harmless diagnosis—had foundered on the rocks of an unlikely, but still possible, and too demoralizing to think about without going crazy, third testicle. The more aggressive approach—tame the bastard into submission by grabbing hold of his neck and throwing him out—had smacked up against a revolving door.

The third solution, the one that I very soon adopted, and which tided me over for three years, was doing my best to ignore him. This was not always easy. The scrotum is designed for two testicles. Mine was accommodating what amounted to three. As a result, as you can imagine, my scrotum felt tight, tense, stressed, overburdened. When I was swimming in cold water, and my scrotum contracted, it felt like my balls, pressing firmly against the skin, might burst through their casing and into the ocean. Imagine dog-paddling and suddenly finding three testicles bobbing near your mouth. Unless I was playing soccer, or taking a test, or watching a movie, that feeling of tension in the groin nagged at me continually, and all I could do was try to shut it out of my mind.

There was a poster on the wall of my Middle Brother's room, which he had left behind when he went to college, which said, "When life gives you lemons, make lemonade." Below the words was a cartoon of a funny-looking man with a bushy mustache, and with the front of his scalp lifted back like the open lid of an auto-drip coffeemaker. Lemons were being poured into the opening of his head, and a stream of lemonade was simultaneously pouring out of his nostrils. It was an inspiring message. The man had been given a head full of lemons, seemingly against his will, and, rather than complaining or crying about it, he was making the best of this intrusion by producing lemonade out of his nose. A fine solution. Make the best of your limitations and move on. I would do the same. Life had given me a possible third testicle, definitely against my will, and I would make the best of this intrusion by asking no girls out on dates until it permanently disappeared, and, in the meantime, re-signing myself to a life of celibacy and masturbation.

At least I could still play soccer. Soccer had been every-thing to me since I was six years old. I had tried at least a dozen extracurricular activities—acting, singing, painting, swimming, baseball, football, tennis, basketball, water polo, surfing, sailing, skateboarding, playing the cello—and soc-cer was the one activity I had settled on as my ticket, so long as I continued to get those straight A's, into the college of my choice. I was so good in soccer, thanks in no small part to my incredible speed, that I was recruited to play for a special traveling soccer club, the same one my Oldest Brother had played for, called the Nomads. And I was so good playing for the Nomads (otherwise known, by oppos-ing players taunting us, as the Gonads) that, at the age of fourteen, I was accelerated to the next highest age bracket, the Under 16s. The extra weight between my legs, easily ig-norable as long as I was distracted by the heat of competi-tion, did not make it any harder to dribble and shoot. So, in some respects at least, I could go on with my life. I would lose myself in soccer, and school, and movies, and the beach, and forget about girls for a while. The one thing I could be grateful for, the lone bright spot in this awful cloud of confusion, was that no one could see through my pants. A cleft palate, a clubfoot, a hunchback—many de-formities were not so easily covered up. As long as I wore pants, my third ball was invisible to everyone but me. My confusion, when I was aware of it, was real and painful. But at least it was a private matter.

When my nose and legs, at just about this same time in my life, also decided to betray me, joining forces with my scrotum in a three-front assault against my sanity, visibility became more of a problem. The nose, unlike the scrotum, is smack in the center of the face. The legs, in a town like La Jolla, where the average yearly temperature is seventy-two degrees and every kid wears shorts or a bathing suit just about every day, are impossible to miss. While in the case of my scrotum, the betrayal was completely unexpected and baffling, in the case of my nose and legs, I was not entirely unprepared. The warning signs had long been obvious. But since there was nothing I could do to defend myself, I had long ignored them. And then, in eighth grade, boom!

As for my nose, I first learned what my genes might have in store for it when I saw Woody Allen's *Sleeper* in the early 1970s, when I was about six. In case you have not seen *Sleeper,* or forget the plot: Miles Monroe, the part owner of the Happy Carrot Health Food Store on Bleecker Street in the West Village, wakes up one day from a state of "cryogenic immersion" to which he had not consented, two hundred years in the future, and eventually finds himself reluctantly working with an underground revolutionary movement to overthrow a dictator, known as the Leader, who is embodied solely by a rather large nose that is housed, for safekeeping, beneath a poorly guarded bell-shaped jar. When Miles sees the nose, he mutters, "Oh, the Leader must be Armenian," and then he destroys the Leader by lifting the jar, kidnapping the nose, and throwing it beneath a steamroller, flattening it. Confused by the reference to Armenians, I asked my dad what Woody Allen meant by that comment, and my dad, still laughing nearly uncontrollably at Woody's joke, explained that "Armenians are famous for their big noses. Your dad and uncle are not alone. But don't worry. Your nose will be just fine."

Well, he was wrong. My nose would not be just fine. What happened to it is that, at the age of thirteen, in keeping with the noses of Armenians generally, and also, as it happens, the noses of Jews generally, and also in keeping, more specifically, with my dad's nose, and my dad's brother's nose, and my Grandpa Sidney's nose, it grew a size too big for my face. Seemingly overnight, and seemingly out of nowhere, a small lump of bone, originating in some unfamiliar cavity behind my eyes, poked its way through the bridge of my nose and set up camp for good.

What is a size too big for my face?

A size too big for my face is I'm not quite the catch around the campus of Muirlands Junior High School that I used to be. Before, girls would pass me notes in class, chase me in the swimming pool at birthday parties, send me little candies on Valentine's Day. After the Great Betrayal of '82, the only things that chased me in the swimming pool were bees.

A size too big for my face is Rusty Beitman (who, I should add, grew up to be a very nice man) drawing mocking comparisons, in a shrill voice that could be heard up and down my row of lockers, between the size of my nose and that of Pete Townshend of the Who.

A size too big for my face is Dr. Jerry Feinberg *not* saying, two years later, when my mother, at my tearful request, agreed to let me see him for a consultation, "Oh, don't be silly! I refuse to take a scalpel to this boy's pretty schnoz!" He would take one look at me and set up an appointment.

A size too big for my face is that I hated my reflection in the mirror, found it excruciating to behold, but couldn't, for the life of me, stop looking at it, so obsessed was I with laying siege to it and getting my revenge.

But a size too big for my face does not mean, so that we don't distort the record in my disfavor, that it was huge. As my mother put it, accurately but not so helpfully, "Dustin Hoffman, who is very handsome and successful, has a much bigger one."

As for my legs, I first learned what my genes might have in store for them when my Grandpa Sidney, in his boxer shorts, sometime in the early 1970s, did a funny dance for me in the living room in Vermont. It was some sort of old-fashioned dance I had never seen before, perhaps of his own creation, involving the raising of each leg a few inches off the floor, one after the other, and the occasional snapping of his fingers, but otherwise not very much movement. It was a pretty simple dance.

"You see these funny legs?" he said. "They're called bowlegs. Or bandy legs. My father, your great-grandfather, had them, and I inherited them from him. They're very good for riding horses."

"But not very good for dancing," I said, at which Sidney started howling with laughter. I was not trying to be clever. I was a five- or six-year-old kid literally describing what I was watching. But my comment thrilled him. Sidney loved to give his grandsons, when we were little, more credit for cleverness than we deserved, as a way of encouraging us to be as verbally interesting as possible. Unclever little grandsons, for any grandfather, can be a bore. So for my unintentional cleverness I got a "That's wonderful, Jonathan! Wonderful! Ann, did you hear what he said: 'But not very good for dancing,'" and then he threw back his head, shut his eyes, and broke out into his trademark high-pitched cackle.

I was reminded of this incident many years later when I read an interview with Grandpa Sidney that appeared in *Commentary* magazine in October 1989, three months after he died. The interview, conducted a year earlier by Norman Podhoretz, was called "On Being a Jew." Sidney requested that it not be published until he was dead because of a statement he made during the interview, which he considered controversial, that the Jews might have been better off had they "gone down fighting" two thousand years earlier, dying out in a "blaze of glory," rather than continuing to live in a seemingly permanent state of persecution. While discussing, more innocuously, during the beginning of the interview, his family history, he said, at one point: "My father was brought up on a farm [in Bohemia], and he had all the superstitious knowledge of European farmers. He attributed his bowlegs to the fact that he had ridden on horses, but was puzzled that I had inherited the same bowlegs without ever being on a horse."

When I read this statement, I was immediately transported back to the living room in Vermont in the early 1970s. Was Sidney trying to hint to me, when he pointed to his bowlegs, and mentioned that he had inherited them from his father, that I had inherited the same unfortunate trait, as a way of gently preparing me for my fate? Were my bowlegs already apparent when I was six years old? Some people are born with bowlegs, and then the legs straighten themselves out. Others are born with straight legs, and then, as the legs grow, they bend. Photos of me as a child suggest that my legs were straight, though it's possible that

Sidney, especially attuned, saw something the photos didn't capture. If my legs were, indeed, already slightly bowed, the likely explanation for why I suddenly became aware of it when I was thirteen is that a sudden growth spurt, when I hit adolescence, made the bowedness more pronounced and, crucially, more visible to people who were inclined to make fun of me for it. This would explain why, after thirteen years of not being called names, a rather long honeymoon period to which I was perhaps not entitled, I was suddenly hearing, in addition to "Hey, there's Pete Townshend's brother" from one end of the hall, "Ride 'em, cowboy," courtesy of a boy named Reggie, from the other.

I recently learned that there is another possible explanation for my bowlegs, other than a genetic predisposition, that would be too absurd to take seriously if it weren't supported by what appear to be reputable scientists. The culprit? Playing soccer! The great love of my youth! In 2006, a group of scientists in the Department of Pediatric Orthopedics at Dana Children's Hospital in Tel Aviv published a paper about a possible correlation between bowleggedness in male children and adolescents and "high-performance" soccer playing. "Little is known," they wrote, "about the interactions of sports-related demands and the human body, in particular on musculoskeletal features, during growth." What they concluded, after comparing the legs of 106 male soccer players, and 68 male tennis players, between the ages of ten and twenty-one, was that there was a "significantly higher prevalence" of bowleggedness among the soccer players, and that *this prevalence was especially pronounced among soccer players ages thirteen and older.* It's interesting to note, in light of this study, that it was at the age of *thirteen,* three years after being recruited to play for the Nomads, the highly competitive traveling soccer club, which required continual grueling training under severely demanding English coaches, that my bowlegs first became apparent. The scientists who performed this study seemed to assume that the physical demands of soccer playing may have caused the legs to bow, but an equally plausible explanation, it seems to me, is that bowlegs are useful for playing soccer, and so boys with bowlegs are more likely to be good at it, and thus more likely to play it.

At the age of thirteen, I didn't care so much where my bowlegs came from, whether from Sidney, or from a recessive gene on my father's side, or from riding horses (though had you told me they came from playing soccer I would have likely quit on the spot); I was just puzzled why my legs, in addition to my nose and testicles, had to make life so embarrassing for me. And my life was only just beginning! Think of the potholes lying in wait for me! On my father's side we had a "family history," so I was told, of diabetes. What that meant, inevitably, as I saw it, was the loss of my vision, the loss of one or both legs, and regular self-injections of insulin. On my mother's side we had a family history of premature baldness. Grandpa Sidney, who, as my maternal grandfather, was the strongest genetic influence, as I understood it, on the fate of my hair, had started to go bald in his early twenties. On both sides of my family we had a history of shortness. My father was barely five feet seven, my Middle Brother was five feet six, Sidney was five feet five and a half, my Oldest Brother was five feet four, and my mother was five feet flat. My paternal grandmother was four feet ten, and shrinking by the hour. At five feet six, and still growing slowly, I was currently tied for second, but that was nothing to be proud of. After all, we were a family of pygmies! It was not difficult, when looking at my reflection in the mirror, to see, looking back at me, a few years down the line, a short, big-nosed, bowlegged, bald-headed, multitesticled freak, and to imagine the insults I had in store for me when I grew up and tried to make my way through the jungles of modern life. A girl might make allowances for one or two deformities, but at a certain point she'd have to draw the line. The heart is only so big. When I watched, around the age of fourteen, on television, Ernst Lubitsch's *The Shop Around the Corner,* there was a scene at the very end that almost brought me to tears: Margaret Sullavan asks Jimmy Stewart to pull up the legs of his pants, so that she can be sure, before she decides to run off and marry him, that a pair of bowed legs is not concealed beneath them. He pulls them up, his legs are perfect, and then, *and only then,* the deal is sealed. Were it not for those perfect legs, she would have dumped him. That scene ruined an otherwise delightful movie for me. I loved Margaret Sullavan until that scene, and have loathed her ever since. Two years later, when I was sixteen, I found myself a few feet away from Jimmy Stewart at the White House. My grandfather had been awarded, by Ronald Reagan, the Presidential Medal of Freedom, for "his commitment to rational thought and civil discourse," and "his devotion to freedom," and Jimmy Stewart, much taller than I had expected, was one of his fellow recipients. Jimmy was now seventy-seven years old, and not looking his best, but he was still the most handsome man in the room. Though I did not lift up the cuffs of his pants to check the angle of his lower legs, I could tell, just by looking at the elegant way he walked, that they were still, forty-five years later, as Margaret Sullavan would have been gratified to learn (had she not died, in 1960, at the age of forty-eight, from what was ruled an accidental overdose of barbiturates, though was generally regarded as suicide), as beautifully unbowed as ever.

At the age of fourteen, having expressed no prior interest in pursuing a career in medicine, and for no apparent reason other than that I had grown up among physicians, I suddenly announced to the family that I wanted to become an orthopedic surgeon. The reason, of course, of which I was unaware at the time, was not far beneath the surface. My bones, in my nose and legs, had suddenly betrayed me. As an orthopedic surgeon, I could tame my bones into submission by breaking them and fixing them. Or so I hoped. (Plastic surgery, perhaps, would have been a more obvious choice of profession, but the subconscious is not interested in being obvious.) In a class exercise designed to teach us how to fill out job applications, I wrote, next to the box titled "Job for Which You Are Applying"—"Mixed internship in internal medicine and orthopedic surgery at Mass General Hospital." With a mixed internship under my belt, my body would be defenseless against me. Wherever it attacked, I'd be ready for it. Next to the box that said "Interests and Hobbies," I wrote: "The development of water-resistant casts." That makes perfect sense. To straighten my legs, I would need to break them in half at the knees, hammer the tibias back into shape, and then reattach them. With water-resistant casts on my sore and healing legs, I could go swimming in the ocean after the operation.

My body, I should make perfectly clear, had no grounds for violence against me. For the previous thirteen years I had been consistently good to it. I ate well, and exercised. I didn't smoke. I didn't do drugs. I didn't sniff glue. I always wore a helmet when riding my bike, and kneepads when skateboarding. I treated my body no less dutifully than the Smithsonian Institution treats the Hope Diamond, watching over it obsessively, guarding it from unclean hands, tending to its nooks and crevices. The famously *cursed* Hope Diamond, I should add. My body, no less cursed, was consumed by a host of grievances that it never bothered to make clear to me. John Updike, in "At War with My Skin," the essay in which he writes of his lifelong struggle against psoriasis, was struggling on only one front. It was a brutal war, but his energies were at least well focused. He had one enemy, and he knew what it was. In my case, I had to contend with not only three enemies, the nature of one of which was a complete mystery, but three enemies simultaneously erupting out of nowhere at just the point in my life when the thrill of sexual exploration seemed within reach. It was the timing, as much as the indignities themselves, that was so awful.

As my friends began to report back from the field—Tommy announcing on the bus that "I made Stacy come with only three fingers up her pussy"; Anthony telling us proudly that "Angela's pussy tasted *exactly* like red wine" —I took my frustration, in my loneliness, out on my teeth. Yes, my teeth. I may have been powerless against my nose and legs and scrotum, but all I needed was a toothbrush, toothpaste, and dental floss to make my teeth whiter, cleaner, and more cavity-free than any other teeth in all of La Jolla. I had good teeth to begin with, and I would make them the best. As the rest of my body rebelled against me at will, my mouth would be my one stronghold. Looking back at my behavior from a distance of twenty-seven years, that's the best I can make of it. A bright white smile, to a kid who feels left out of the action, can make up for an awful lot, I suppose. So, from brushing two times a day in the past, I moved on to four times a day. Four became six. Six became eight. Eight became ten. To brush your teeth ten times a day and not get noticed by the other students and made fun of for it, you have to do it surreptitiously. This required excusing myself from class to go to the bathroom four or five times a day, and very often switching bathrooms more than once until I found one that was unoccupied. If no bathroom was free, I went to a drinking fountain that was on the far side of campus, so remote that no one ever used it. Occasionally, when desperate, if I didn't have time to make my way across the campus to the drinking fountain, and I couldn't find an unoccupied bathroom, I would use either the janitor's hose or that one broken sprinkler, near the Natal plum bushes on the back side of the playground, that always dribbled water out of its spout. I would crouch down next to the sprinkler, wet my toothbrush, and use a pocket mirror to see what I was doing. To make sure I always had a toothbrush within easy reach, I owned eight of them, and kept two in my gym locker, two in my hall locker, two in my backpack, two at home. To make sure that the toothbrushes did not become encrusted with bacteria and small particles of food, I would continually replace them.

Whenever you attack an enemy with far more force than is necessary, there is a high risk of collateral damage. That is what happened, unfortunately, in the all-out assault against my teeth. Just as the firing of a dozen missiles, from unpiloted drones, and F-14s, and warships stationed in the

Arabian Sea, will occasionally result in the death not only of the one or two Taliban soldiers we were targeting but also of the ten or twenty children in the hospital next door, which then results, in turn, in the loss of potential support for the American invasion on the part of the local villagers, so did the carpet bombing of my teeth, from the hard bristles of my toothbrushes applied ten times a day, result not only in the whitest teeth in La Jolla, and not a single cavity to my name, but also in collateral damage to the tissue that surrounded them and, in turn, the loss of potential support on the part of my gums. You can imagine the look of surprise on the face of Dr. David Green, D.D.S., when, at the age of thirteen and a half, I went to see him for my semi-annual checkup. Instead of pronouncing me patient of the month, and, as my prize, taking a Polaroid of my mouth and tacking it to the wall, he scolded me for being a maniac, and promptly shot me up with Novocain. A narrow strip of flesh was then extracted, with a knife, from the roof of my mouth, and reattached, with stitches, to the base of my lower gums, to shore up the gaping recession beneath my front teeth. The jagged wound in the roof of my mouth, almost unendurably painful after the anesthetic wore off, throbbed and bled for days. The little strip of flesh, with no flow of blood to it, immediately turned white, like a tiny sliver of chicken breast, and stayed white forever, never assimilating the pink color of the neighboring tissue. (I've since learned from many dentists that this failure to assimilate, on the part of the transplanted piece of flesh, is common, and harmless, and no fault of Dr. Green's.)

With my lower gums now compromised, the transplanted piece of flesh potentially visible if I opened my mouth too widely, a big proud smile was no longer an option. People would see a strange growth on my gums. I would see their faces darken, and hear them thinking, *Ew! What* is *that?* The possibilities were horrific. A giant canker sore, a tapeworm, trench mouth, herpes! Instead, they would see nothing. I would make sure of that. Whenever I was about to break out into a smile, I took care not to open my mouth too widely and, for good measure, instinctively covered my mouth with my hand. So much for my one stronghold.

Did I learn my lesson and never again use disproportionate force when taking out my frustration on my body? No. When my face, in ninth and tenth grades, started breaking out in the occasional pimple, maybe one or two pimples a month, nothing for a reasonable person to get excited about, I interpreted these eruptions, in my paranoia, as an obvious sign that a brand-new front was opening up in my body's ongoing campaign against me. To control this front before the tide turned against me, I started washing my face ten times a day, and spending up to six hours a week in various saunas around town, sweating out the grease. But it didn't seem to work. The one or two pimples a month, far from disappearing, became three or four. Three or four became five or six. In my panic, I began to attack each pimple as if it were an army of thousands, going mano a mano with it in one of those special mirrors that my mother had in her bathroom, which enlarged the face by a factor of five. For a whole hour, as I poked at it and picked at it and doused it with alcohol, I was grappling with a pimple that was five times its actual size, assuming that everyone in the world saw that same gargantuan pimple and was continually staring at it as fanatically as I was.

As we all know, when you go mano a mano with a pimple, what would have likely disappeared in three days becomes a festering wound, and lingers on the scene for two weeks, damaging the pigment in the skin and often leaving behind a scar. But instead of relaxing my efforts and pulling back, in my desperation for total victory I went further. I resorted to every means possible known to dermatologists in the mid-1980s, shy of Accutane (which is prescribed only for what is known as "severe recalcitrant nodular acne," which I never came close to having), to destroy the occasional two to six pimples that refused to go away, including clindamycin, erythromycin, tetracycline, and, when it became available, Retin-A. There was also a foul-smelling sulfurous cream that one doctor prescribed for me that dried out my skin so severely it turned my face into a mask of white flakes. My own special remedy was covering my entire face with a white mask of Clearasil, one or two bottles' worth, and lying on a lounge chair in the privacy of the backyard of our house, with a fan pointed toward me so I wouldn't sweat and further clog my pores, and then baking my face in the sun for up to four straight hours, burning it to a bright and crispy red, thereby camouflaging, or outright obliterating, the red bumps. In La Jolla, chronic sunburns were common among teenagers with acne. A sunburn is a natural form of makeup. It's also a dangerous form of makeup. But since the risk is not immediate, the danger is easily ignored. For most teenagers, the risk of getting skin cancer twenty years in the future is a risk well worth taking for the sake of not being ugly right this second.

Many years later, when I was in my early thirties, I read an article in a women's fashion magazine that explained why the ruthless campaign against my skin was not only futile but self-defeating. Drying out your skin, as I was doing in every way imaginable, actually *increases* the odds of getting pimples. Why did no one tell me this at the time? What happens is that the skin, having been drained of its oil, essentially gets parched and, in order to remoisturize itself, produces more oil than it would have otherwise. This explains why my face, for much of my late teens and twenties, looked wet. It was covered with a glistening sheen of oil, and every time I tried to wash it away, the wetness came right back. Cleaning your face compulsively, as I was doing, in an effort to take arms against your pimples, actually encourages the skin to recruit reinforcements.

I was obviously not the only person I knew of whose body had stopped behaving during adolescence. I am not claiming to have been the only teenager in La Jolla singled out by God for mistreatment. One girl at school, known, thanks to Rusty Beitman, by the horrible nickname of Sasquatch, suddenly found herself, around the age of thirteen or fourteen, with a swath of dark hair above her upper lip, and thick carpets of dark hair on her forearms. In class she would always keep her elbow on her desk, and her hand in front of her face, so that she could lean into it with her mouth, and keep her mustache covered. The pose looked natural enough if you didn't know any better. But everyone knew. Her forearms she kept covered with long-sleeve shirts, even in hot weather. She had a tendency to pull violently at the ends of her sleeves, deliberately stretching the material. She would then grab hold of them, and clutch tightly, as if to keep the sleeves from rising up her forearms and uncovering the thick coils of hair that were concealed beneath them.

It is Sasquatch who comes back to me as I recall my own

huge arsenal of tics that I gradually built up over the years to defend myself against my body. I wasn't consciously emulating her, but I can't help but wonder if wearing a turtleneck, and pulling the neck up to my mouth, and then chewing on the border of the neck so that it wouldn't slide back down, in an effort to conceal the one or two pimples on my chin, was not, on some level of awareness beneath the surface, borrowed from her playbook. Always resting my elbow on my desk, and keeping my hand in front of my face, and leaning into my hand with my nose, to conceal it from observation and potential ridicule, also appears, in retrospect, Sasquatchian in origin (as is my habit, lately, when I don't have the energy to shave my forearms, of wearing long-sleeve shirts, even in hot weather, and clutching tightly at the ends of my sleeves). My tendency to stand with my right leg thrust slightly forward, the heel of the right foot at a right angle to my left foot, in a sort of modified fourth position, to conceal the bow in my legs, was definitely a tic of my own creation, as was my tendency to tack back and forth, in a series of frenetic diagonal movements, when I walked across the quad. You see, bowlegs are most pronounced if you are facing them head-on. If I am walking in a straight line, and you are either directly in front of me or directly behind me, you will notice my legs bending away from each other below the knees. But if you are facing my legs at an angle, or a rapid series of angles, the bow is obscured. My goal, when tacking back and forth, was to create a blur of movement, much in the way of Duchamp's *Nude Descending a Staircase,* so that no one on campus, spying on my legs, could possibly make out where one of them ended and the other began.

When, at the age of fifteen and a half, I asked my mother if I could get a nose job, I had no reason to believe that she would say yes. "Your nose is fine the way it is" was an equally plausible answer. "And nose jobs are very expensive. To pay a few thousand dollars, or whatever it is, for nothing is absurd. We're not made of money, you know."

I wonder how my life would have been different, if at all, if that had been my mother's response. A woman I know who dabbles in therapeutic literature, and fancies herself an analyst of sorts, once told me, without my having asked her opinion on the matter, that the answer my mother actually gave—"If a nose job is important to you, then of course your father and I will pay for it"—is partially responsible for my continuous inability, to this day, to make peace with my body. "She shouldn't have legitimized your self-consciousness," this person said. "Had you not gotten that nose job—had your mother insisted that you were perfectly beautiful as you were—you would have learned to love your body and accept it for all its flaws, rather than fighting against it for the rest of your life." Maybe. The other alternative is that I would have continued to be miserable every single time I looked in the mirror, and eventually killed myself. Not a gamble most mothers want to take. And not a gamble that I would choose to take if I could do it all over again. Since my mother wasn't in the least bit surprised by my request, and didn't hesitate at all in granting it, she must have been well aware how miserable I was. It must have been as distressing for her to watch her baby boy squirming in discomfort every time he faced a camera as it was for me.

The expense of the operation I was prepared for. But not

the pain. In my zeal for victory, I had forgotten about that part. The operation, worth briefly describing to the extent I remember it, began with a series of excruciating injections. There were about seven of them, placed at regular intervals around the circumference of my nose. The final shot of this series, in the shallow depression between the upper lip and septum, otherwise known as the philtrum (or, as I understood it as a child, the delicate mark of the angel's touch), caused a surge of pain up through my head so violent that it felt as if my skull might break at the seams. I flinched, and the nurses tightly held my wrists. Swabs of pure cocaine, to further deaden the nerves, were then shoved so deeply into my nasal cavities that I could feel the tips of the swabs between my eyes. A fantastic stillness, and woodenness, quickly set in across my face. As Dr. Feinberg vigorously chipped and filed away at the bump, the cocaine went to my brain and I began to babble excitedly, the words bumping into each other and climbing over each other and wrestling with each other to get out, about how much more handsome I would look when it was all over. The nurses started giggling, and Dr. Feinberg had to take a quick break to join them.

When the swelling went down, the feeling of triumph was intoxicating. My delicate face, unjustly taken away from me when I was thirteen, had been restored. No longer would I have to worry about people stealing a glance at my profile and snickering. No longer would I walk ten minutes out of my way, between classes, to avoid running into Rusty Beitman, or instinctively turn away, and cover my face with my hand, when someone tried to take my picture. After three long years of being weighed down by my face, I could finally stand tall again. My legs might have needed some refashioning below the knees; my skin might have been a little pimply, and way too shiny; my smile wasn't as broad as it could have been; and I would have loved, even at five feet, eight inches, now the tallest member of my family, to have been four or even six inches taller. And of course there was Signor Quasi Testicale still lurking between my thighs. But all of that aside, I did, at last, and the glances thrown my way confirmed me in my impression, feel like a pretty little boy again.

Not everyone, alas, shared my sense of intoxication. Twenty-four years later, in 2008, when looking at my college application, which was still on file at Columbia College, I read, for the first time, the recommendation that my eleventh-grade history teacher, Mrs. Soriano, wrote for me at my request, and was struck by the negative effect my

The author, four months after his first nose job, with his mother.

newfound feeling of liberation apparently had on her opinion of me. Though her recommendation was positive in
most respects, she couldn't help but note, without perhaps
realizing the degree to which this observation might make it
more difficult for me to get into college, that I had a "giant,
swelled head," an impression derived, I suspect, from my
new tendency to admire my reflection in any mirrored surface I could find, including silverware, fingernail clippers,
the face of my watch, the protective Mylar covers of library
books, the rearview mirror of my parents' Volkswagen
Rabbit, which I twisted and turned so aggressively to bring
my new face into proper view that it finally cracked off at
the base, and, when they became available, the shiny surfaces of compact discs. After three years of despising my reflection, I suddenly felt good about myself again. My head
might have swelled up a bit, I plead guilty to the charge, but
when we consider how contracted it was to begin with, the
swelling wasn't really much cause for concern. It was not
the ballooning of my head Mrs. Soriano was observing but
its equilibrium. If Mrs. Soriano could only have known
how far my head would once again contract, in near-
suicidal despair, when, as I had feared, I began to go prematurely bald at the age of twenty-two, she might have cut
me some slack.

My feeling of triumph, post-op, was short-lived. As is
common with nose jobs, the final results, not evident for
many months, were less perfect than the patient had hoped
for. It is simply impossible to predict, no matter how much
care the surgeon takes in shaping it, how a nose will eventually heal. You can control the body only so much. In my
case, it took about six months to realize that the tip of my

nose veered slightly to the left. The bridge of the nose, when viewed from the right, could have been smoother. That gruesome bump, hacked and pounded into submission, had apparently dug itself in rather deeply, and already seemed to be mounting a counterattack. I soon developed a new tic—always trying to position my body so that no one in my near vicinity could view me from the right, so that my right profile, my weak side, would be concealed. All that money, all that pain, and I was once again, only six months after my nose had healed, contorting myself to elude my face. It would be another eight years until I could build up the courage, and money, to take another crack at it. My mother refused to pay for it the second time. "Don't be silly," she said. "Your nose looks fine. If you want another one, you'll have to pay for it yourself." Which I did. And which I'll do again. If a third time was the charm for Michael Jackson, may he rest in peace, why can't it be the charm for me?

A ringing in my ears, and a mild feeling of dizziness, both roughly coinciding with the reemergence of the bump on the bridge of my nose, brought to mind a variety of possibilities, including delayed, residual trauma caused by the pummeling of my nasal bones, Ménière's disease, and tinnitus. From a report on Beethoven I had written many years earlier, I remembered that he had heard a buzzing in his ears shortly before going deaf. There's a fine line between a buzzing and a ringing, so the hypothetical causes of Beethoven's deafness, ranging from lead poisoning to syphilis, were also brought into the mix of possibilities, syphilis alone being ruled out definitively on the grounds of my virginity. When I told my mother my symptoms, she had a different diagnosis: earwax. Dr. Schoenberg, the pediatrician who had been giving me periodic once-overs since I was five, agreed with her. After looking in my ears, cleaning out some wax, asking me to touch my fingertips to my nose as I walked in a straight line, one foot directly in front of the other, and then giving me a hearing test, Dr. Schoenberg, for not the first time in my life, was unimpressed.

"You're fine. When you hear that ringing noise in the future, just let it keep ringing. Eventually, they'll hang up. If they don't hang up, stop listening!"

The examination was over. He was about to send me home. This was my one and only chance.

"Dr. Schoenberg?"

"Yes?"

"I have a strange bulge in my scrotum."

He stared blankly at me for a moment. "Is that what this visit is really about?"

I didn't know the answer to that question then, and I don't know now. I do remember, during the second semester of my junior year of high school, hearing ringing in my ears, and feeling dizzy. That much is true. But I also remember that the bulge in my scrotum, which I had managed to shut out of my head for about a year, had become increasingly difficult, over the course of the previous two years, to fend off, and had finally managed to push itself up out of the recesses of my mind and into the surface of my consciousness, first the back of it, and then the middle, and then the forefront, where it lodged itself and refused to budge.

"Well," said Dr. Schoenberg, when I didn't answer, "let's take a look. I'm sure it's nothing."

I pulled down my pants. He reached down, grabbed hold of my scrotum, and gave it a good squeeze.

"Whoa!" he said.

"What? What is it?"

He squeezed again before responding. He was focusing intently, checking to make sure of something. Finally, Dr. Schoenberg relaxed his grip and let go. "You've got an inguinal hernia, my friend."

When I heard these seven words, the last two not registering very strongly, I was immediately certain of two things: (1) I was going to die, and (2) my father was going to be upset with me for not having brought the bulge in my scrotum, when it first appeared, three years earlier, to his attention.

As for my certainty that I would die, it was the word *inguinal* that put me over the edge. *Hernia* I knew. At least I thought I did. I associated it with the word *ulcer,* a relatively innocuous ailment, as I understood it, of the stomach. But *inguinal* completely threw me. A *hernia* might be innocuous, but what purpose could *inguinal* serve but to make it deadly? It was like the *non-Hodgkin's* part of *non-Hodgkin's lymphoma.* One too many words for comfort.

"My God!" said Dr. Schoenberg. "Your pulse is racing. Don't worry! You'll be fine!"

"What's an inguinal hernia?"

"It's harmless. The chicken pox is worse, and you made it through that okay, didn't you? So relax."

"What's an inguinal hernia?"

"An inguinal hernia is just a break in the wall of the abdomen and, in your case, a small piece of intestine poking through that opening into your scrotum."

"A piece of my intestine is in my scrotum? That doesn't sound harmless at all."

"Trust me. You're fine. A surgeon will push it back in no time."

"I need surgery?"

"The sooner the better. Definitely sometime in the next week. Because as long as it's not fixed, there's a small risk— Don't get excited! It's a very small risk—that the opening in the abdominal wall will close up tight, thereby cutting off the circulation to the piece of intestine that's poking through it. This causes what is known as strangulation, which is dangerous if you don't take care of it immediately. So don't go on any camping trips in the middle of the desert until it's fixed. Because if the opening closes up, and you're not within easy driving distance of a hospital when it happens, you could have problems. The longer you go with an unrepaired inguinal hernia, the higher the risk of strangulation. That's why it's good we caught this so soon! You've probably had it, I would guess, at worst, what, a few weeks or so, maybe a month? And now we got it!"

———

So here I am, a week later, lying in a cold bed, staring at the ceiling, thinking of my warm room back home, and my bed full of stuffed animals, and waiting for the redhead, with her pretty freckled arm, to finish shaving off my pubic hair with her dull razor and no cream. She finishes. The skin above my penis, red and chafed, burns. She hastily pulls the sheet up to my chin and disappears.

"There he is!" says a cheerful man with a bushy mustache. It's Dr. Proukosh. Eleven years later, in 1996, he will die of pancreatic cancer, but today he is the picture of strength. He pats me vigorously on the shoulder. "You're not worried, are you? This is nothing! Nothing! In about forty-five minutes, you'll be a new man."

The surgery is painless. A curtain separates me from the

action, so I see nothing, but I can feel Dr. Proukosh reaching in and roughly grabbing the bastard by the nape of his neck and dragging him outside my tent. He gives him a good kick in the ass, sending him sprawling into my gut, and slams the door in his face. Proukosh was right. In forty-five minutes of yanking and pulling and shifting and stitching, he has restored me to my proper manhood.

An hour after the surgery, in the recovery room, Proukosh drops by to see how I'm feeling, and to wish me the best of luck in what he assures me will be a long and fruitful life ahead, and to inform me, casually, that my enemy's departure might not be permanent.

"When you've had a hernia," he explains, "especially when you're young, the odds are greater than average—about ten to fifteen percent—that you'll get another. Not likely, but greater than average. No need to dwell on it. I'm sure you'll be fine. Just don't lift up any cars or buses on your own." And with that, he gave me a wave and left.

"Greater than average," he said, as high as a fifteen percent chance, I'll get another. And that was probably a lowball estimate to get my hopes up. The chances are probably higher, as high, possibly, as twenty-five percent, and maybe, if you've got an especially weak gut, as I probably do, as high as fifty percent. If you are bowlegged, and continually tack back and forth when you walk in an effort to mask the curvature in your tibias, as I do, thereby putting excessive strain on your groin muscles, the chances probably go up to seventy-five percent. I had a three in four chance, according to my calculations, of getting another hernia, thereby incurring the risk of strangulation, which, if not treated immediately, would cut off the flow of blood to my intestine and result in my death.

Dr. Proukosh my savior? How could I be so naïve? He was my doomsayer! Those casual words of his—"the odds are greater than average . . . you'll get another"—have haunted me for twenty-four years and counting. Not a single day in my life has gone by since he cursed me that I haven't worried about a piece of my intestine breaking down the door to my scrotum and once again setting up camp.

CHAPTER 2

Vertigo

T IS THE FALL OF 1985. A letter arrives in the mail from my Granny Shammy, my dad's eighty-six-year-old mother, who lives, all by herself, four feet, ten inches tall, in a fifth-floor walk-up in Bronxville, New York. Her real name is Shamiram. Maiden name: Mzrakjian. *Mzrak,* in Armenian, means "spear." When I tell you about Granny Shammy's trip to America, you'll understand why the spear in her name is gruesomely appropriate. Her journey started in 1899, the year of her birth, in Diyarbakir, a city in southeastern Turkey. Facing predatory Turks on their left, and predatory Kurds on their right, her family, in 1910, decided to move to Baghdad and then, in 1920, to escape to America. The trip to America, as she described it to me, with a big globe in her arms to jog her memory, slowly tracing the route she took with a shaky, deformed, arthritic finger, was arduous, wet, dangerous, and frightening, and seemingly impossible to survive without something horrible happening along the way:

> *On a beeg, beeg, beeg, beeg raft we sailed down Tigris River. Then we stopped in Bombay for three months. To make money to keep going. Then we went up the Red Sea to Alexandria. Again, stopped to make money. To keep going. Then we went across the Mediterranean to Marseille. Again, stopped to make money so we could keep going. And then to Calais. And then, after making money to keep going, in a beeg, beeg, beeg, beeg ship, we went chug, chug, chug, chug, chug [I'll never forget those adorable squeaky* chugs *for as long as I live] across the Atlantic Ocean.*

The spear? Not yet. The trip isn't over.

After chug-chug-chugging across the Atlantic Ocean, Shammy and family arrived at Ellis Island on February 16, 1921. A few months later, while she was taking a class on portrait painting at the Art Students League in New York City, an Armenian admirer, a boy in her class, upset that she had rebuffed his advances—"No thank you; I'm not interested"—tried to kill her! He stabbed her with a knife, narrowly missing her heart and spearing her shoulder instead. Every time Granny Shammy visited us in La Jolla, I would ask to see the big scar that ran from her shoulder down the side of her chest. Can you imagine? Your family uproots itself from its homeland, spending years escaping from those murderous Turks, and those murderous Kurds, and those murderous sharks in every port and sea along the way, finally arriving in the land of peace and freedom after sailing

halfway around the world, and what greets you on arrival?
A murderous Armenian!

Well, some good came of it, for my sake at least. A man
named Dicran Goulian (*Goul,* in Armenian, thank God,
means "rose") read about the stabbing in some local newspaper in New Jersey and recognized the last name of the
woman who was stabbed, Mzrakjian, as the name of a family he had known back in Diyarbakir. So he visited her in
the hospital to introduce himself, and the rest—including,
indirectly, Yours Truly—is history.

Grandpa Dicran, who, among other things, ran a small
dry-cleaning business, while my grandmother worked twelve
hours a day as a seamstress for rich people in northern New
Jersey, died in 1963, before I could meet him, but Granny
Shammy lived on and on and on, long enough to spend two
wonderful months a year with me in La Jolla, California,
and long enough to send me the letter I'm holding in my
hand.

Which I can't, which I'm too scared, to open. It's the first
letter—the very first letter!—she's ever sent me in my whole
life. What could be so important that she has to put it in a
letter? If the matter is urgent, she can call me. If the matter
is not urgent, she can wait to tell me face-to-face. I just saw
her in August, and I'll see her again in January, and she can
talk to me all she wants, because whenever she's visiting I
never leave her side. Her tiny body, her squeaky voice, those
shuffling, slippered feet you can barely see because that
shiny, colorful, exotic bathrobe she wears always rubs
against the floor, and those thousands of years of Armenian
wisdom impressed on her wrinkled cheeks are irresistible!
It's like having Yoda, or E.T., living in the guest bedroom.

Grannies do not get better than this! We play backgammon together. We sunbathe together. We hunt for pretty shells on the beach together. We cook all her Armenian treats from the old country (*lahmajun, dolma, kufta, borek, baklava*) together. The filo dough is never store-bought! She makes it from scratch, rolling every layer individually, and she lets me baste it with safflower oil instead of butter.

So why, out of nowhere, out of the deepest, darkest blue of Bronxville, New York, does Granny Shammy suddenly put pen to paper? Is she worried about something? Did my father happen to mention to her that, although I am a senior at La Jolla High School, and ostensibly preparing to apply to college, I am taking no math, no history, no foreign language, and—the straw that breaks my father's heart—no *science,* but, instead, a series of Mickey Mouse courses that require very little effort, an unmistakably clear sign, as my father sees it, to any decent four-year college, that I am not putting my best foot forward?

Or did my father say nothing at all? Perhaps Granny Shammy, despite her failing eyesight, could no longer fail to acknowledge the gradually mounting evidence, over the previous twelve months, that Grandson Number Three appeared to have hopped on a different ship from that of Grandsons Numbers One and Two, their ship heading for Ellis Island, and mine heading into an iceberg.

I refuse to open this letter. Granny Shammy is my one ally in life. She's my one safe harbor in a sea of stress and pain. To lose her support would be the end of me!

———

In late August 1981, two weeks after my thirteenth birthday, my two older brothers, whom I will continue to refer to as Oldest Brother and Middle Brother (less out of a concern for their privacy than out of the desire to not overdignify them by naming them, their achievements in life sufficiently dignifying), simultaneously abandoned me. My Oldest Brother, who had been a star soccer player at La Jolla High School, left home for Yale College, where, in addition to playing on the varsity soccer team, he would study philosophy. My Middle Brother, who had been a star science student at the Bishop's School (a rigorous private school in La Jolla), taking organic chemistry at UCSD at the age of fourteen, and skipping both eighth and eleventh grades, left home, at the age of sixteen, for Harvard College, where he would study theoretical physics. My Oldest Brother, in studying philosophy, was following in his grandfather's footsteps, and my Middle Brother, in studying science, was following in his father's footsteps. Goulian Sons

The author, age three, in a clown suit, with his two older brothers. On the left, in a devil's mask, is his Middle Brother; on the right, holding a skull, is his Oldest Brother.

Numbers One and Two, it was clear to all who cared to notice, were very good boys, models of discipline and purpose, and everyone in the family was very proud of them.

I, too, was proud of them, but also sad for their absence. Family dinners, always served at six o'clock on the dot, were no longer quite so convivial. In response to the question "So what did you learn today?" it was no longer possible, when I couldn't come up with anything good, to shrug and deflect the answer to the others. What I, alone, learned that day, or didn't learn, became the subject of the next five years.

In June 1984, when I received my score on something called the Achievement Test in Math, it suddenly became clear, to all who cared to notice, that Goulian Son Number Three was not made from the same stock as that of Goulian Sons Numbers One and Two. Where their stock was thick and meaty and could easily serve a family of ten, mine was basically dishwater.

What is the Achievement Test in Math, you ask? For your ignorance I would give ten years of my life. As the eruption of Mount Vesuvius, in A.D. 79, was to the inhabitants of Pompeii, so was my performance on the Achievement Test in Math to the happiness, and cohesiveness, of the three remaining inhabitants of the Goulian household.

A brief primer: to get into college in America in the mid-1980s one had to take, along with the SATs, three Achievement Tests, one in math, one in English, and one in history or science or a foreign language. (They are now known as Subject Tests.) The purpose of all these tests, collectively known as the College Boards, was to provide colleges with a uniform basis for comparing applicants from thousands of high schools, ranging wildly in quality and competitiveness, from all over the country. The tests were scored from 200 to 800. Anything below a 700 and your chances of getting into Harvard or Yale dropped significantly.

In late May 1984, at the end of tenth grade, I was preparing to take the first of my five College Boards, the Achievement Test in Math. This was earlier than normal. Generally, one takes these exams in the second semester of eleventh grade, or in the first semester of one's senior year, so that one has had time to take the classes required to prepare for them. But in my case I was taking my first College Board at the end of my sophomore year, a year early, because in seventh grade I did so well in math that my teachers insisted I take classes a year ahead of most of my peers. "He's not being challenged enough," they said to my mother, and the matter was settled. No one consulted me. No one said to me: "Do you mind if we push you to the limits of your mathematical capacities? Or would you prefer, and there's no shame in admitting this, to relax a little bit, to coast through life in comfort, to be, in the end, an Average Person?"

Three and a half years later, the day before the Achievement Test in Math, I recorded a few thoughts in a journal of misery that I was hiding beneath my bed. There are times in life to be subtle, and there are other times in life, such as when the fear of not living up to your parents' expectations has given you a case of vertigo you can't shake, when you've got to come right out, for the sake of clearing your head, and say what's on your mind: "I hate to admit that my brothers' academic successes are finally beginning to pressure me," I wrote. "It seems that these pressures I speak of remain dormant for about nine months. Only to be rekindled at the end of May, as Harvard and Yale send their scholars home. It wasn't always this bad, but as my sophomore year comes to an end, the test-taking is just beginning." Three days later, checking back in with my journal, I wrote: "The Achievement Test has been over for twenty-six hours. A preoccupation of mine for many weeks is gone. The mental torture has been assuaged, and that's the last I'll speak of it."

Not so fast! The mental torture was soon reignited, when I received my test score in the mail. Where my brother had gotten an 800, a perfect score, on the "Level Two" Achievement Test in Math, the harder version, I had opted to take the "Level One," the easier version, and gotten a 650.

Was it unmanly of me to cry when I received that score in the mail? Absolutely. And not just crying. Bawling! Banging my fists against the pillow! All I can say in my defense is that I was not a man. I was a boy, caving in beneath the pressures of modern life, on the verge, as I put it quite explicitly in my journal, of a "nervous breakdown." "Maybe I can't handle this intense life," I wrote. "Maybe I'll just drop out of school and marry someone wealthy."

My mother, seeing the streaks of dried tears across my cheeks, looked on the brightest side possible and tried to help me see the light. The Achievement Test in Math, she explained, was only one of many factors that the colleges took into consideration when evaluating the strength of a candidate's application. At the end of my junior year, I would have many other chances to prove myself—on the two remaining Achievement Tests, in English and history;

and on the three or four or even five Advanced Placement tests that I would likely take; and, most important of all, on the SATs. By that time, the Achievement Test in Math would be a distant memory, easily explainable, and over-lookable, as an aberration, a case of sophomoric, pretest jit-ters. My grades, all A's since kindergarten except for a pair of shameful B's in fourth-year Spanish, were excellent. And my extracurricular life was superb. Like my Oldest Brother, who had been recruited to play soccer at Yale, I was a star athlete, a member of the varsity soccer team, the varsity cross-country team, and the junior varsity track team. What was the Achievement Test in Math when measured against all of that!

My mother's argument was a strong one in June 1984. Two months later, when I informed my parents, while at Andover summer school, that, for no reason at all, I would be quitting sports forever, the part of my mother's argument about my extracurricular life being "superb" was effec-tively obsolete.

Quitting soccer was not what my parents had expected from me when they suggested I attend Andover summer school for six weeks. The reason I was sent "back east" to Andover, just as my Oldest Brother, in the summer between his junior and senior years of high school, was sent "back east" to Harvard summer school, was to give my college application a sheen of East Coast respectability, and to help convince Ivy League schools that, although I grew up in what was essentially a theme park on the beach, with an art-house movie theater called the Cove, and streets with names like Sea Lane, Avenida de la Playa, and Whale Watch Way, and with a high school newspaper that was called *The*

High Tide, and with the only legally sanctioned nude beach in the country, I had the mental toughness to survive, academically, outside my element.

My parents, who had not been privy to the scribblings in my journals, had every reason to believe, when I called them from Andover to tell them that I was quitting soccer forever (preferring to tell them on the phone, while three thousand miles away, so that I wouldn't have to deal with their upset and bafflement in person), that the pressure to survive, academically, outside my element had, in fact, been too much for me, and that I had mentally disintegrated. What else could explain, to the rational observer, my sudden decision to quit soccer, after playing it superlatively well for ten straight years, just eighteen months before applying to college? We sent him "back east," and he went crazy!

DAD: You're *what*?

ME: I'm quitting soccer.

DAD: Why?

ME: I just don't feel like playing anymore.

DAD: But you play so well. And you've been playing so long.

ME: But I just don't feel like playing anymore.

DAD: I'm not sure I understand. This must be only part of the story.

ME: No, it's the whole story.

MOM: Is there something else going on? Is there some problem you're having with your team?

ME: Nothing else is going on.

DAD: Jon, this doesn't make much sense. You don't play soccer for ten years, and play it very well, and then give it up just like that with no explanation. Something else must be going on.

ME: I don't know what else to tell you. I'm giving it up just like that, and nothing else is going on.

MOM: But what will you now put on your college application? What will your extracurricular activities be?

ME: I don't know. I haven't thought that far ahead yet.

DAD: That far ahead? "That far ahead" is a year and a half from now. Jon, that's not far. It's around the corner. Why don't you give this decision a little more thought? There's no need to be rash when you don't have to be. Soccer season doesn't begin again until September.

ME: I'm not being rash. It's been on my mind for a few weeks.

DAD: A few *weeks*? A few weeks is not even a blink of an eye. Why not continue to mull this decision over, and see if it continues to make sense to you at the end of the summer?

ME: Dad, there's nothing to mull over. I've given it a lot of thought.

DAD: What is "a few weeks" when you've been playing soccer for ten years? I don't understand your logic.

ME: Fine! I'll keep mulling it over!

DAD: Jon, there's no need to get upset. All we want you to do is keep in mind that what makes sense to you today might not make sense to you two months from now. It might not make sense to you *two weeks* from now. In fact, it wouldn't surprise me if it stopped making sense to you tomorrow.

In fact, it continued to make sense to me tomorrow, and the tomorrow after that, and thirty tomorrows later, when

I returned to La Jolla and announced, to my friends, who were no less baffled than my parents, that I was hanging up my cleats and shin guards forever.

"You're *what*?" said my friend Skipper, who had been playing soccer with me since we were ten and who went on, a year later, to play for the U.S. national team against the Soviet Union. Two years later, as a freshman at UCLA, he was one of the leading scorers in the league, and he would definitely have gone on to play professionally in Europe had he not, as a sophomore at UCLA, been hit by a car while sitting on a motorcycle at an intersection in Los Angeles, the impact shattering his leg into many pieces and permanently ending his career.

"I'm quitting."

"Why?"

"I'm burnt out, I guess. I don't know. I need a break."

Skipper nodded but didn't fully understand. Nobody did. The inscriptions in my high school yearbook for the year 1983–84, inscriptions written by my friends shortly before I left for Andover, included this from Mark Ople (who went on to play soccer at Yale and is now an immigration lawyer in San Diego): "Varsity soccer next season is going to be great. With La Jolla's awesome defense, we'll be unstoppable"; this from Kevin Benson (who went on to major in physics at Harvard, and then get a Ph.D. in physics at Oxford, and is now working in finance in New York City): "I can't believe all your achievements—academic and athletic. Keep up the work. Sweat a lot. After Andover, I expect you to be a scholar"; this from Howard Greer: "You are good at sports, and you still get killer grades. Keep it up! Call me this summer and we'll party!"; this from Amy

McKnight (who is now living in Spokane, happily married, and with two sons): "Congratulations on track, soccer, and all your other achievements this year—keep it up!"; and this from my best friend in high school, Macky (who went on to become a winning contestant on the dating show *Studs,* in 1992, and is now a successful real estate broker in La Jolla): "You did killer in soccer this year, and you're a killer athlete. Have fun at Andover. Take it easy and stay barreled [a term used in surfing to describe the point at which you are riding, in a crouch, through the tunnel, or barrel, formed by the lip of the wave breaking over you. Used here, it is a general term that means, 'stay cool, stay chill, keep shredding']."

When I left for Andover, I was, to all appearances, well within the barrel, cruising in a crouch through everything life threw my way. "You motivate me to do the best I can in school," wrote Wendy Brazier in my yearbook a few weeks before I left for the East, "and I'll always appreciate your example." When I returned from Andover two months later, I had, to all appearances, wiped out. The example I now provided Wendy (who still lives in La Jolla, and is happily married, with two children, one of whom, as I write this, is about to graduate from La Jolla High School) was no longer *Always do the best you can in school; nothing ventured is nothing gained; shoot for the stars and you're bound to hit at least one of them,* but instead *If you can get away with taking an easy class, rather than a hard class, then take the easy one; if you are facing a hard exam for which you haven't studied, and it is still possible to convince the vice principal to let you drop that class and take a different one, then drop the class and take a different one;*

since the risk of failing rises in direct proportion to the degree to which you challenge yourself, by not challenging yourself, you reduce the risk of failing. Or, in sum, loosely borrowing a phrase from Bartleby the Scrivener: *If you prefer not to do it, then don't.*

The author, age sixteen, a few months after returning from Andover.

The first thing I preferred not to do was to continue living up to the limits of my mathematical capacities, as I had been doing against my will since seventh grade. In my tenth-grade yearbook, Jennifer Segal, a year older than I was, wrote: "Good luck at Andover. . . . I'll see you next year when you're in Calculus and I'm in dumb shit math!" By "dumb shit math" she was referring to a course called *Pre*calculus, a remedial class designed for the mathematically uninclined (or, as we referred to it less indirectly back then, the mathematically retarded). When, at the beginning of my junior year, Jennifer Segal walked into "dumb shit math," she was bewildered to find that a seat had been saved for her. By me. It would be the last math class I would ever take *in all my life.*

Having tasted the fruit of not challenging myself, and finding it delicious, I continued nibbling. Instead of taking Advanced Placement Chemistry, the hardest chemistry course offered at La Jolla High School, which my Middle Brother had taken when he was thirteen or fourteen, I decided, at the risk of bringing shame upon my family, and with the juices from that first bite of Precalculus still running down my chin, to take only the second hardest chemistry course offered at La Jolla High School, the name of which, twenty-four years later, still makes me sweat with guilt. There are many ways in life to break a father's heart. You can get caught making out with, and fondling the breasts of, your thirteen-year-old second cousin, as my friend Jonah did; or you can get caught smoking pot on the morning of your Bar Mitzvah, as my friend Jacob did; or you can get caught shoplifting two six-packs of Coors beer, and four bags of Cheetos, as my friend Simon did; or you can get caught being on a surfing trip in Baja California and not, as you told your parents, at the "Model UN championships in New York City," as my friend Brent did. Or, in my case, you can get caught—and though I didn't have the courage to say "I'm sorry" at the time, I'm man enough to say it right now: Dad, I'm sorry! I'm sorry! I'm sorry!—not taking Advanced Placement Chemistry, as you should have been, since you grew up eating your meals on a place mat with a picture of the periodic table on it, but only *Advanced* Chemistry or, as it was informally known among the more ambitious students at La Jolla High School, many of them the children of doctors and scientists at UCSD—Chemistry for People Who Speak English as a Second Language.

The knife was plunged yet deeper into the family's back when a curt letter from the principal soon arrived in the family mailbox. Two notes were enclosed in this letter, the first from my chemistry teacher, informing the principal that I hadn't done any homework for six weeks, had gotten C's on a number of pop quizzes, and was barely pulling a B-minus, and the second from my "choral ensemble" teacher, saying that I had missed seventeen straight classes and therefore was currently getting an F. When these notes arrived, I was on the second floor of our house, in my bedroom. I had never heard, and have never heard since, my father yell so loudly. In fact, it was the first of only two times in my entire life that he has yelled at me, the second occurring about two months later, when, at forty-five miles an hour, I accidentally crashed my parents' 1976 Buick station wagon into the rear end of a car that was waiting to make a left turn on Nautilus Street, totaling the front third of the Buick, and the rear half of the car in front of me, after which I drove home and parked the car in our driveway as if nothing had happened, hoping that, by the time my parents noticed it, they would have forgotten I had driven it.

When the letter arrived from the principal—his name was Principal Tarvin, and he was generally a very nice man; sandbagging me, as he did with this letter, was unlike him— my father was downstairs in the kitchen, and I was between fifty and seventy-five feet away from him. And yet it was as if his mouth was pressed against my ear. The force with which he screamed my name, twice, stretching each

Jonathan out to three big and booming syllables, seemed to disturb the very foundation of the house:

"Jon . . . a . . . than!!! Jon . . . a . . . than!!!"

I stood at the top of the stairs and looked down at him. It was at this moment that the meaning of the term *livid,* which my mother always liked to use when someone's irresponsibility had caused her an inconvenience—"This makes me just *livid.* I paid this bill weeks ago, and they still have no record of it"—finally penetrated. As I watched my father smack his Birkenstocked foot four times on the tiled floor at the base of the stairs, I now understood that the word *livid* served its own purpose, that it was different from just *angry* or *annoyed* or even *furious,* that my mother had been using it incorrectly all these years.

Slacking off in chemistry was not nearly as disturbing to my parents as my skipping "choral ensemble." By taking only Advanced Chemistry, I had prepared my parents for the possibility that my achievement in the sciences might be less than they could hope for. They felt, they *insisted,* that I could do better, that if I did my homework in chemistry I could bring my grade up to an A, as the teacher said I could, and, with head hung low, I promised to try harder.

But skipping "choral ensemble," which I had elected, eagerly, to take, and which required nothing more, to get an A, than showing up, singing in key, and showing some enthusiasm, made no sense. With head hung low, I promised to try harder, but why not try hard to begin with, my parents wondered, unless, in a fit of masochism, I was out to destroy myself? Not only did I have a very good singing voice, with a wide range, from bass to high tenor, and even a decent falsetto, but I clearly *enjoyed* singing. I was always doing it, in the shower, while doing my chores, while setting the table for dinner. My eleventh-grade history teacher, Mrs. Soriano, when asked, on my college recommendation form, "What has been the candidate's most valuable contribution to your class?" responded, in part, that "he is quite a singer, and always entertains us with show tunes." By "show tunes" she was referring, primarily, to one show tune in particular, "If I Only Had a Heart." The song had been committed, to my heart and memory, since the age of eleven, when I played the Tin Man in my sixth-grade class's production of *The Wizard of Oz,* a production that, because of affirmative action, was lacking in one crucial respect. For the sake of ethnic diversity, a Chinese girl named Lydia Chen was chosen for the role of Dorothy, even though Michelle Berman, the first girl I ever kissed (on the cheek, at the age of ten), was a much better singer and actor than she was. Take a quick look, if you would, at the following photo:

Lydia is there in the rear, on the right. Crooning, in the foreground, is Yours Truly, wearing a silver Danskin leotard so that none of my skin would show through the joints of my costume. To Lydia's right are Seth Rosen, as Toto; and Staci Cerrudo, as the Scarecrow. Teddy Janowsky, the Lion, is not visible. If Michelle, and not Lydia, had been chosen, four of the five leads (Seth, Teddy, Michelle, and I) would have been Jews. Instead, thanks to affirmative action at Torrey Pines Elementary School in 1979, we had a Chinese Dorothy who often forgot her lines and said things like "Oh no! He's gone! He's melting away!" when the Wizard flew away in his balloon at the end of the musical, which, if you've seen it, you know is not the case at all; the Wizard remains intact in his balloon and does not melt in the least; it is the Wicked Witch of the West who melts away, much earlier in the production, when Dorothy douses her with water.

In February 1985, three months before the SATs, my father, keeping one eye on my efforts at self-destruction and trying to cut them off at the pass, suggested, in order to get my reading comprehension muscles into better shape, that I start to read more rigorously in the months leading up to the test, and toward that end he placed copies of *The New Yorker, The New Republic,* and *The New Leader* on my desk. I told him I would consider reading them. With no indication that I was putting this thought into action, he bought me a copy of *Word Power Made Easy,* and suggested that we study vocabulary words together each week. I told him that that would not be necessary, since my vocabulary was "in good shape." At this point, rather early in the race, he gave up and passed the baton to my mother.

When my brothers and I were babies, and continuing

until we were two or three, my parents had a special agreement concerning bodily related crises. Every other week my mom and dad would take turns, one of them taking care of vomit-related crises, the other taking care of feces-related crises. Obviously, there were far fewer vomit-related crises than feces-related crises, so this agreement was just another way of saying, "Let's take turns taking care of feces."

My mother, in agreeing to relieve my father of the burden of having to oversee my admission to a respectable college, got stuck with far more shit than she bargained for. She signs me up for a Kaplan SAT course, at considerable cost, and I refuse to do the homework. She signs me up for another one, and I refuse to go. "Enough is enough," she says, and I stare blankly out the window. My poor mom! Here she is trying to potty-train me, and I'm throwing my shit in her face.

So she sat me down, on the L-shaped couch in the family room, to have a "serious talk" with me, every word of which seems indisputable in retrospect, about the strong correlation between the quality of the college one attends and the chances of getting ahead in life; about the silliness of permanently jeopardizing one's future because of a momentary bout of stubbornness; about the unpleasantness of the task she has willingly assumed, to oversee my admission to a respectable college; about her moral obligation, as a responsible mother, to not let her youngest son destroy his life; and about the importance, given all of the above, not only of studying as hard as I could for my College Boards but also of taking them, *all five of them,* before the end of my junior year, so that I could apply, in late October, to the college of my choice under what was known as the early decision policy.

By the time she finished speaking, I had shifted my body, very gradually, in subtle increments of two to three inches, to the point farthest removed from her on the L-shaped couch, so that, with my mother on the top of the L, I was essentially catty-corner from her. With arms folded, head bowed, staring blankly at her, I said, "Okay. Is our talk over now?"

"Okay? That's it?"

"I don't know what else to say. My vocabulary's in good shape. So there's no need to study."

A month later, when the SATs were over, I sought out, for consolation, a group of stoners, surfers, and burnouts who had congregated in a corner of the parking lot outside the center where the test had been taken. They were eating carne asada burritos, sipping Slurpees, and commiserating with one another about how "fuckin' neckin' " the test had been, especially the verbal section of the SAT.* "At least we knew *stymie*," said Mark McReynolds. "Yeah," said Greg Brouse, laughing, "at least we knew *stymie*." Apparently, Mark and Greg, in the hour before the test had begun, had studied a few vocabulary words at the back of the Barron's guide to the SAT, and *stymie* had been one of them. And then, as luck would have it, *stymie* was on the test.

The rest of us, including me, had been stymied by *stymie*,

---

* *Neckin'*, which had two slightly different meanings (when referring to one's parents, it meant "bitchy, naggy, absurdly strict"; when referring to an exam, it meant "difficult, painful, impossible to complete"), was one of the seven Most Popular Sayings at La Jolla High School in the year 1983–84, as determined by a poll of the students. The results of the poll, considered notable enough to publish in the yearbook, also included *killer!, and . . . like . . . , what's up?, no problem, no way,* and *err!*

as we had been stymied by many other words before and after it. It's been twenty-four years since I took that test, and that one word—*stymie*—has never left me. It's the only word I've ever remembered from any test I've ever taken.

A week later, when it came time to take my two remaining Achievement Tests, I had not come close to recovering what little strength of purpose I had to begin with. My morale had taken a deadly hit. The knowledge that Greg Brouse and Mark McReynolds had gotten a word right on the verbal section of the SATs that I had gotten wrong, had surmounted *stymie* while I had been stymied by it, was a mortal wound to my confidence. After slogging my way through the Achievement Test in English, I had nothing left to give. As the rest of the battalion kept marching in step toward the front, I collapsed at the rear. Instead of answering the questions on the Achievement Test in History, I drew cartoons on the answer sheets, and then canceled my score immediately afterward to avoid getting a zero. I would now have to take the test again in the fall. What this meant, I knew from my mother's discussion on the L-shaped couch, was that my application to the college of my choice, under the early decision policy, would be jeopardized, it now being impossible for the college to which I would be applying to make a fully informed assessment of my qualifications.

When I returned home, and parked my parents' white Volkswagen diesel Rabbit (impossible to confuse with the Buick, which was three times as long, and got one-fourth the gas mileage) in the driveway, and strolled inside the house, my mom, who was washing dishes at the kitchen sink, said, "How'd it go?" and I said, "It went great! I think

I did just fine on the English test, and I ate both granola bars you gave me, and I think I canceled my score on the history test."

When I think back to my mother's reaction to this news, I am reminded of a description I once read of John Ruskin's reaction to the news, brought by messenger, and read aloud by a servant, that his favorite nephew had drowned at sea. Loosely paraphrasing from memory, it went something like this: "As the message was read aloud, Ruskin, as if suddenly turned to stone, froze where he stood on the living room carpet. Not a muscle twitched. Not a lip trembled. His eyes, wide open, saw nothing. Finally, the servant stopped speaking and left the room, but Ruskin, still frozen, remained exactly where he stood, perfectly impassive and immobile, like a statue. He remained that way, in some part of his heart, forever after."

As the water kept running out of the kitchen faucet, my mom, just like Ruskin, seemed turned to stone. Not a muscle twitched. Not a lip trembled. Her eyes, wide open, saw nothing.

When, a few weeks later, my scores on the four College Boards that I did manage to take arrived in the mail—including a 580 on the verbal section of the SAT; a 570 on the Achievement Test in English, and a 2 out of 5 (a failing score) on the Advanced Placement test in American History—my father, like Ruskin, and like my mother, whose face, as livid as the whitest marble, had yet to soften at the news that all of my College Boards would not be taken by the end of my junior year, was turned to stone. Their eyes, wide open, saw a man bearing a striking resemblance to their son in ten years, with a mop in his hand, and an empty bottle of Wolfschmidt vodka in his back pocket, cleaning up bathrooms for a living at Penn Station.

———

So here I am, in the fall semester of my senior year, taking no science, no math, no history or foreign language. I am, to all appearances, not putting my best foot forward. Two months ago, my two older brothers, the best foot on each one of them so far forward that you would need a good pair of binoculars to see it, entered graduate school. My Oldest Brother, the one who went to Yale, entered Harvard Law School. My Middle Brother, the one who skipped two grades and entered Harvard College at the age of sixteen to study theoretical physics, entered, at the age of twenty, Harvard graduate school in physics, where he will continue to theorize, in ways that he is unable to make intelligible to his family, about the possibility that the universe is made up of strings. Between their undergraduate and graduate educations, my brothers, by my count, have three Harvards and one Yale between them. Put another way: My two older brothers, before I have had a chance to even *apply* to college, have done as well as you possibly can in the American educational system. And they have done it *simultaneously*.

And here, in my hand, out of the deepest, darkest blue of Bronxville, New York, is a letter from my Granny Shammy, the first letter she's ever sent me in her whole life.

Can you blame me for being suspicious and not wanting to open it? Why now, why a formal letter, when she could just as easily pick up a phone and call or, even better, wait to see me in January and speak to me in person? You always tell me, Granny Shammy, "Do not waste money, sweetie pie," and "Never waste paper," and here you are wasting money on a stamp, and two pieces of paper, one for the envelope and one for the letter itself.

Finally, after holding it up to the light repeatedly, trying to get a sneak peek at the contents, I open the letter. Here are the first four lines, the lines that cut a hole in my heart, exactly as she wrote them, the ellipses, the misspellings, the grammar, all her own:

Dear Jonathan Matthew

Hi my youngest Grandson. How are you. are you working very hard. to make your Grade. So you can go eny where you wount to. . . . As your brothers. . . . I am proud of them. . . .

And the reader thought I was being paranoid. Spare us the melodrama, you thought to yourself. Enough with this holding the letter up to the light, mumbling to yourself, "*Et tu,* Granny Shammy? *Et tu!*" when all she was doing, you thought, was sending me a nice little check for my piggy bank. Ha! Now you'll trust me in the future when I tell you of my problems. My one safe harbor in a sea of stress and pain, and she deserts me. And you wonder why I have vertigo.

I take a breath. I calm down. I read the rest of the letter. And the hole in my heart is healed.

Here's the whole letter, exactly as she wrote it:

Dear Jonathan Matthew

Hi my youngest Grandson. How are you. are you working very hard. to make your Grade. So you can go eny where you wount to. . . . As your brothers. . . . I am proud of them. . . . I just send them a note <u>that</u>. that *they have to be very carfull of their diet too . . . they are on their own. and they have to be very carfull . . . to eat a lot of fruits and vegetables too . . . to stay healthy . . . when they get old like me. not to have Arterithis like me . . . that I can not get-rid of it . . . so I am sending you to put this [ten-dollar] check to put in your pigy bank . . . too so long dear one I miss you all . . . May God bless you and Guide you all the way. . . . . . .*

with all my love and prayer
with you all your Gramma
<u>*Shammy Goulian . . .*</u>

A ten-dollar check for my piggy bank! You were right! That was the real point of the letter. Why it couldn't have waited until she saw me in January I have no idea, but I'm very glad to have it.

The author, age seventeen, with his Granny Shammy.

CHAPTER 3

Boy Meets Girl

T IS EARLY JUNE 1986. Prom night. I am wearing white tights, black pumps, a black skirt, a red bow tie, and red lipstick. And a Viking hat, which I bought for ten bucks at a costume shop. It's basically a football helmet with two horns on the top, and a strip of rabbit fur that fastens beneath the chin. You can question my taste in tuxedos, but you can't question my school spirit. Our school colors, after all, are red and black. And our mascot is the Viking. Are you telling me that not a single Viking ever wore a skirt and pumps? Prove it. I happen to have it on good authority, from a scholar of medieval history at the University of Oslo, that Eric the Red had a split personality. After a night of slaughter and mayhem, he was known to repair, for some quiet time, to his boudoir, where, door locked, he would take off his chain mail, put on a G-string and some red lipstick, and become Erica the Red.

When my mother reads this book, there are four or five

passages that will cause her to experience what is known as angina pectoris, which the *American Heritage Dictionary* defines as a "severe paroxysmal pain in the chest associated with an insufficient supply of blood to the heart." One of those passages is the opening paragraph of this chapter, for it is here, for the first time in her life, that she will find out what I wore to my high school senior prom. On the day of the prom, you see, I left the house, wearing nothing but a bathing suit and flip-flops, at three in the afternoon, and told my mother I would be back home the following morning, by which time the "after-prom"—the takeover, by La Jolla High School students, of an entire Motel 6—would have terminated.

"But . . . I don't understand," said my mother. "Are you wearing a bathing suit to the prom?"

No, I explained, I was going swimming at the beach first, and then, time being tight, since the prom started at eight, I would be going straight from the beach to my friend Macky's house, where a group of ten of us, five boys, five girls, would be assembling for pre-prom snacks, such as pretzels, carrot sticks, and Coke, before the limo picked us up.

"But . . . how am I supposed to take a picture of my son with his prom date if he's not here?"

"Mom, don't worry! Macky's mother will take a picture of me. And I'll make sure you get one."

"But . . . I don't even know who your date is."

"Her name is Courtney Buffington. She's a very popular and beautiful girl."

"Is she your girlfriend?"

"No. Just a friend. She's a little Waspy for my taste. You need a magnifying glass to see her nose."

"Do you *have* a girlfriend?"

"At this particular moment? No."

"Have you *ever* had a girlfriend?"

"Mom, this is not the time for this. I gotta go! I'm late for the beach! I'll see you tomorrow! And don't wait up!"

So my mother, on the day of her baby boy's prom, saw nothing. Nothing but a boy with long hair, bleached yellow from the sun, wearing a bathing suit. My heart goes out to her as I write this. What kind of a monster doesn't let his mother take a picture of him with his prom date!

In the course of writing this book, I managed to get in touch with five people in my prom group, hoping to track down a picture of me that night, so that the reader can see for herself that some Vikings are more in touch with their feminine sides than others, and that not every single Viking in history—behind the plunder, the war cries, the eating of mutton without a fork or knife, and not even a napkin in his lap!—had a hairy chest. My efforts came to nothing. No one had a picture. Their memories of that night were enough for them. This is unfortunate for the reader, who could have used a picture, but very good for my mother, who is much better off without one. My description of Erica the Red might break her heart. But a picture of him would definitely kill her.

———

In early August 1984, as Andover summer school was drawing to a close, I found myself, on a warm afternoon, lying flat on my back, on a woman's bed, with hot wax being poured on my chest, and my nose two inches from the first fully unshaved armpit I had ever seen on a female body in all my life. And I mean *fully*. This was not peach fuzz.

This was not the armpit of a thirteen-year-old girl whose mother had not yet told her, "Honey, now that you've reached puberty, I think it's time we learned how to shave." This was the armpit, willful and dangerous, and smelling of at least two of the following four spices—cumin, basil, oregano, and chili powder—of a *woman,* dark and dense and mossy and wet and begging, at my peril, to be eaten. Not mincing words, it looked almost exactly like a vagina, a highly bohemian and Semitic vagina, circa 1973, before electrolysis, laser removal, and Brazilian waxes turned every girl in America into a mannequin.

The woman to whom this pit belonged was named Shoshanna. She was eighteen years old, about five feet, ten inches tall, with long, thick, dark hair, and bare feet. Always bare feet. Always a pair of Birkenstocks carried in one hand. Always a long skirt, or long dress, which you could rest assured said HECHO EN GUATEMALA somewhere on the inside of it, and—until that afternoon in her bedroom, when she put on a tank top, unveiling the pits—always a baggy, long-sleeve, tie-dye shirt that looked hideous. She was by far the oldest student at Andover that summer, and kept to herself. Most of the kids found her irritating. The humming to herself, the smiling, the peace signs, the gentle rocking of her body, while she walked across the quad, to some bootleg tape of a Grateful Dead concert that played constantly in her head. They couldn't stand it. The mutterings behind her back, always at least a few millimeters out of her hearing, just to be safe, were unremitting: "Why does she bother carrying her Birkenstocks if she's never gonna put them on?" "Why is she wearing a Mexican blanket on her back in eighty-five-degree weather?" "Why does she refuse to wear deodorant? I can smell that chick all the way from here." "Why does she have a button on her dress saying 'Make love, not war' if she hasn't fucked a single person this summer?" And, the most commonly asked question: "Why is that chick so old? What is she doing here?"

This was my only exposure to Shoshanna, occasional glimpses across the quad, and mutterings here and there, until that warm afternoon in early August, a few days before going back to La Jolla, when we met, by chance, in the infirmary. I don't remember why either of us was there, but I do remember that neither of us had a very good excuse to be there, and that we were both pretending to be sick in order to get out of doing something onerous. Laughing at how pathetic we were, and wondering if there would ever come a time in our lives when we would no longer have to pretend to be sick in order to avoid doing things (I won't speak for Shoshanna, but the answer, from this end, is no), we were best friends within an hour. I imagine that at least one of us said to the other, as kids always say to each other when they get very close very quickly: "This is *so* weird! It's like we've known each other our *whole lives*. And we only met like an hour ago!"

In that first hour, in the infirmary, sick and writhing in pain on our respective beds, before we were discharged and headed back to her room, she explained that, because of a childhood devoted fanatically to ballet, she had fallen two years behind academically, and so would be only a junior, at a public high school in San Francisco, in the fall. Her plan was to graduate a semester or two early, the credits from Andover coming in handy here, and go to Mills College, the all-women's school in Oakland, and study midwifery.

When I asked her why she gave up ballet, she put her hands next to her head, in mock horror, and opened her mouth like that guy in Edvard Munch's *The Scream,* and then whispered, in a deliberately absurd tone of shock: "Because my butt . . . got . . . huuuuge."

When we got back to her dorm room, she put on a Joni Mitchell tape and, keeping her back to me, though letting me see the back of her bra, changed into a tank top. When she turned around, it was impossible for me not to fixate on the pits. When a woman has what appears to be a vagina growing under each arm, how does a sixteen-year-old boy not stare? She caught me gawking and smiled.

"My mom freaks out when I don't shave," she said. "It's hilarious. 'Mom, relax! It's natural! Why does it bother you so much?' 'It's not natural! It's disgusting!'"

"Your mom's wrong," I said. "Your pits aren't disgusting. You definitely pull it off." Which was true. Had Shoshanna been very short, or very blond, or wearing slacks and a blazer and high heels, I might have felt differently. But on a gypsy hippie earthy Amazonian, dark and mysterious and dangerous, hair, everywhere, seemed to have its place. She definitely pulled it off. Not every girl could. There were many girls, many women, in La Jolla, California, including my mother, whom I would not want to see with three vaginas.

"If I had as much hair as you do in your pits, I wouldn't have shaved my own," I told her. A few days earlier, not long after deciding, definitively, that I would be quitting soccer, I had shaved off my armpit hair, what few pathetic tendrils I had of it, for the first time in my life.

"Let me see!" said Shoshanna, excitedly, and forgetting instantly about her mother.

So I took off my shirt and raised my arms. Where there

had been wispy patches of hair a few days earlier, there were now abrasions, cuts, and scabs.

"Oh, my God!" she said, laughing. "What did you use? A kitchen knife?"

"I used the same razor I use for my face, but the blade was too wide, I guess. I was gonna shave my chest next, but I decided to wait till I got a different razor."

She was doubled over, giggling. I was blushing. She gave me a hug and a kiss on the cheek.

"You should have waxed it, silly!"

Wax? I had heard of Nair, which supposedly didn't work very well, sometimes causing painful irritation and ingrown hairs. And I had obviously heard of bleaching, with either peroxide or lemon juice, but that didn't work very well either. It didn't get rid of the hair, and it didn't conceal the roots. But wax, for some reason, was new to me.

"Can I wax off your chest hair?" she said, clearly excited by the prospect, and lightly pulling at the hairs on my chest as if to show how easy it would be. "*Please?* It will only hurt for like a second. I promise."

Why did she have wax? I asked. What on her body did she wax, that she had wax?

For the first time that afternoon, she blushed. "My 'stache," she said. "I'd let it grow, but my mom would crucify me. My pits are already too much for her."

Sure, I told her. Go ahead and wax my chest. If getting my chest waxed was even half as exciting for me as the waxing of it would clearly be for her, then it would definitely be worth it. My reasoning, unfortunately, turned out to be shaky. When she poured the hot wax on my chest, her dark and wet pit just two inches above my nose, it felt good. When the wax hardened, and she pulled it off, it felt like my skin was being torn off my body, precisely the same way it felt when I got a tattoo on the base of my trachea twelve years later. There is a scene in Haruki Murakami's *The Wind-Up Bird Chronicle* in which a Japanese soldier, on patrol in Outer Mongolia, is skinned alive by a group of Mongolian soldiers who are trying to force him to give up crucial information about the purpose of his mission. The scene was more traumatic for me than it might have been for other men, those other men in this world who have not had their chests waxed, or their tracheas tattooed, and I kept pleading with the man to come to his senses. "Talk to them, dammit! Tell them what they want to know! Loyalty to your comrades cannot be worth the amount of pain I know, firsthand, you are dealing with right now."

When Shoshanna, after laughing and patting my head like I was a little puppy—"You poor thing!" "So fragile!" "Awwww!"—asked me if she could now wax my legs, I said, "No . . . fucking . . . way!" And thank God for my resolve. The painful ingrown hairs, all over my chest, that resulted from that waxing took months to heal.

"You cannot wax my legs," I told her. "But you *can* keep me company when I get my ears pierced. I've been dying to get my ears pierced, but I'm too afraid to go by myself."

"Afraid of *what*?"

Blushing, I avoided her eyes. "The pain. The needle. The people staring at me. Everything." She gave me a hug and a kiss on the cheek, and the next day, at a jewelry store in Andover, with Shoshanna, as a joke, literally holding my hand, I got a gold stud injected into each earlobe and spent the rest of the day, every ten minutes, dousing my ears with alcohol. "You look beautiful," she said, every time she caught me looking at my reflection. And gave me a hug and a kiss on the cheek.

Shoshanna and I spent as much time as we could together during the one day of summer we had left, but we never went any further than *a hug and a kiss on the cheek*. Whenever I was lying next to her on her bed, I had to force myself, painfully, to suppress my erection, in the same way that you'd have to suppress an erection if a hot doctor was giving you a physical. I wasn't convinced that Shoshanna wanted me sexually. There was something faintly patronizing about the way she interacted with me, like a protective older sister—the patting of my head, for example—that made her seem off-limits. Also, I felt it would have somehow compromised the trust we had placed in each other, the openness with which we had talked about our bodies, to show that I was turned on by her. I had never been this open about my insecurities with another person. Though I did not tell her about my third testicle, which I felt no woman on this planet wanted to hear about, I did tell her how embarrassed I was about my bowlegs, and about how anxious I was, whenever I was playing in a soccer game, that all the people on the sidelines were staring at them.

"Your legs are adorable!" she said. "You're overreacting." Of course she would say that. What else could she say to make me feel better? What she did not say, I noted, as I had said to her concerning the hair in her pits, was that I could "pull it off." Bowlegs you don't "pull off." Bowlegs are ugly no matter what you look like.

In the final hour we spent together, as I watched her pack up her things, I finally said to her, "By the way, is your butt really that big? For two days I've been looking at it, and it looks normal to me."

Without so much as a pause, she turned around and lifted up her skirt.

"It's big, but it's nice," I said. "You definitely pull it off."

She turned around with a big smile on her face, and gave me a hug and a kiss on the cheek.

"Just so you know," she said, "I don't pull up my skirt for just anybody. But you seemed like a safe bet."

I nodded and smiled, assuring her that of course I was a safe bet, and crossed my legs to conceal my burning erection.

"Bye, sweetie," she said. "I gotta go."

We hugged, and kissed each other on the cheek, and said we would definitely keep in touch, and, as was true with most of my other friends at Andover that summer, we didn't keep in touch. Life back home takes over in no time, and before long the summer is a distant memory.

Ten hours later, I was back in La Jolla, applying alcohol every ten minutes to my earlobes, and hiding from my parents in my bedroom. When I think back to my mother's reaction, when I returned from Andover summer school, where I had been sent, at considerable cost, for some East Coast enlightenment, looking much less boyish than I had when I had left for Andover six weeks earlier, I am reminded of the final ten minutes of *Rosemary's Baby,* when it has finally dawned on Mia Farrow that it might have been the Devil, and not John Cassavetes, who impregnated her. At that point in the movie, Mia's complexion has already turned a very sickly white, thanks to the special baby devil food that Ruth Gordon has been feeding her, but when she learns that she is about to give birth to the Devil's child, Mia's complexion gets even *whiter*. It is *that* shade of whiteness, the second shade, the whitest shade of white possible, whiter even than *livid,* that my mother's complexion turned when she saw me with my ears pierced, my eyebrows plucked, my chest waxed, my underarms shaved, and wearing a touch of lip gloss that Shoshanna had given to me as a parting gift. And just as Mia Farrow, had she become aware, during either of the first two trimesters, that she was about to give birth to the Devil's child, would have tried to get an abortion (which would have been impossible, since her obstetrician, like her husband, was in league with the Devil), so would my mother, had she known, when carrying me inside of her, during the winter through summer of 1968, what kind of a monster I would turn into sixteen years later, have, understandably, tried to abort me. And there is not a single mother, Catholic or otherwise, in the whole world, who would have blamed her. For Catholics, it is only the killing of embryonic *human beings* that is a problem. The killing of embryonic devils is warmly encouraged.

That first night home, after dinner, after *MacNeil/ Lehrer* was over and the dishes had been cleared, my mother, staying as restrained as possible, and affecting a tone of the most casual curiosity, as if she were asking about the height of the tide that day at La Jolla Shores Beach, asked my father what he thought of my earrings.

"Earrings?" he said. "What earrings?" From across the dinner table, through his bifocals, my earrings looked like specks of dust.

"Look at your son," said my mom. So he looked.

"Oh!" he said. And then he turned back to my mother. "What did you ask me?"

"What do you think of them? Would you like some yourself? I'm sure Jonathan could tell you where you could get your ears pierced."

"Well," said my dad, giving it some thought. "I won't need my ears pierced this evening. And I will not need them pierced at any point tomorrow. And probably not next week. But I will keep giving the matter thought, and get back to you both."

Now, you may be asking yourself: Did Mrs. Goulian really get flustered because her son had an earring in each ear, and a tiny bit of lip gloss on the lips, and overly groomed eyebrows, and no hair on his chest or underarms, where, if memory served, there had been hair before? Was this all it took, in 1984, in La Jolla, California, to get under a mom's skin? Answer: Yes.

But don't be so quick to make fun of her. After all, it was enough to get under *everyone's* skin. Let's put this in perspective. In 1984, in La Jolla, as was true in most places in this country, a huge amount of significance was attached to *which ear* an earring appeared in. If it was in the *left* ear, that meant you had a liberal conscience, and that you wanted people to know it. It was essentially like having a bumper sticker on the back of your VW bus that said, NO NUKES. It was a gesture. Nothing more. So no one took it seriously.

An earring in the *right* ear, on the other hand, meant that you were gay, and that you wanted people to know it. That, people took more seriously. An earring in the right ear could get a bag of Tater Tots thrown at your head, which I saw happen to a gay kid at La Jolla High School. In La Jolla, Tater Tots. Other places, bats and bullets.

Earrings in both the right ear *and* the left ear were unclear. They meant that you were (a) gay; or (b) that you were *not only* gay *but also* a budding transvestite; or (c) that you were *not* gay but *only* a budding transvestite; or (d) that you were *not* gay, and *not* a budding transvestite, but just weird and confused and in need of some sort of psychological counseling.

When my mother set eyes on me, the same thought ran through her mind as would have run through the mind of any middle-class Jewish woman who grew up in Park Slope, Brooklyn, in the 1940s and '50s—"Oh, my God! I don't understand! Is he a or b or c or d? Or all of the above? This is not a fair test! I don't understand the question!" When I went to Andover, on her bill, in order to give my college application a gloss of respectability, so that the admissions committees at Ivy League colleges would be fooled into believing that I had not grown up on Fantasy Island, what I spent my summer doing instead, without realizing it, was designing a multiple-choice question from hell for my mother. It was a question in which every single answer seemed plausible. And for the next twenty-four years, as if she had died and gone to Hell and was forced to take a horribly difficult test for the rest of her life, she would be forced to answer that *one question*: What *is* he?

Fortunately for my mother, she had many other things in life, more important than my appearance, to worry about. Unlike Shoshanna's mother, who did not work, and therefore had lots of time on her hands with which to obsess about Shoshanna's fall from grace, my mother was a busy lawyer, with many difficult cases to deal with, and, like my father, she worked up to fourteen hours a day. And my parents had an active social life, going to plays or concerts or dinner parties every weekend, which further helped to distract them from Jonathan's new fixation on his reflection, and from his fixation on altering that reflection, and from the electronic music (primarily men singing like women) that was constantly seeping under the door of his bedroom. So that *one question*—What *is* he?—was not constantly ringing in her head.

A more important question concerning her youngest son—namely, *Why is he sabotaging his promising academic career by taking easy classes, skipping classes, and not doing his homework?*—took all the maternal energy she had to spare. When you are faced with two serious dangers, both in need of your intervention but only one of which you have time for, you have to choose one over the other. The word for this, from the French word *trier,* meaning "to sort," is *triage.* When a physician is on duty in an emergency room, for example, and two patients are wheeled in, one of them with a tropical skin disorder—exotic, puzzling, and troubling, but not apparently life-threatening—and the other with *necrotizing fasciitis,* a bacterial invasion that will literally devour all the patient's flesh within days, turning him into a gray, oozing, foul-smelling corpse, you focus on the patient with the *necrotizing fasciitis.**

For my mother, who had taken upon herself the obliga-

* I have Atul Gawande's wonderful collection of essays *Complications: Notes from the Life of a Young Surgeon* to thank for bringing me up to speed on the horrors of *necrotizing fasciitis,* as well as the horrors of dozens of other diseases and ailments about which I had previously been ignorant.

tion of overseeing my admission to a respectable college, my sudden lack of interest in my academic future, just like *necrotizing fasciitis*, was a threat to my well-being that had to be cut off at the pass, or else. Jonathan dressing like a girl, in halter tops and stirrup pants from Wet Seal, and a pair of furry Ugg boots rising halfway to his knees, as exotic, puzzling, and troubling as it was, would have to wait its turn.

Meanwhile, there were occasional glimmers of hope that Jonathan's flirtation with androgyny was not as serious as it had initially seemed. Since I had pulled the starter studs out of my ears prematurely, without first letting the holes properly heal, out of my impatience to replace those studs with earrings that were snazzier and more exotic, the holes in my earlobes got infected. So I had to remove the earrings and let my ears heal before getting them repierced. This pattern—premature removal of studs, followed by infection of earlobes, followed by not wearing any earrings for a few months—was repeated several times during the two years before I left for college. And during these occasional two- or three-month-long interregnums of relative masculinity, my mother was encouraged to believe that, perhaps, I had outgrown this fascination with androgyny and moved on.

Furthermore, it was never entirely clear to my parents to what extent my clothing, and my zoned-out behavior in general, was simply a routine part of what they perceived, from afar, having nothing to do with it themselves, as *beach culture*. My parents never went to the beach. In the sixteen and a half years I spent as a child in La Jolla, my parents spent a total of zero minutes in the ocean. They had left Chicago, in 1970, for La Jolla, California, not because they were dying to go boogie boarding, but because my dad got a good position on the faculty of UCSD Medical School, which happened to be located in a beachside resort.

So, as we see, it was not difficult for my parents to put my mysterious physical transformation out of their minds, and to focus their attention on their own lives, and on making sure that I sent my application to Columbia College, where I was applying for early decision, before the deadline lapsed.

Early in the second semester of my senior year, however, with my admission to Columbia having been secured (more on this incredible occurrence in the next chapter), my mother's maternal energies were freed up to address that exotic disease with which I had returned from Andover summer school a year and a half earlier and which, based on a rational comparison of my appearance with the appearances of the male children of all her friends, had become increasingly impossible to excuse as a routine part of La Jolla beach culture. In eight months, when I would be heading off to New York City, my mother's youngest cub would be leaving the den forever, and so this seemed as good a time as any to find out, as he made his way through the wilds of life, what sorts of bears, whether female or male, he would be copulating with. To get as much information as she could about the nature of his copulatory future, she called, for help, a man named Mr. Carey, a teacher at La Jolla High School who, she had good reason to believe, might know what was going on inside his head.

When I arrived at La Jolla High School in the fall of 1983, as a sophomore, it was common knowledge that one should try as hard as possible to avoid taking a course with the notoriously cranky, obese, tyrannical, and delusional

Mr. Carey, otherwise known, far behind his back, as Jabba the Hutt, the giant, menacing, toadlike character in *Return of the Jedi*. After teaching at La Jolla High School for twenty-five years, Mr. Carey had apparently come to view his position on the faculty, with good reason, as impregnably secure, and from this position of security he supposedly tormented his students as much as possible. His temper, so we had all been warned, was entirely irrational and unpredictable, usually ignited by provocations that he had invented, and the force of his voice, when he chose to use it at full strength, could send shock waves through your body and lift you out of your chair. So we had all been warned. And that was all I needed to hear. When I signed up for classes in tenth grade, I took every precaution to make sure that Mr. Carey would have no place in my life.

A month into the first semester, my English teacher, Mrs. Morrison, became violently ill and had to take a leave of absence. To fill the vacancy she had left behind her, in waddled Mr. Carey. Grinning viciously from his perch at the head of the classroom, the first thing he said to us, in that rumbling, grumbling, monstrously resonant voice of his, was this: "I am sorry to inform you all that you've been the victims of what is known as a bait and switch. Mrs. Morrison was the bait. The fish was hooked. I am the switch. Ha!"

Two and a half years later, by the second semester of my senior year, I had not only gone out of my way to take as many classes with Mr. Carey as possible—four of them in all, three English classes and a course he invented, called Exploration in Arts—but had also gone out of my way to spend as much time with him as possible *after the school day had ended,* either by working on the school literary magazine, *The Devil's Wine,* of which Mr. Carey was the adviser, or by hanging out with him in the announcer's booth of the high school stadium, when, solely to hear the sound of his own voice booming over the loudspeaker, he would spend an afternoon of his time calling plays during football games. I even went to his house on a number of occasions, an hour's drive east in a dusty town called El Cajon, to go over final galleys of *The Devil's Wine* before it went to the printer. My friends were of course bewildered. "Why do you spend so much time with that freak?" they kept asking me. "The dude's disgusting."

He was only a disgusting freak if you did not appreciate, as I did, that behind the fantastic edifice of pathologies he had erected for himself was the fear that his life had amounted to nothing. What else could explain his famously ridiculous fantasy life, the stories of his achievements and triumphs that he had been sharing with his students for twenty-five years, but that no one but he took seriously? The lesson of "The Secret Life of Walter Mitty," which I'm sure Mr. Carey had read, was simple: When your life is disappointing, make up a new one. When life gives you lemons, why make lemonade when you can make vodka? What Mr. Carey did not choose to emulate, however, when he looked to Walter Mitty for inspiration, was the "secret" part. For where Walter Mitty kept his fantasies within the confines of his own head, Mr. Carey unleashed his fantasies on the public. And where Walter Mitty concealed his interior fantasy life behind a mask of diffidence, and ineffectuality, Mr. Carey, by means of his ferocious temper and tremendous girth, seemed to go out of his way to try to force you to take his fantasies seriously. The message was clear: "If you so much as doubt my stories, I will squash you."

The threat of being squashed notwithstanding, it was hard not to doubt. It was very difficult to imagine Mr. Carey fitting into a wet suit, which would have been essential during his "four or five years" working as a "professional scuba diver," mapping out "subterranean coasts for the military," or fitting into a tuxedo during the "two or three years" he spent working as an "escort to socialites and models in New York City." Equally difficult to believe was that he had been a "perfume tester in France" for a "number of years"; that he had read "two books a day since the age of sixteen"; that he had read his "first full-length novel" when he was three years old; that he had two Ph.D.s, one in anthropology, the other in either physics or history, depending on which year he told the story; that he had been "a drummer in a jazz band"; that he had been an "amateur astronomer"; that he had worked as a "magician at Coney Island"; that he had successfully patented "numerous items"; that his father had "invented the credit card," for which Mr. Carey was still receiving royalties; and that he had "brawled" his way "around the world for years," for the most part unsuccessfully, having been "kicked to the curb in Rhodesia," "spat on in Syria," and "left for dead in just about every single country in Europe and Asia." And this is hardly an exhaustive list.

Mr. Black, the journalism teacher at La Jolla High School, had feuded with Mr. Carey many years earlier, over something no one could remember, and he had hated Mr. Carey ever since. To spite Mr. Carey, and for his private entertainment, Mr. Black asked his students to keep track of Mr. Carey's claims, and to report them back to Mr. Black, who kept a record of them, going back many years, on a large index card that he kept in a special drawer in his desk, with a running calculation of how old Mr. Carey would have to be in order to have accomplished everything he claimed to have accomplished. According to Mr. Black's calculation: 285 years old.*

Just as Mr. Carey's temper, consistent with his reputation, was irrational and unpredictable, so was his capacity for looking the other way if he was confronted with behavior for which he had a right to get angry. When I was a sophomore, for example, not long after Mr. Carey first made an appearance in my life, four seniors, in the middle of the night, distributed hundreds of copies of an eight-page magazine, called *The Gag Reflex,* which they had written themselves, typed up at home, and Xeroxed at Kinko's. Copies of the magazine were distributed all throughout the campus, in students' lockers, on benches, and in giant stacks all over the quad. The next morning, every single person at La Jolla High School, including members of the faculty, had a copy. The centerfold was a picture of two enormously fat people, a man and a woman, kissing and embracing in the shower, the folds of their fat blending into each other like giant mounds of bread dough. The caption read: "The Careys at Home." The faculty was scandalized by this, and by other naughty bits in the eight pages of the magazine, and when the identities of the four pranksters were discovered, they were suspended for a week. Mr.

* It is interesting that, considering how much delight Mr. Black took in calling attention to Mr. Carey's craziness, it was Mr. Black, and not Mr. Carey, who, one month into my senior year, as a result of what everyone interpreted to be a nervous breakdown, abruptly quit teaching forever and never again returned to campus, leaving six journalism classes without a teacher.

Carey's reaction? He thought their suspension was absurd, and that they should have been rewarded for their creativity and initiative. "The Careys at home," he muttered to himself, shaking his head and smiling. "My wife looks nothing like that."

And they said I should avoid taking this man's courses? A man with the psychological complexity of a Mr. Carey comes along only once in a lifetime, and I was determined to study him. If my life ever fell short of my expectations, or other people's expectations, and I needed to invent a new one to protect myself, Mr. Carey's big bag of tricks might come in handy.

And boy was it lucky for him that I stuck by his side. For in the spring of 1986, during the second semester of my senior year, Mr. Carey's big bag of tricks, on a night I will never forget, came up empty. On the night in question, Mr. Carey and I were both wearing tights and makeup. The occasion for the tights and makeup was a lavish production of Shakespeare's *Twelfth Night,* which Mr. Carey was helping to oversee as part of the course he had invented, Exploration in Arts, the sole purpose of which, as far as we could tell, was that he could put on the play, and then star in it as the enormous Sir Toby Belch. Naturally, I auditioned for the role of Sir Andrew Aguecheek, Sir Toby Belch's skinny, and somewhat effeminate, sidekick, which I won, not only because the falsetto voice in which I spoke my lines was perfect for the role but because no one else auditioned for it. On the night of the play, after two months of rehearsals, during which he screamed at everybody for not remembering their lines, Mr. Carey confessed to the entire cast, while standing in his tights, that he couldn't remember his own. He was so ashamed of himself that he was actually shedding tears. This giant, fearsome man, an icon at La Jolla High School for twenty-five years, the indomitable Jabba the Hutt, was breaking down before our eyes. The entire cast, sitting on the floor of the stage, stared at him in stunned silence. Canceling the performance was inconceivable. People had already entered the auditorium and begun to take their seats. Thousands of dollars of the school's money had been invested in the production. A professional costume designer had been hired. A professional set designer had been hired. A professional instructor in old wind instruments had been hired to teach a group of students how to play the recorder. And Mr. Carey—whose desire to play Sir Toby Belch, a lifelong dream, was the sole reason that this lavish production had been brought into existence to begin with—couldn't remember his lines? Was this an episode of *Candid Camera*? Or *The Twilight Zone*? We kept waiting for the punch line—"Ha! Fooled ya! I was just preparing for my role!"—but it never came. He just stood there, tears rolling down his fat pink cheeks, and stared back at us.

When it finally became too embarrassing for the students to stare back at him, they all turned and stared at *me*, for Mr. Carey's inability to remember his lines, although problematic for everyone, would be especially problematic for me, since Mr. Carey and I were in just about every scene together. Sir Andrew Aguecheek is Sir Toby Belch's *sidekick*, and I had memorized my lines by reference to specific cues—namely, *his* lines.

So I went to my dressing room to think things over. I

needed a plan. A cast of dozens, in tights and makeup, not to mention a full audience of expectant parents and faculty and students, was relying on me to come through. Eventually, Mr. Carey hunted me down. He came into my dressing room and closed the door. Between the two of us, there was no room to spare. It was the closest I had been to another male body since I was fifteen.

"This is catastrophic," said Mr. Carey. "I've let everyone down. I don't know what to do." At that moment, with tears once again welling up in his eyes, it was clear what had to be done. We had to wing it. If he let everyone down, he would never recover. He would go bonkers. He would either eat himself to death or devour his students.

"Don't worry!" I said. "Don't worry! Just say anything at all vaguely Elizabethan, 'doth this,' 'doth that,' and the crowd will be fooled. I've read this play twenty times, and I barely understand it. Do you think these people will know what the hell is going on? Just do me one favor: when you're finished muttering, look me in the eye and wink. That'll be my cue to start speaking. I know my lines, and I'll make up for both of us."

That was all it took to buck up his courage. He rallied. He mumbled his way through the lines, "doth this," "doth that," looking me in the eye and winking when it was my turn to speak, and we pulled it off. At one point, I got a huge laugh from the audience at his expense. I couldn't help it. After a long stretch of his mumbling, during which he was showering my face with saliva in his effort to say "doth this," "doth that," I turned to the audience and made a face, as if to say: "I have no idea what he's talking about. Do you?" As we took our final bow, to a standing ovation and seemingly endless applause, he turned to me and yelled, "I owe you big-time, kid!"

Not at all! The college recommendation he had written for me eight months earlier, and that I read for the first time many years later, was so thoughtfully deceitful that I already owed him a big favor without realizing it. Instead of telling Columbia that I had gone seemingly crazy when I went to Andover, going there a Jock and Scholar and coming back a Budding Androgyne, Mr. Carey told them that "[Jonathan] handled the preppie scene at Andover with distinction, so I believe he will have few problems in adjusting to life at Columbia."

Mr. Carey, as you can see, was much more than just a teacher to me. So when my mother, before her baby cub left the den, wanted to know what was going on inside his head, it is no wonder that she turned to Mr. Carey for advice. As English class was getting out one day, Mr. Carey motioned me over with a wave of the hand. He waited until the last student had left the room, then cleared his throat, mopped his sweaty brow with a napkin, sighed, fiddled with some No. 2 pencils on his desk, then cleared his throat again.

MR. CAREY: Your mom called me.

ME: About what?

MR. CAREY: She wants to know what's going on inside your head. I told her, "I have no idea, and I'd rather not know." She told me not to tell you she called, but I'm telling you anyways because I think you should know she's worried about you, and you should find a way to make her less worried. But however you do it, please don't tell her I told you she called me. I promised her I wouldn't tell you.

ME: There's nothing going on inside my head. Nothing to be worried about at least.

MR. CAREY: Look. I don't care. It's none of my business. The only reason I'm telling you this is so you know your mother's worried.

ME: Does she think I'm on drugs? I think she might think I'm on drugs. My eyes are bloodshot a lot. But it's not from drugs. It's from chlorine. I spend a lot of my time in swimming pools.

MR. CAREY: Look. What you do in your private time is none of my business. And to be frank, I'd rather not know. That way they can't get it out of me if they try to torture me.

ME: I can't believe she called you.

MR. CAREY: Look. Give her a break. A mom's a mom. If my son looked like you, I'd throttle him. And then I'd send him to boot camp. You should be thankful your mom is so civilized. Do your mother a favor, do yourself a favor: tone it down a bit while you're still at home, and then you can ratchet it back up when you get to college. Even David Bowie, one of your muses, I suspect, dresses like a normal human being during the day.

Tone it down while I was still at home? Mr. Carey, of all people, who had been ratcheting it up for the past twenty-seven years, telling me to tone it down? Why did Mr. Carey think that I was any more capable than he was of casting off my disguise at will? Why did Mr. Carey believe that my disguise was any less crucial to my well-being than his was to his? When, at the age of sixteen, I decided to quit soccer, and resolved not to push myself academically as hard as I had in the past, in order to relieve myself of pressures I couldn't live up to, what I hadn't realized was that athletic and academic superiority had been the chief sources of my self-esteem. So, to a degree I hadn't consciously anticipated, the very mystery of my transformation, from Jock + Scholar to Budding Androgyne, was all I now had going for me. Where my mother was unnerved about what might be going on inside my head, my classmates were intrigued. And this sense of being intriguing was, it is clear to me now, affirming for me. People were noticing me, paying attention to me, wondering about me.

The problem, unfortunately, was that the novelty of a costume, no matter what it is, eventually wears off. People get used it. Just as Mr. Carey had to tell increasingly outlandish stories, and make himself increasingly bigger and angrier, to keep people impressed and intimidated, so did I have to "ratchet it up," to use his words, wearing more and more makeup—from lip gloss to eyeliner, eyeliner to mascara, mascara to a touch of rouge, a touch of rouge to teardrops painted on my upper cheeks—and more and more girlish clothing and accessories—bright pink overalls; women's handbags; fake pearl necklaces; long, dangling rhinestone earrings; and my mother's perfume, Joy by Jean Patou—to keep my classmates impressed and interested. Many years later, in the mid-nineties, when I decided to quit the law, and, to symbolize my break with conventional respectability, I decided to get a tattoo (tattoos, in the mid-nineties, still having the power to raise eyebrows), the same thing happened to me. Initially, people were impressed. And then, as is true of any costume or shtick, they gradually got used to it. They got desensitized. Whether it's a boy in earrings and makeup, or Mr. Carey telling tall tales, or a girl with purple hair and ten piercings in her lips, people will stop noticing anything. And then they will stop caring. And, in the case of tattoos, they will stop recognizing them as symbols of anything other than a pathetic need for attention, and simply feel sorry for us for having permanently disfigured ourselves. This puts tattooed people in an awkward position. We don't want any more tattoos. Most of us regret the ones we already have. But we are forced to get more of them, and then more after that, to keep reminding people that we have them. When our friends, reminded that we have them, plead with us to come to our senses—"No more! You already have too many!"—we see this as a provocation to keep going. Unfortunately, there's only so much skin on the body. The tattooed man at the Coney Island amusement park in the early nineties, covered from head to toe, didn't foresee this problem. Having run out of space with which to prove himself, he killed himself.

By the end of the second semester of my senior year, the need to remind my friends and classmates that I was still intriguing, that the mystery of my transformation, from Jock + Scholar to Budding Androgyne, was still worth wondering about, forced me to go one step further than I had gone before. I had no choice. Other than the mystery of my transformation, what else did I have going for me?

So here I am, in white tights, black pumps, black skirt, red bow tie, red lipstick, and a Viking hat, on prom night, early June 1986, preparing to make my grand entrance into the

Marriott Hotel and, as four hundred heads turn to look at me, about to experience one of the greatest horrors of my life.

The horror? No one cares! La Jolla High School's very own Budding Androgyne has chosen this evening to mark his important passage to Fully Blossoming Androgyne, and no one cares. Not a single person seems in the least bit fazed by my outfit. No *ooh*s, no *ah*s, no *whoa*s, no *ohmigod, look at him, he's taken it to the next level*s. Just routine hugs and high fives. I don't want hugs and high fives. I want gasps of shock and horror. There is a conspiracy of indifference against me, and I can't take it. Almost two years ago, when I was sixteen, for reasons I don't entirely understand, but hope to understand many years later, when I write a book about it, I changed the subject of my life from soccer + school to earrings + lip gloss, and then to halter tops and stirrup pants and Ugg boots, and then to perfume and purses and teardrops and pearl necklaces, and now, the pièce de résistance, a Skirt to the Senior Prom, complete with lipstick and pumps, and I want that change of subject recognized! Instead, they're treating me like a little brother who's playing dress up in his older sister's bedroom. They're trying to be accepting, nice, and tolerant. They've known me since I was five. Between soccer games, Little League, swimming lessons, and picnics at the beach, every kid who grew up in La Jolla is part of an extended family of sorts. They're trying to show me that they accept me for *who I am*. But how can they accept me for who I am, if I myself don't know who I am? The old subject—soccer + school—I understood. I was a jock who was hoping to go to Yale, so that he could play soccer there like his Oldest Brother.

This new subject—earrings? makeup? tights? pumps?—is as much a mystery to me as it is to my mother. Is he a or b or c or d? Or all of the above?

The Man in the Gray Flannel Skirt, by the time it's finished, will be the crib sheet we never had.

CHAPTER 4

"Are You *Gay*?"

T IS LATE AUGUST 1989. My grandfather, whose philosophical positions I've always had trouble sorting out, because he's had so many of them and it's often difficult for me to tell one from another—over the course of his life, as far as I can tell, beginning at the age of thirteen, when he first declared himself a socialist, he's been a socialist, a Marxist, a communist, a pragmatist, a Communist, an anti-Communist, a Trotskyist, a Social Democrat, a democratic Socialist, a naturalist, an experimentalist, an instrumentalist, an experimental naturalist, a pragmatic naturalist, a humanist, a rationalist, a Jew, and an atheist, a *fearless* atheist I should add, unafraid of dying, and unafraid of going head to head with God, in case there happens to be one—died six weeks ago. I'm on my knees, on the floor of his study, in his summerhouse in Vermont, sorting, at my grandmother's request, through fifty-four years of his papers. What is imme-

The author, age two, with his Grandpa Sidney.

diately shocking to me, in looking over these mounds of articles and books and correspondence, is how my grandfather managed to avoid getting carpal tunnel syndrome. He complained of many bodily ailments during his last twenty years, the years in which I knew him, but hand pain was not one of them. His eyes, weak since he was a teenager, caused him problems; his legs, the muscles of his calves often cramping up, caused him problems; his voice, and sense of taste, both weakened by a stroke, caused him problems. But his right hand, the knuckles white with the urge to instruct, correct, and *rebuke* if you were lucky, *excoriate* if you were not, was seemingly indomitable. A man named Corliss Lamont, a copy of a letter to whom sits among a heap of rubble on the floor, was not among the lucky:

Dear Corliss:
    Voltaire once remarked that everyone has a natural right to be stupid, but that beyond a certain point it was

a privilege that should not be abused. Your letter of June 30 replying to my attempt to reason with you has gone far beyond that point.

I did not suggest that you hang yourself. Nor did Max Eastman. He merely expressed the fear that you would do so after Khrushchev's revelations of the crimes of Stalin whom you had so zealously supported against the criticisms of John Dewey, Norman Thomas, and other democratic and socialist thinkers. Your thunderous silence as our charges against Stalin were being confirmed seemed to indicate a state of despair. That you should read this fear as a suggestion on our part is such an obvious projection of your own state of mind that it is tantamount to an acknowledgment. I predict that more revelations about Stalin's barbarities will come to light. The longer you live—and I hope you live a long time because personally I bear you no ill, objecting only to your defense of terror—the greater will be your punishment. . . .

In your heart of hearts you . . . know how deeply you committed yourself to Stalin's regime, and how lucky you are to live in a free culture that does not purge by concentration camp, frame-up trials, and death those that were proved wrong, not even those who like you betrayed its ideals by pleading Stalin's cause. Bless your stars you live in the U.S. and not the U.S.S.R.!

Whenever your name is mentioned, some one is sure to ask: what did he say when the Russians themselves exposed Stalin? I bet members of your own family don't mention Stalin's name for fear of embarrassing you!

Did Corliss manage to avoid hanging himself after receiving this letter? If not out of guilt for supporting Stalin then out of the fear of getting another letter from Sidney Hook? As much as Corliss deserved, I'm sure, to be punished for his defense of terror, why is it Corliss, and not the victims of Stalin's crimes, to whom my heart goes out when I read this letter? Am I reflexively coming to Corliss's defense, and siding against my grandfather, even though my grandfather just died and my loyalties should be with him, because this letter to Corliss reminds me of the last time I was in this study, two years ago to the day, when it was not poor Corliss on the receiving end of Sidney's white-hot temper but *me*?

———

To put my visit to Grandpa Sidney in late August 1987 into proper perspective, so that you don't judge him too harshly when I tell you how roughly he treated me upon my arrival, and during the three days of my stay, until I said, "Enough is enough!" and left in a huff, I must first tell you about the Famous Drought of 1952, and about a few other things that explain why Sidney was already in a foul mood, for reasons having nothing to do with me, when I showed up on his doorstep.

In the summer of 1952—or was it the summer of '32, '42, or '62, all three of these dates also having been mentioned as the year of the Great and Insufferable Drought (the summer of '32 having occurred, as it happens, three years before my grandparents bought the house, which would have made it difficult for them to have experienced this traumatizing event firsthand)—it did not rain in South

Wardsboro, Vermont, for "many weeks," sometimes even "many months," as a result of which all the wells in South Wardsboro went dry. Since my grandparents owned an apartment in New York City, and therefore were not obliged to stay put and suffer, they quickly packed their bags and left, only to return a few weeks later, after the drought was over. The effect this drought had on my grandparents—a few days of inconvenience before being forced to retreat to the comforts of civilization—was deep and permanently scarring. From that moment forward, until the days they respectively died, it was impossible for either of them to open any one of the seven faucets in their house in Vermont, or hear someone else opening one of these faucets, without flinching.

It was also impossible for them to flush the toilet, or hear someone else flushing the toilet, without flinching. The house rule, common in country homes with wells constantly on the verge of going dry, was "If it's yellow, let it mellow; if it's brown, flush it down." It's a fair rule if you have what is known as an *archaic* well, a well that was dug by hand, and that is operated by means of a hand pump, as my grandparents had during the time of the Famous Drought. But if you have what is known as a *modern* well, which my grandparents had installed in the early 1960s, which is drilled through otherwise impermeable rock, and which taps, by means of an electric pump, into springs far beneath the surface, then no amount of wastefulness, whether by taking a shower for longer than five minutes or flushing the toilet ten times in a row for kicks, will have any effect on your water supply.

Whenever I reminded Grandpa Sidney of the distinction between an *archaic* well and a *modern* well, in defense of my request to take a seven-minute shower, I was always reminded of the Famous Drought of '52:

"If you had been there, Jonathan, as we were, during the drought, the drought of 1952, and experienced the hardship of having no water, then you'd understand why we take these precautions."

"But we have a modern well! With an electric pump! Our water comes from the center of the earth now!"

"It doesn't matter, Jonathan. The purpose of a luxury is not to *abuse* it."

"Who said anything about *abusing* it? I just want to *use* it by taking a seven-minute shower."

"A five-minute shower, even a *two*-minute shower, is more than sufficient. One minute to wet your body. Then you turn the water off. Then you soap yourself. Then you turn the water back on. And then one more minute, at most, with the water now running, to wash the soap off your body. And then you're done. To ask for seven whole minutes, on the grounds that you need seven minutes to clean yourself, is absurd. To ask for nine minutes, as you did the other day, is obscene!"

Now you understand what Alfred Kazin meant, in *Starting Out in the Thirties*, when he wrote that

> when it came to close argument, [Sidney] Hook was unbeatable; one saw that he could not imagine himself defeated in argument. The concentration of all his intellectual forces upon the point at issue was overwhelming, the proofs of inconsistency on the part of his opponents were unanswerable; to watch Hook in argument was to watch him moving in for the kill. Socrates may have persuaded his opponents, but Hook invari-

ably shamed them. He was the most devastating logician the world would ever see.

The ever-dawning water crisis, requiring everyone to be
in a constant state of nerve-racking alert, and the careful ra-
tioning of water, as if it were the monthly allotment of butter during World War II, were just two of the many rigors
of country life with which Sidney, by late August 1987, had
long since tired of contending. Though the house was no
longer quite as "primitive," as he had called it, as when he
had bought it, in the summer of 1935, at the age of thirty-
two, it was still more primitive than an eighty-four-year-old
man could be expected to put up with.

Yes, the house had electricity now, but it was unreliable,
the power going out at least once a week, sending everyone
scurrying for flashlights and candles. Without power we
had no water, since our drilled well, that modern luxury not
to be abused, was powered by an electrical pump, and so if
the power outage coincided with a call of nature, then you
had to do your business in the woods.*

Yes, the house had a telephone now, but our phone line
was known as a *party line,* which meant that we shared it
with two neighbors, each of us with our own ring (one long
ring for neighbor A, two short rings for neighbor B, two
long rings for us). The problem with this system was that
only one member of the party could use the phone at any
one time, and so when a neighbor's girlfriend was on the

---

* Doing one's business in the house, while the power was on, was only
marginally less uncomfortable than doing it in the woods, since the
septic tank, the location of which no one could remember, dated from
the 1950s, and, to avoid overburdening it, all toilet paper (unless you
were a favored guest) had to be placed not in the toilet but in a brown
paper bag, which was then used as kindling.

phone all the time, gabbing away with her friends in New York, as happened one summer, Sidney couldn't use the phone, and no one could reach him.

Yes, the delivery of mail was more reliable than it used to be, fewer letters disappearing into the jungles of New England, but it still took a letter five days to arrive when it should have taken three, and you still had to drive your car two miles to the mailbox to pick it up.

Yes, the trip from New York, thanks to the arrival of the interstate highways in the 1950s, had been reduced from eight hours to four or five, but that was still a long trip, long enough to worry about something awful happening every time people were visiting and hadn't shown up exactly when they were supposed to, which they never did, since most of the roads in the area, including ours, were un-marked.

And the roads near the house had been barely touched in a hundred years. So it was still a fifteen-minute trip, at the rate my grandfather drove, going very slowly on the slip-pery dirt, and honking three times around tight curves to alert oncoming cars, to the nearest general store, six miles away. Which meant a fifteen-minute drive, every morning, just to get *The New York Times*. A trip to the nearest decent hospital, more relevant when you're eighty-four than when you're thirty-two, took a good *forty* minutes.

And then there were all the chores and expenses to keep the house in order: the mowing of the lawn; the haying of the fields; the killing of vermin; the chopping of wood; the repair of broken storm windows, and of holey screens, and of the electric fence around my grandmother's garden, which was always humming away but never seemed to keep anything out.

When Sidney was a younger man, three months of roughing it, in the wilds of Vermont, 250 miles from the grime and bustle of New York City, was romantic. It was a test of character. When he was an old man, beginning around 1975, it was a pain in the ass, and put him on edge. When my brothers and I visited Vermont together as children in the mid- to late 1970s, we called Sidney, behind his back, Oompus Grumpus, the Grumpus derived from *grumpy* obviously, and the Oompus, for reasons no longer clear to me, probably borrowed from the Oompa-Loompas in Roald Dahl's *Charlie and the Chocolate Factory*. Calling him Oompus Grumpus was our silly way of trying to make light of his near-constant irritability, which would have otherwise been unbearable. You don't travel three thousand miles to hang out with a grumpy grandpa unless you can turn his grumpiness into something entertaining. Sometimes, taking our irreverence a little too far, we would deliberately provoke him. One of our favorite pranks, which we pulled once every summer, just infrequently enough for him to forget by the next summer, was to put his favorite candy, called a *hopje,* a hard, dark brown, Dutch confection made out of sugar, butter, coffee extract, and salt, into his coffee cup when he wasn't looking. Besides burnt toast with ginger marmalade, the *hopje,* which came in a white wrapper with a picture of a windmill on it, was his only regular indulgence in life. Some people smoke when they write. Some people drink. Sidney sucked on *hopjes.* After he died, when my grandmother asked me to go through the pockets of his coats and pants, all I found were pennies, pieces of string, and *hopje* wrappers. Putting a *hopje* in his coffee cup was tampering with the sacred.

"Ann," he would say after a few sips, "this coffee doesn't taste quite right. Did you use the same Chock Full O'Nuts as yesterday, or is this from a different can?"

"Sidney, it's fine! It's from the same can. Drink it!"

So he would continue drinking, and would eventually discover, after the last gulp, a dark brown square sitting at the bottom of his cup.

"They put a *hopje* in my coffee!" he would scream, and then he would bound up from his chair and chase us, trying to hit us with a rolled-up copy of *Commentary, Encounter,* or *The New Leader,* and we would run away from him, laughing and screaming and singing, "Oompus Grumpus, Oompus Grumpus," over and over again, to the tune of "Oh, My Darling, Clementine."

"You boys are extremely fresh!" Sidney often said to us. "If I had behaved as you do when I was your age, my grandfather would have smacked me." At the time, I thought nothing of it. Years later, after I had stopped going to Vermont every summer, preferring to let my grandparents visit me in La Jolla, where I could use all the water I wanted, my "freshness," as Sidney had put it, haunted me. Toward the end of my sophomore year of high school, in early June 1984, while I was still reeling from the Achievement Test in Math, I wrote, in my daily journal of misery, that "my relationship with my grandfather has greatly disturbed me lately. I have to explain it fully . . . to relieve myself of some mental strain." I then spent over a thousand words expressing my regret for having treated Sidney so irreverently when I was a child, putting *hopjes* in his coffee, and flushing the toilet when the water was still yellow for no other reason than to antagonize him, and my further regret for not having attended a large celebration in New York City, two years earlier, for my grandfather's eightieth birthday. When I was fourteen, a gathering full of stuffy old people—including Jeane Kirkpatrick, Edward Teller, Murray Kempton, Norman Podhoretz, Irving Kristol, Daniel Patrick Moynihan, and a telegram from President Reagan—was less important to me than playing in a soccer tournament called the Tuna Bowl, which conflicted with the party. Although I clearly had not shown my grandfather "proper love and respect" by attending his birthday party, I hoped that I had redeemed myself by attending his Jefferson Lecture in the Humanities, in Washington, D.C., just a month before recording these thoughts in my journal. I confessed that I "did not understand a word" of his one-hour lecture but that at least "I understood what he was," namely "great and important," and that, finally, after years of treating him as "just an average grandfather," I was now appropriately "proud of him." I closed my journal entry by bringing up, as was usual for me at that time, the subject of death: "If my grandfather had died before I could show him how I felt, I don't feel I would have ever gotten over it, and now I have."

My concern that Sidney might have died before I could show him how I felt was not hypothetical. Two years earlier, at the age of seventy-nine, he had suffered a powerful stroke that seemed likely to kill him. My mother had rushed up to Palo Alto, where he was living at the time, to say goodbye. For many days he was in a state of such unbearable discomfort, with the left side of his body paralyzed, and violent and unremitting hiccups making it impossible for him to swallow food, that he begged the doctors to end his life. They refused, and he eventually, for the most part, recovered. Six years later, in March 1987, in an op-ed piece published in *The New York Times* entitled "In Defense of Voluntary Euthanasia," he recalled those many days of "agony" in the hospital—"I felt I was drowning in a sea of slime," he put it—and argued that, despite his recovery, and his ability to resume his writing and research, he should have been allowed to die. The constant dread of suffering another agonizing stroke or illness in the near future and, even worse, of possibly lingering on interminably in a state of "crippling paralysis" or "comatose senility," in which case he would have to suffer the further indignity of being a burden on his family and friends and society, outweighed, he argued, whatever pleasure he still derived from life.

Further compromising his happiness was his belief, when he was feeling especially disillusioned, that his life-long defense of freedom had come to nothing. In 1979, in a letter to Henry Regnery, the conservative founder of the Regnery Press, Sidney wrote: "The older I grow the more formidable grows the challenge to freedom and enlightenment. The historical ignorance of the young is appalling. The situation is too serious to allow oneself to be discouraged. One must keep on fighting." By 1985, the year he caught me reading, uncritically, Lillian Hellman's *Scoundrel Time,* "a book full of lies by an unrepentant former Stalinist," as he put it to me, the situation had certainly not improved: "I am not very optimistic about the prospects of the survival of the free and open society," he wrote to a professor at Caltech. "But of course the struggle must continue—even against odds."

In the fall of 1985, when I announced to the family that I would be applying to Columbia College, the best school I thought I had a chance of getting into that was three thousand miles away from home, Sidney immediately offered to send a letter of recommendation. It was clear to him, from what he had heard from my mother about my scores on the College Boards, and from what he could infer from the drastic transformation in both my appearance and my academic priorities upon returning from Andover, that my application would need a boost. I thanked him for the offer but told him I didn't think a letter from my grandfather would help. Columbia couldn't possibly take it seriously. He was my grandfather, after all. Of course he thought I was very special.

"Don't worry," he said. "Everyone's prominent friend or relative sends a letter, so they all cancel each other out. But if no one sends a letter, it looks pathetic."

Twenty-four years later, while writing this book, I went up to Columbia and tracked down the letter. When I opened it, the first thing I saw, at the top of the page, in thirty-six-point type, about six times the size of the type of the letter itself, were the words THE HOOVER INSTITUTION ON WAR, REVOLUTION AND PEACE. In case you're not familiar with it, the Hoover Institute, as it is more commonly known, is one of the two most conservative think tanks in America. In 1973, when Sidney stopped teaching philosophy at NYU, he was offered, by the Hoover Institute, because of his uncompromising anti-Communism, his opposition to affirmative action, and his defense of academic freedom against the efforts of student radicals to suppress it, a salaried position as a senior fellow.

What shocked me, when I first set eyes on this letter, was not that my grandfather was affiliated with the Hoover Institute, which of course I knew, but that he had chosen, in a personal matter that had nothing to do with this affiliation, to send a letter of recommendation to an admissions committee that he very well knew could be packed with liberals, on the stationery of such a famously conservative institution. It was not only foolish but misleading. My grandfather was not, on balance, conservative. There were many other sides to his politics. In fact, when forced to label himself, he always maintained that he was a "Social Democrat," and, consistent with this claim, he supported universal healthcare, a tightly regulated market, a robust welfare state, and a "steeply progressive income tax." In support of his liberalism more generally, he was in favor of campaign finance reform, against the death penalty, and "a firm supporter of freedom of choice with respect to abortion" and euthanasia. In defense of an active government, and in opposition to what he called a "fetish for the free market," he wrote, in 1978, in an article titled "A Response to Conservatism":

> It was not the operation of the market that extended and protected the rights of the Negroes in the South but the government, and the central government at that. It was not the operation of the market but of the government that guaranteed the rights of the American working class to collective bargaining.

It was *this* side of Sidney Hook that liberal members of an admissions committee should not have been encouraged to forget, assuming they were aware of it to begin with. So why go out of your way to advertise your nonliberal credentials by sending your letter on Hoover stationery, with the words THE HOOVER INSTITUTION ON WAR, REVOLUTION AND PEACE printed at the top in blindingly large letters? For one of the greatest rationalists of the twentieth century, it was an act of astonishingly poor reasoning.

The only explanation for this blunder is that my grandfather was so proud of his association with the Hoover Institute, felt so at home there, that to send a letter on Hoover stationery was a natural, reflexive, unthinking act of loyalty and identification. The stationery was near at hand, and near at heart, so he grabbed it.

But that is not the case. Less than four months later, in March 1986, he referred to himself, in a private letter to a journalist, apropos of his position as a senior fellow at the Hoover Institute: "I am a Social-Democratic Daniel among a lion's den of mainly Republican and Jacksonian Democrats" (the Jackson here referring not to Andrew Jackson but to Henry "Scoop" Jackson, the conservative Democratic senator from Washington State). In other words, my grandfather felt politically *at odds* with his fellow scholars in residence at Hoover, which was all the more reason *not* to use Hoover stationery for a private letter of recommendation on behalf of his grandson.

As for the letter itself, it was better left unread. Sidney first addressed the issue of his credibility: "I should declare at the outset my special interest. Jonathan Goulian is my grandson and my judgment is probably influenced, despite my philosophical objectivity, by my blood tie." This blood tie notwithstanding, Sidney went on to inform Columbia, about midway through his letter, after lightly praising me in terms far too general to make any impression at all, that "[Jonathan] has resisted my efforts to induce him to specialize early in science and philosophy as well as to complete his education at a local institution and do his graduate work in the East." What Sidney was saying here, in essence, in a letter of recommendation that he insisted on sending to Columbia, was that he didn't think I should go to Columbia.

What he was also saying, by implication, was that I was the only grandson who had failed to live up to his expectations. It's interesting to note that my Oldest Brother, Grandson Number One, had majored in *philosophy,* the first of the two disciplines in which I had refused to specialize; and my Middle Brother, Grandson Number Two, had majored in *science,* the second of the two disciplines in which I had refused to specialize. Colleges "back east," Yale and Harvard respectively, were appropriate places for Grandsons Numbers One and Two, who had not resisted Sidney's efforts, to attend. Only Jonathan, rebellious Grandson Number Three, should go to college at a "local institution," by which he meant any one of the branches of the University of California, which at that time cost almost nothing for in-state residents, and thereby not waste his parents' money on an Ivy League education. For Jonathan, a school "back east" could wait until graduate school, for which, one could only hope, he would receive funding.

There's only one way this letter could possibly have benefited me, and if this is what Sidney had in mind when he wrote it then I tip my hat to him: after reading it, and realizing that Sidney Hook, Senior Fellow at the Hoover Institute, clearly preferred that his grandson *not* go to Columbia, the admissions committee would have gone out of its way to accept me solely to *spite* him. The only problem with this theory, I finally realized, after poring over my application file for hours, was that Sidney did not send his letter until two and a half weeks after the deadline by which all application materials had to be received, and, by all indications, it was never read. He insists on sending a letter, and then sends it too late to be considered.

The admissions committee, after observing, in notes of their meeting that were still on file with my application, that my College Boards were indeed only "so-so," though not seeming at all concerned, as my mother insisted they would be, by the fact that my score on the Achievement Test in History had yet to be reported by the Educational Testing Service, went on to note that I was worth taking a chance on, in part because they hoped I would "add a little spice" to the campus, and in part because I was "a legacy, and a Californian," two groups, apparently, that received preferential treatment. My grandfather had fought obsessively against affirmative action for twenty years, going so far as to found an obscure organization called the Committee on Academic Non-Discrimination, and his grandson was given not one leg up by Columbia on the grounds of affirmative action, but *two*.*

---

* It may seem odd to you that a "Californian" would be in such high demand at a college like Columbia—where, in the year 2007, 20,000 students from across the country competed for only 800 slots—that he would be held to a lower academic standard than students on the East Coast. But remember: in 1985, the year I applied, when only 8,000 students competed for 750 slots, Columbia was not nearly as popular as it is today. New York City, for most Americans, was still known as a war zone back then, and Columbia, which had begun to admit women only as recently as 1982, was still known as heavily male. Columbia getting a student from La Jolla, California, was like the Bronx Zoo getting a panda bear from China. The cost might have been heavy—that's one less kid from Dalton or Trinity—but you made allowances. Today, much less desperate for Californians than it used to be, Columbia would take one look at my College Boards and toss my application in the trash.

What Sidney perceived as my lack of intellectual focus at Columbia, indicated primarily by my decision to take five film courses, which Sidney felt an Ivy League college had no business offering ("Columbia should be ashamed of itself," he said to me), confirmed his belief that I should have saved the cost of tuition and stayed in California. When I took a course at Barnard College called Women and Religion, it almost killed him:

"*Women and Religion?*" he screamed at me on the phone. "That's the most inane title of a course I've ever heard! What will you be taking next? *Blacks* and Religion?"

Sidney was equally frustrated by my continual switching of my major, from English, to comparative literature, to art history, to anthropology, to art history, to comparative literature, and finally back to English:

"It's clear, Jonathan, that no course of study will satisfy everything you're looking for. That is not unusual. Most things in life, including one's job, or even one's marriage, have their share of tedium. But if you stick with something, Jonathan, it might grow on you."

Knowing that I harbored vague ambitions of becoming a writer, and that a literary pursuit of some kind might be the one thing in life I could "stick with," Sidney always asked to see what I was working on, and he was generally encouraging. Even when he thought something was terrible, he tried his best to be positive. Sometimes, his best could have been a little better. When, in my junior year of high school, I sent him a short story I had written for *The Devil's Wine,* the school's literary magazine, about somebody who got killed in a car crash and went to Hell, with lots of colorful descriptions of his mutilated body, Sidney said to me: "Your metaphors are interesting and creative. But there's no point to your story. It's basically gibberish." When I got an A plus on a short story in a fiction-writing class in college, and proudly sent it to Sidney, he immediately called to tell me: "This woman was much too kind. It's one thing not to treat a student harshly if he tries his best and gets it wrong; but it's another thing, as in this case, to overpraise. Neither is the right course. A student should be encouraged to perform to the limits of his intelligence, not to rest on laurels that were undeserved."

In all the years I knew him, the only novel that Sidney ever recommended to me, shortly after I arrived at college, was Saul Bellow's *Mr. Sammler's Planet,* about a curmudgeonly old Jew, living on the Upper West Side of New York, who spends a good part of the book being disgusted by the sights, smells, sounds, and political idiocy of the unwashed, unread, ignorant young people in his midst.* I doubt Sidney read the whole book. He had no patience for novels. As Bellow himself observed: "Sidney confined himself entirely to politics. No literature for Sidney Hook." But Sidney clearly knew enough about the book to know that Artur Sammler, in his alienation from the hedonism, androgyny, and intellectual shallowness of the hippies and yippies and God knows what else, was as good a model as he could hope for, in literature at least, for his dangerously unfocused, and increasingly girlish-looking, youngest grandson.

So, as you now understand, when I showed up in Ver-

---

* On the inside cover of my copy of the book, which I read shortly after Sidney gave it to me, I noted five separate places where Mr. Sammler, by all indications Bellow's alter ego, expressed his distaste for female odors, including this on page 36: "Females were naturally more prone to grossness, had more smells, needed more washing, clipping, binding, pruning, grooming, perfuming, and training."

mont in late August 1987, to spend a week with my grand-parents at their summer home for the first time since I was fourteen, I was visiting a man who did not want to be in Vermont, the rigors of country life no longer pleasant to contend with; a man who was in physical discomfort, the aches and pains of his eighty-four years wearing down his strength and spirit; a man who was living in daily dread of the prospect of having to suffer, once again, a painful stroke or, worse, a debilitating one; a man who felt that his life-long struggle for freedom and enlightenment had largely been futile; a man who felt politically "isolated," as he put it to me, at odds with both the Left and the Right; and, fi-nally, a man who had long seen me not as a grandson in the course of healthy intellectual and sexual development but as a symbol of what had gone irretrievably wrong in the 1960s, when rebellion, for its own sake, took the place of a serious engagement with ideas. So when Sidney said to me, upon setting eyes on me, with a rolled-up copy of *Commentary* in his hand, "My God. Look at you," this com-ment was the product of numerous sources of irritation, only one of them having to do with me.

Was I aware, at the time of my visit, of all the reasons why I shouldn't have taken my grandfather's irritation per-sonally? Of course not. All that I saw, for the first time since the summer of 1982, the last time I had been in Vermont, when I couldn't take a seven-minute shower without getting scolded, was Oompus Grumpus. In La Jolla, when my grandparents visited us for the holidays, Oompus always stayed out of view. La Jolla was not his turf. To be invited back, he had to be on his best behavior.

But Vermont was his turf. And so for three days we were

locked in combat, with Sidney looking disgustedly my way and muttering under his breath to my grandmother, and with me, arms folded, staring balefully in his direction. I distinctly heard: "need for attention," "emaciated," "pathetic," "vain," "Michael Jackson," "nose job," "*faygeleh,*" and "that *shmatte* he wears on his head" (referring to my turquoise bandanna). There was also a reference to my "limp-wristedness," which was true. I was limp-wristed. But wouldn't you be, too, if you were stuck in a house with a grandfather who didn't like the way you looked?

Everything came to a head, nothing but a *shmatte* to protect me, three days into my stay, when I went to my grandfather's study to get a *hopje* from his bowl of *hopjes,* not to put in his coffee, which he deserved, but to put in my mouth. All this tension had put me on edge. I needed a pacifier. While sucking on the *hopje,* I saw a book on the shelf that seemed interesting. I do not remember the title of the book, but I do remember that when I pulled it off the shelf a gigantic moth, the size of a small bird, came flying in my direction. At just the moment that I squealed in terror, my grandfather walked in.

"What's the *matter* with you? I've never heard a man squeal like that before."

"I had no idea what it was! It could have been a bat!"

"Do you have any idea what you sounded like? You squealed like a girl."

"I didn't squeal like a girl. I screamed like a man who thought he saw a bat."

"What bat? There was no bat. It was just a moth."

"That was not initially clear. I heard fluttering wings, saw a burst of movement, then lost my composure for a moment."

"Are you *gay*?"

Was I *gay*? Because of my squealing at the sight of a five-inch moth, he thinks I'm *gay*? Finally, after three years of wincing in my direction, watching with horror as his grandson transformed from a Healthy Jock + Scholar into a Budding Androgyne, he had come out with it!

I needed to stall for time. I didn't want to give him the satisfaction of telling him that I was not gay, nor did I want to give him a heart attack by lying to him and telling him that I was. So I did what children have been doing for centuries when caught in a jam; I repeated the question.

"Am I *gay*?"

"Yes!"

That didn't buy me much time. Uh . . .

"Gay, straight, bisexual, pansexual, who cares anymore, Grandpa? It's 1987, for God's sake."

"What does 1987 have to do with anything?"

"1987 has to do with it no longer being 1957, or 1927, or 1887, or 1487. This is the modern age!"

"That's exactly what they said in the 1960s. It's the modern age! And because of that anything is permissible. Drown yourself in LSD. Burn down classrooms. Blow up banks."

"I see a bat-size moth flying out of the bookcase, and I do what 99.9 percent of human beings would do under the circumstances—I scream in terror—and suddenly I've been inducted into the Weather Underground. I burned down no classrooms! I blew up no banks! And as for my sexual orientation, even assuming for the sake of argument that I were gay, why would that be a problem?"

"It would be a problem!"

This was the second time, in just *one month,* that a man over the age of eighty had told me that my gayness, if, in fact, I were gay, would be a problem. A month earlier, during a summer trip to Israel, while in Jerusalem, at a youth hostel called Heritage House, run by Orthodox Jews, I was confronted about my sexual orientation by a small man with a long white beard who bore a striking resemblance to Rumpelstiltskin. One of the purposes of Heritage House, maybe the only purpose, was to convince nonreligious Jews to stay in Israel and become more observant. By offering free room and board, and lectures on the Bible and Jewish history, they hoped to lead us down the path of enlightenment.

On the fourth day of my stay, the rabbi overseeing the hostel took me aside and asked me to leave. I apologized for speaking up too much in class and said I would be more reverent in the future.

"Your spirited participation in class is not the problem," he said. "To learn, you must question. We are not here to brainwash. The problem for us is your sexual orientation."

"In what sense?" I asked.

"In the sense that you are a homosexual," he said.

"But I'm not a homosexual," I said.

"But you seem to wear women's clothes," he said.

"Yes," I said.

"Why?" he said.

"Because I like the way they look on me," I said. "That does not mean I sleep with men."

The rabbi was struck dumb by this. He stared at me in silence. The veins in his temples began to throb, his heart pumping faster and faster to get blood to a brain on the verge of meltdown. Over sixty years of Talmudic training had not prepared him for the notion that a man who wears women's clothes does not, ipso facto, sleep with men. He stared at me and said nothing for a very long time, pulling at his beard and considering the problem. I stared back at him in silence. Finally, sighing heavily, he said: "Well, then I suppose I have no basis for asking you to leave. You can stay."

So I stayed, continuing to attend classes, and participating no less spiritedly than I had before.

In Vermont, I did not stay. After the squealing, and the indictment that followed, I cut my visit short. My Middle Brother was also visiting at the time and was sufficiently aware of what was going on to report back to my mother that Sidney had behaved outrageously toward me. She called him, so she told me later, to complain. When your grandson goes out of his way to visit you, she explained to him, and you want him to visit you in the future, you have to keep your mouth shut about his clothing even if his clothing is objectively hideous. Perhaps this was what prompted his letter of apology six months later, which included, as I quoted in the Introduction, the following lines:

"I hope you will one day forgive your Grandpa. It's not your fault, it's mine. I'm an antediluvian fuddy-duddy, an old stick-in-the-mud, and it's not always easy for me to keep up with the behavior of young people."

Whether prompted by my mother or not, the letter seemed to come from the heart. It must have been hard to write, and I felt bad for him. I was embarrassed that our relationship—spirited, contentious, even combative at times, but fundamentally loving—had come to this. Instead of calling him, or writing him, and saying, "Grandpa! You went much too far in your apology! Even I don't know what the hell I'm doing with this *shmatte* on my head!" I did nothing. I let it go. Eventually, we resumed our bi-weekly phone conversations, but neither of us brought up his letter, or the incident in the study in Vermont.

Eight months later, when I was in Madrid, during the fall semester of my junior year of college, I sent my grand-parents a long and loving letter about my experiences thus far in Spain, about the food, the language, the architecture, the clothing, anything and everything I could think of to give them a vital sense of the life I was living in a foreign city. I hope, looking back at that letter, that it was my at-tempt, at least implicitly, to make it clear to Sidney that his apology was accepted. After all, if I still harbored a grudge, I wouldn't have gone to such trouble to write. That is the spirit in which I hope, looking back, he received it.

When my friends sent their grandparents long letters like this, they got letters in return that said things like "Thanks so much for your letter! It really made my day." That was not Sidney's style. The object of a letter, for a man who had spent his entire life doing battle against the unenlightened, was not to waste time with platitudes. It was to instruct:

We have just received your long and newsy letter of Sep-tember 28, and enjoyed it immensely. . . . You certainly have a natural knack for writing, with a wonderful sense for detail. You have an observant eye and orga-nize your material effectively. By now you yourself must be aware that you have a natural gift for writing but like all natural gifts, e.g., for song, or athletics, art and training can take it to great heights. In your case, I hope you develop with it your capacity for logical inference which used to impress Ann and me when you were quite young, and exercised it in those games. Although you don't seem interested very much in formal or mathematical expressions, you have an analytical grasp, knowing what follows logically from what.

Which *used* to impress Ann and me!
Sidney continued:

Most of the American writers with great reputations, like Norman Mailer, E. L. Doctorow, Joseph Heller, and their like, can't think from a to b, and are always harnessing their purely literary talent to some unworthy cause. This is also true for a whole group of South American or Central American novelists like Marquez (Brazil?), who has become an apologist for that ruthless Stalinist braggart, Castro. One of the reasons that Saul Bellow and Robert Penn Warren are several cuts above the gentry I named above is that they can think, and one respects them for it even when one disagrees.

Grandpa, I just wanted to bring you up to speed on my life in Spain! Can't we leave Castro out of the picture for just five minutes?

Later in his very long letter, Sidney expressed regret that his own children, my mother and uncle, had become "depoliticalized," a reaction, he suspected, to "the baptism of fire to which the children of controversial thinkers are usually subject." The implicit message I took from this: since the *grandchildren* of controversial thinkers are at a safe distance from these flames, especially grandchildren who grew up in a resort on the coast of Southern California, there was no reason why I should continue to harness my talents to purely literary endeavors and shy away from political engagement.

After discussing, apropos of Jesse Jackson's campaign for the presidency, Jackson's "opportunistic dealings with Farrakhan, and his brotherly embrace with Castro, Arafat, and Kadaffi," Sidney continued:

> *Some day when you have the leisure, but only after you have completed your college and graduate work, I hope you will read my* Out of Step *in an independent and critical spirit. Unfortunately, it contains little or no personal data, which probably intrigues the budding novelist in you.*

That I would pursue graduate work, and complete it, was not open to question, nor was it open to question that until I completed my graduate work I would not have a sufficiently independent and critical spirit with which to properly appreciate his autobiography.

He closed his letter, the last letter he ever sent me: "You are always in our thoughts."

Nine months later, he was in a hospital in Palo Alto, dying of heart failure. I was at Berkeley summer school, so I drove down to visit him for what I knew would be the last time. When he saw me, his eyes lit up. He asked me how my classes were going, and then he asked me to read him his mail. He loved to hear me read out loud. "You have a wonderfully resonant voice," he always said. "You'd make a great senator or trial lawyer." Not a great actor? Or stand-up comic? Or pop singer?

A nurse walked in and handed him a disgusting blue milk shake, then left. "Sidney, drink your milk shake!" said my grandmother. "The nurse said you have to drink it!"

"Fuck the shake," said Sidney, the first time I ever heard him cuss in the presence of a woman. "At this point in my life, I don't have to drink my milk when I'm told to." This little show of defiance ("At this point in my life, I don't have to . . . ," borrowed from Albert Einstein) was clearly for my benefit. He wanted me to remember him at his best, feisty and fearless, not as someone hanging on to life by a tube. And I was grateful for it. When David Rieff, many years later, writing of his mother's last days, quoted her as screaming in terror, "I don't want to die!" I couldn't sleep for days afterward. If Susan Sontag, who had had numerous opportunities to come to terms with death, and who seemed as mentally tough as anyone who ever lived, couldn't face it stoically at the end, how could the rest of us hope to do better?

I finished reading Sidney his mail. And then I took one last look at him, kissed him on the cheek, and left. The last thing he said to me, the last thing he shouted to me, as I waved goodbye to him, was "Continue your studies, Jonathan! Your studies first, everything else can come later."

So here I am, in Grandpa Sidney's study, six weeks after he died, going through fifty-four years of his papers. My grandmother tells me lunch will soon be ready, and hands me a stack of obituaries and condolences. "Put these in a box. Then take a shower and come to lunch. You're filthy!"

I find a box, and as I'm gathering up all these obituaries and condolence letters—even a Western Union telegram from Richard Nixon!—I can't help looking them over. One of them, an obituary written by William Buckley, Jr., called "Fond Remembrances of Sidney Hook," is impossible not to keep reading. Even Buckley, just like me and Corliss Lamont, had felt the sting of Sidney's temper:

> Many years ago (I was 26) on a balmy afternoon late in the spring I rattled northward on a train to engage in a debate at Bennington College. I knew my adversary was a tough hombre, but I was simply unprepared for the ferocity with which he scorned me, my arguments, and (even) one or two of my friends. I did some counterpunching, but found myself unable to handle the sheer hot fire from the other end of the platform.

Ferocity . . . scorn . . . sheer hot fire. "His mind attacked a problem or an enemy," wrote Buckley, "as an acetylene torch would tackle dumb concrete."

I keep reading. It's a lovely piece, admiring and respectful, and even, at times, touching. But then, toward the end, coming directly on the heels of a discussion of Sidney's atheism, *this:*

> Ten years ago a longtime friend of Sidney Hook confided to me the most wonderfully humanizing story of the lacuna in Hook's knowledge. They were lunching at his apartment by Washington Square and Hook asked his guest if they could walk together in the park after lunch. Hook sat down on a park bench and said to him, "Ralph, I want you to tell me something I don't know.

What exactly do homosexuals do?" "So," my friend told me through his laughter, "I told him. His glasses came down a bit on his nose, and then he said, 'That's disgusting!'" From the prince of rationality—reason.

After coming to Corliss's defense against my grandfather, I now find myself coming to my grandfather's defense against Buckley. For I find this strange anecdote open to question for many reasons. To begin with, it's difficult for me to believe that my grandfather, at the time of this conversation with Ralph, did not know what buggery was. Sidney was not an idiot. He was a cultured, sophisticated person. He knew what Oscar Wilde went to prison for. He knew what the ancient Greeks supposedly did in their spare time. If the conversation occurred as this person Ralph related it, then the only explanation is that my grandfather was posturing. By exaggerating his ignorance of what, exactly, homosexuals *do,* he would be able to make it clear to Ralph not only that he was not a homosexual but that he was so far removed from the homosexual frame of mind that he wouldn't even know what to do if he were, in fact, a homosexual. "What exactly do homosexuals *do*?" would be a way of asserting his masculinity, much in the way that a frat boy, standing on the front stoop of Sigma Chi, says to another, "Yo, check out that faggot in the skirt across the street!" loudly enough so that I can hear it.

But why would my grandfather feel a need to assert his masculinity? After fifty-six years of hunting down, flushing out, and attacking, with his acetylene torch, Stalinists in all their guises, what did he have left to prove? The anecdote doesn't seem right to me. Who is this person Ralph, and why should we trust him?

Also, what is this anecdote, even assuming for the sake of argument that it's true, doing in a *fond remembrance* of Sidney Hook? My grandfather was not known for his homophobia. It was not a prominent part, or even a visible part, of his worldview. In all his writings, running to thousands of pages, I don't recall a single word on the subject. My grandfather's feelings about homosexuals, and what they do in the sack, were typical of his generation, and unworthy of comment in an account of his life. That Buckley went out of his way to include this anecdote, devoting a whole paragraph to the subject of buggery in an obituary that ran to only nine paragraphs, says more about Buckley's homophobia than my grandfather's.

And yet . . . in light of the run-in I had with Sidney when I arrived in Vermont looking like a *"faygeleh,"* in which he essentially said "That's disgusting!" to my face, the anecdote in Buckley's obituary is, if accurately reported, illuminating. If Ralph's story is true, then my grandfather's distaste for homosexuality (or, at least, what homosexuals *do*) was far more deep-seated than I realized. What puzzles me most of all, now that I think about this anecdote more fully, is why Sidney believed that what homosexuals *do* was exclusive to homosexuals. Was he really as naïve as he claimed? When Sidney told me, in his letter of apology, that it was difficult for him to keep up with the behavior of young people, perhaps he was right about this in ways he never, ever, could have imagined.

CHAPTER 5

"Remember: Always Carry a Dime to Call the Police!"

T IS LATE OCTOBER 1986, about a minute past midnight. I am eighteen years old, standing on the corner of Avenue C and Ninth Street in New York City, wearing pink lipstick, a pink halter top, five-inch heels, and a long pink skirt. My oldest friend from La Jolla, Danny Berman, visiting me from Yale, is standing next to me. I've never seen him this livid in my whole life. Shifting his weight from foot to foot, clenching and unclenching his hands, he keeps muttering, under his breath, over and over and over, "Where the *fuck* are we? Where the *fuck* are we?"

I have no idea where the fuck we are. Avenue C and Ninth Street means nothing to me. It's in the East Village. That much I do know. But I thought the East Village stopped at First Avenue.

"Where the *fuck* are we?"

"Shhhh," I whisper. "Relax. If they see that we're scared, they'll attack."

Ten minutes ago everything was fine. We were in Times Square, at the Marriott Marquis hotel, trying to get into the revolving bar up at the top. Danny wanted me to show him a good time when he came to New York, something spicy he could tell our friends back in La Jolla about, and that was my idea of a good time. Get one or two Shirley Temples at the revolving bar, check out the view, make fun of the tourists, and then go home. But the doorman wouldn't let us in.

"Your girlfriend's too young," he said.

"He's not a girl," said Danny.

"It doesn't matter. I don't care *what* he is. You guys aren't coming in."

So where did that leave us? As Danny stood glumly on Forty-fourth Street with his hands in his pockets, wondering if his trip to New York would be a total bust, I frantically looked over the listings in the back of *The Village Voice*. Ah! There, in a small box, I saw an ad for *Gidget Goes Psychotic,* written by, directed by, and starring Charles Busch, the famous drag queen playwright. If Danny wanted something to tell the kids back home, this, I figured, was it: a show full of drag queens, singing and dancing and maybe even having sex with each other onstage; freaks of all colors and genders and transgenders in the audience, maybe even having sex with each other in the aisles; the curtain not opening until midnight, by which time even the alley cats in La Jolla have gone to sleep; and all of this happening not in some red velvet playhouse on lily-white Broadway but at an *avant-garde, experimental, underground,* and possibly even *guerrilla* theater in the East Village, where the 1960s began and never ended. Good times in New York could not possibly get better than this!

When I hailed a taxi and told the driver the address, he seemed skeptical.

"You guys know what you're doin'?" he said.

"Yeah," I said. "We're going to a play."

"Okay," he said, and he started the meter. "As long as you know what you're doin'."

"You guys know what you're doin'?" was my first clue that we were not headed toward the best part of town. When the driver peeled away immediately after dropping us off, that was my second clue. I instantly regretted not asking the man to please wait until we had gotten safely inside the theater. But it was too late. He was gone.

It was now 11:55. The show started in five minutes. But there was no one in sight. I pulled on the theater door. It was locked. Did I have the wrong night? It was definitely the right address. The sign above the door said, GIDGET GOES PSYCHOTIC. And then I saw a little white note, affixed with Scotch tape, to the makeshift ticket booth, dark and empty, to the right of the theater door. "Sold out. Next showing tomorrow night: midnight."

It was at that point, at 11:56, that I heard peals of high-pitched giggling, and the sound of mountain bikes bouncing over curbs. I wheeled around and saw six or seven teenage boys, all of them black, riding bikes in the street in front of us, and around us, and seemingly through us. They seemed to be circling us. Nobody else was in sight. No cars, no cabs. It was just these five or six or seven boys on bikes, jumping off the curb, jumping onto the curb, and the two of us boys from La Jolla, one of them in a gray sweatshirt saying YALE on it, in nice big blue letters, the other in a pink skirt. I backed against the theater door, and put my hands against it for support.

"Awwwwww," one of them said in a creepy falsetto voice, as if speaking to a baby. "The poor lesbian boys can't go to the showwww." Another one immediately chimed in, deliberately lisping the *s* in *lesbian* to sound as grotesquely queer as possible: "Awwwwww, poor little lethbian boys. Locked out of the showwww. Now where will they goooooo?"

Although Danny was clearly perturbed by the fact that all the boys on bikes were black, and that their blackness, as he clearly saw it, increased the possibility that they would kill us, this was not, I should clarify, a problem for me. When I was eleven years old, toward the end of sixth grade, I applied to a school called Gompers, located twenty miles southeast of La Jolla in an all-black neighborhood called Southeast San Diego. Gompers, which ran from seventh to twelfth grade, was known as a magnet school, because it tried to attract kids from wealthy neighborhoods of San Diego by offering highly advanced courses, in this case courses in science and computers. The purpose of the school was voluntary racial integration. I was accepted, and, in seventh grade, I went. It took forty-five minutes, by yellow bus, to get there. I was the only white kid in my PE class, and the only kid who had actually paid money for the regulation Gompers PE shorts, little dolphin shorts with my name written on them. The kids loved it. They couldn't believe that someone had actually paid money for those shorts. I became something of a mascot to them. It did not hurt that, because of my speed, I immediately earned their respect on the football field, and soon became the linchpin of every running play. I loved Gompers, but unfortunately I couldn't stay. The long bus ride home made it impossible for me to make it to my soccer practices on time, which irritated my coach. Since soccer was everything to me, I left Gompers behind.

What bothered me about these boys on the bikes on Avenue C and Ninth Street was not that they were black but that they were behaving like psychopaths on the verge of spilling blood. It was clear to me that they must have been hovering near the theater for some time, watching the crowd line up and wait to get in. This was the opening night of the play. A crowd of mostly white people, many of them gay, many of them in drag, was probably a novelty in this neighborhood. The boys, sitting on their bikes, must have watched the crowd disappear into the building, and then the light in the ticket booth go out, and then our cab pull up. The sight of me pulling on the handle of the locked door, and Danny standing nearby in his Yale sweatshirt, was too pathetic to resist.

So now, at 12:01 A.M., on a crisp October night, this creepy harassment. But is that all it is? Do they have something else in mind for us? I look at Danny. He's looking at me, for the first time in our friendship, with hatred in his eyes. "Where the *fuck* are we?" he says to me, under his breath, barely moving his mouth. I ignore him. He's asked me that question ten times already. And then again, for the eleventh time, moving his mouth more violently this time, clearly going crazy before my eyes: "Where the *fuck* are we?"

"I don't know," I say, keeping my eyes on the kids. "Stop asking me that. We'll figure something out." The farthest east I've ever been is the Palladium, near Third Avenue. Avenue C is east of it, but how far? And which way is west? I tell myself not to panic, but I'm suddenly so scared, Danny's lividity not helping me, that I am having trouble getting air into my lungs. If these boys on bikes see me hyperventilating, they'll smell blood and move in for the kill. I can take off my heels and run for cover, but there's no cover in sight. Banging on the theater door and shouting for help would be absurd, because no one's attacking us. No one is even explicitly threatening us. What am I supposed to say if someone comes to our rescue? "These boys are riding their bikes in a menacing fashion, and saying very mean things to me. Make them stop." The only rational plan I can think of is to stay put until the show gets out. But I don't know how long the show is. If the show lasts two hours, that plan is ridiculous.

Danny's lips are trembling. His whole body is quivering. Now he's hunched over, staring at his feet, opening and closing his hands like a crazy person, opening them as wide as they will go, stretching the webbing between the fingers, then closing them tightly into fists. Why does he keep doing that? Is he getting ready for a fight? That would not be a good idea. It would be two against seven, and one of those two is wearing five-inch heels and has never thrown a punch in his life. Oh, my God! Wait a minute! Is it possible that Danny's getting ready to fight not them but *me*? Is Danny, out of rage toward me for bringing him not to a show full of dancing drag queens, something to tell the boys back home, as I had promised, but, instead, to the jaws of death, going to sacrifice me? Oh, my God! He's going to side with them to save his skin! He's going to push me to the ground and kick me and scream, "Where you goin' now, you little lethbian freak! You goin' *nowhere*!"

I should never have left La Jolla. I should have listened to Grandpa Sidney and gone to college at a local institution, and put off going "back east" until graduate school. I had been warned, amply warned, but still I left. . . .

———

In the early spring of 1986, not long after I was admitted to Columbia College despite Grandpa Sidney's wishes that I stay in California, he sent me a book in the mail called *The Victim's Song,* which had been published the previous fall, and which had an ominous picture of a subway station on the back. The author was a professor of English named Alice R. Kaminsky, who had known my grandfather since the 1940s, when her husband, Jack Kaminsky, the head of the philosophy department at SUNY Binghamton, had been a graduate student of his at NYU. Ms. Kaminsky quoted my grandfather twice in the book, and sent him two courtesy copies, perhaps hoping he would review it. He kept one copy for himself, barely reading it before shelving it, and sent me the other, suggesting I take a glance at it before leaving for Columbia.

"Just a glance," he said to me on the phone. "It's not a good book. It's too angry, and poorly argued. The author was driven mad with grief. But a quick skim should give you a good sense of the degree to which New York City has gone to pot."

Instead of quickly skimming it, I stuck it in the bookshelf in the playroom without opening it, and quickly forgot about it. I didn't want a good sense of the degree to which New York City had gone to pot, I wanted a good sense of the degree to which I was making the right decision in leaving La Jolla.

On the night of August 25, 1986, less than twelve hours before leaving for Columbia, I finally took *The Victim's Song* off the bookshelf. Why I did this, all of a sudden, after ignoring the book for so many months, is a mystery to me. All I can remember is taking the book off the shelf, and then lying down on my stomach, on the plushly carpeted floor of the playroom, and, for the first and only time in my life, reading a book cover to cover without moving.

On September 13, 1980, Alice Kaminsky's son, Eric, a twenty-two-year-old piano student at the Manhattan School of Music, was waiting on a subway platform at Eighth Avenue and 181st Street, near the school's campus, when two Dominican men entered the subway station and held him up at knifepoint. He didn't struggle with them. According to one of the two men, who testified against his co-defendant at trial, Eric kept repeating, over and over, as the other man held a knife to his neck, "Take my money, but don't kill me." First, they took his wallet, which had twenty-two dollars in it. Then, for reasons unclear, since Eric was not resisting, the man holding a knife to Eric's throat stabbed him deeply in the back, twisting the knife while he did it, and then the two men tried to push Eric onto the subway tracks. Eric, bleeding from his back, now tried to fight back. As one witness described it, Eric tried to protect his hands during the scuffle, which would have made sense, since he was a gifted pianist and his hands meant everything to him. The two men were too strong for him and succeeded in pushing him over the side of the platform. Bystanders, a group of fourteen-year-old kids, jumped down to the tracks and helped him up, but the knife had pierced both his lung and his aorta, and he quickly bled to death. Eric was Alice Kaminsky's only child. She and her husband had to identify his body at the morgue, which she describes in detail in the book. *The Victim's Song* is her response, full of hatred and rage and a desire for vengeance, to what she considers an epidemic of liberal rhetoric about the humanity, and the rights, of criminals, exemplified, in her mind, by Norman Mailer's *The Executioner's Song*. Her son's killers were sent to prison, one for twenty-five years to life, the other for less because he cooperated and testified against the first one, but she wants them both dead. She confesses to fantasizing about them being sodomized repeatedly, and having their eyes gouged out, while they await their execution in prison.

One of Ms. Kaminsky's goals in writing this book was to convince the reader that to live in New York City was to risk, on a daily basis, getting mugged, raped, or murdered. She successfully convinced me of this by describing one gruesome crime after another, such as the murder of Caroline Isenberg, twenty-three years old, "graduate of Harvard and aspiring actress," who was stabbed to death on the roof of her apartment building in 1984. In a chapter called "The Rotten Apple," Ms. Kaminsky appeared to make a strong case, supported by various statistics, for why New York City was the most disgusting and dangerous place in the world, full of rats and rapists and robbers and murderers, and why only an idiot, indifferent to the threat of bodily harm, would choose to live there.

The reason I wasn't repelled by this book, either intellectually or emotionally, as my Grandpa Sidney had been, is that in Eric Kaminsky I saw a kindred spirit. We had just enough in common for me to identify with him, and to find myself, against my will, vicariously reliving the horror of his death. In the picture of him in the book, he looked slender and pretty, with delicate cheekbones. He was wearing a T-shirt saying PROPERTY OF UCLA ATHLETIC DEPT. I had the *exact same T-shirt.* His arms were thin, like mine. His neck was delicate, like mine. Like me, he was a fast runner, a track star in junior high school, and, just like me, he quit playing sports after his sophomore year. In my case, I had taken up wearing earrings and makeup and stirrup pants and looking in the mirror all day. In his case, he fell in love with a girl, and devoted more time to practicing the piano.

Like me, he had had a hernia in junior high school, and in both our cases the ruptures in the linings of our guts had had uncommonly profound effects on our lives. In my case, not going to a doctor right away, putting it off for three years, trying to repress, day after day, the fear that I might be dying and even the awareness that there was anything wrong with me at all, made me deeply, painfully, even morbidly self-conscious about my body, a self-consciousness that still plagues me as I write this. In his case, the hernia was repaired as soon as it was discovered, but he blamed his poor recovery from the surgery for the loss of his speed. If he hadn't lost his speed, he wouldn't have taken up the piano so strenuously. If he hadn't taken up the piano so strenuously, he wouldn't have gone to the Manhattan School of Music. If he hadn't gone to the Manhattan School of Music, he wouldn't have been waiting on the platform of the subway station at Eighth Avenue and 181st.

Grandpa Sidney, at least a half dozen times over the previous eight months, had called me from the Hoover Institution on War, Revolution and Peace to tell me two important things: "Remember: Always keep your wallet in your front pocket! And always carry a dime to call the police! Two dimes! Just in case you get cut off." But what good would a dime have done Eric Kaminsky, who was stabbed and thrown on the tracks before he had a chance to make it to a phone booth? The one advantage I had over Eric was that I didn't have to protect my hands. I could throw a punch, or at least put up my arms to defend myself, without worrying about ruining my career. But putting up my arms to defend myself wouldn't do much good if it was a knife or gun I was facing. And I had never thrown a punch in my life. I didn't know *how* to throw a punch. I didn't *want* to throw a punch. My wrist and hand bones were so thin and fragile that, upon contact with a skull or cheekbone, they would shatter. The only rational plan I could come up with, if someone attacked me and I couldn't run away, was to fall to the ground and curl up in a ball like a pill bug, with my eyes tightly closed, and my little hands, in tightly coiled fists, in front of my face. Only a sadist would kill a man while he was in a fetal position. A casual murderer, someone who hadn't yet been hardened by a life of killing people to the point of enjoying killing people just for the sake of it, would recoil from me, and maybe even call an ambulance.

The next morning, August 26, 1986, less than twelve hours after reading *The Victim's Song,* I left for Columbia. The reason I remember it was August 26 is that early that very same morning a young woman—eighteen years old, Jewish, middle class; she might as well have been my twin—was found murdered in Central Park, not too far from the Met. Having lunch with my parents at the Popover Café the next day, the twenty-seventh, I saw, over the shoulder of the woman at the next table, who had the *New York Post* or *Newsday* in her hands, the picture of the crime scene, on the cover. "The Metropolitan Museum of Art," my Uncle Ben had said to me a few days before I left La Jolla, "is one of the greatest cultural institutions in the world. You must pay a visit as soon as possible." By the time I paid a visit, a week or two later, to that great institution, what was running through my mind, as I walked up the seemingly endless flight of steps, was a six-foot-four-inch Robert Chambers, 220-plus pounds, and a five-foot-four-inch Jennifer Levin, leaving another institution, called Dorrian's Red Hand, and stumbling their way across Eighty-sixth Street into the park, where, in a fit of incomprehensible brutality, Chambers strangled her, leaving her dead on the lawn behind the Met, her shirt and bra pushed up above her breasts.

In the following photo, taken of me at Eighth Avenue and Twenty-eighth Street a few months after moving to New York, is it any wonder, after all the stabbings and blood and dead young bodies I had been exposed to so recently before this photo was taken, that I have taken cover, in my mother's arms, for protection?*

* It's interesting to note that a few months earlier, in August 1986, the rather gentle-looking boy in this photograph had filled out a draft registration card, as I was legally obliged to do upon turning eighteen, and had thereby become eligible, in the case of war, to be forced to kill people. A mere fourteen years earlier, had my lottery number been picked, I could have been sent to Vietnam, where I would have been forced to wade through leech-infested swamps and blow the heads off of Vietcong. The draft had been abolished in 1973. But in 1980, when the Soviet Union invaded Afghanistan, President Carter, wanting to send the right message in the face of Soviet aggression, reinstated the draft registration process, just in case. I was twelve when that happened. I soon developed a fear, which often kept me up at night, that in the course of battle my skin would be singed off by a nuclear bomb, exposing my organs.

When most young people move to New York City for the first time, they experience a sense of exhilarating liberation. With me, it was just the opposite. When I arrived in New York City, on August 26, 1986, I experienced a sense of psychological, physical, and existential suffocation, with a crushing fear for my life mixed in for good measure. In La Jolla, my horizons, literally, were quite broad. I looked out my bedroom window and saw a great expanse of shining sea. In New York, in Room 910 of John Jay Hall, on the southeast corner of the Columbia campus, which doubled as the northwest corner of Amsterdam and 114th Street, I looked out my window into the brick wall of the adjacent dorm, ten feet away from me. Where, in La Jolla, I had been rocked gently to sleep by the sound of the waves lapping against the shore far down below the hill beneath my house, in Room 910 of John Jay Hall, I was violently kept awake all night by the sound of sirens from St. Luke's Hospital.

Yes, there were more things to do in New York than in La Jolla, over one hundred movies playing at any one time, but only if you had the courage to do them. For those newcomers to New York City who had not read *The Victim's Song,* this courage, I imagine, was not hard to come by. But for me, who had Grandpa Sidney looking out for my best interests, telling me to "remember: Always keep your wallet in your front pocket" and to "remember: Always carry a dime to call the police! Two dimes! Just in case you get cut off," and to make sure to give *The Victim's Song* a quick skim before I went off to Columbia, so that I would have "a good sense of the degree to which New York City had gone to pot," this courage had evaporated before I left my house, and had been supplanted long before I landed at JFK, while I was still high above the Mississippi River, by an informal list I began to compile in my head, with *The Victim's Song* by my side as a reference, of Potentially Perilous Places and Things to Be Avoided.

Thanks to my great-uncle Morris, who took me aside at a family gathering on the Upper West Side, soon after I arrived in the neighborhood, to fill in some of the gaps that Alice Kaminsky had left in her parade of horrors, walking on the sidewalk near tall old buildings was added to the list. Sometime in the late 1970s, so he explained to me, a student at Barnard College, doing nothing more dangerous than walking on the sidewalk, was killed when a piece of stonework broke off from the façade of an old building and hit her squarely in the head. It was difficult to imagine a more senseless death. Was it negligent to simply walk on the sidewalk in New York City? Was it unreasonable of this young woman not to assume that the wing of an angel—or was it the ear of a gargoyle, or the nose of a cherub, or an ugly hunk of mortar and stone?—might, at any moment, fall out of the sky and end her life in an instant? The building was not owned by an anonymous slumlord. It was owned by Columbia University! Did pieces of stone fall out of the sky at Harvard, or Yale, or Stanford? Thanks to that little tidbit from Morris, I have never been able to walk on the sidewalk in New York City near tall old buildings, not in the twenty-two years since he told me that horrible story, without reflexively putting my hand over my head at least once every twenty paces, and continually preparing myself for the end.*

---

* Uncle Morris, as it happens, saved his own life by reflexively putting his hand, while in the course of reading Solzhenitsyn's *Cancer Ward*, on his neck about once every twenty pages, to casually check for tumors. Eventually, toward the end of the book, he found one and, according to the surgeon who removed it, none too soon!

The Ramble, located smack in the center of Central Park, roughly between Seventieth and Eightieth streets, was also added to my list. As it was explained to me during my first week at school, by many students who had grown up in New York City, the Ramble was the Sodom and Gomorrah, primarily the Sodom, of Central Park. If you were a man, and wanted to have sex with another man without paying for a motel room, you went to the Ramble. Since it was densely wooded, and full of hidden trails, secret crannies, and big rocks to hide behind, it was a good place to have sex in public without being seen. Unfortunately, since the Ramble was no secret to cops and homophobes, it was also a good place to go if you wanted to bust someone for public indecency, or bust someone's head open for being gay. One night in the late seventies, for example, it was often further explained to me, just in case the risk of walking through the Ramble had not been properly understood, a gang of maniacs, carrying baseball bats, prowled through the Ramble looking for heads to break open and, when they finally found some, repeatedly shouted "faggot" while they did it. The only reason this particular incident, not uncommon apparently, was so widely publicized, is that Dick Button, the ice-skater and sportscaster, who almost died from his wounds, was one of the victims. As one boy in my dorm, who, despite having gone to a fancy prep school on the Upper East Side, considered himself a tough and savvy veteran of the streets, put it to me crudely: "Believe me. Stay out of the Ramble. The queers will try to fuck you, and everyone else will try to kill you."

But would steering clear of the Ramble give me a large enough margin for error? Where the Ramble ends, and Sheep Meadow begins, seems obvious enough on a map, but would these fuzzy distinctions, trees blending into trees, boulders into boulders, be obvious enough to me when I was taking a stroll through the park? More important, would these distinctions be obvious enough, or even relevant, to maniacs roaming through the park looking for people to beat up? If you're a psychopath, out for blood, you don't promise to stay within the formal boundaries, as determined by the Central Park Conservancy, of the Ramble. You bash in the head of anyone, anywhere, you want.

Central Park, *all of it,* would have to be avoided.

Taxicabs, not only gypsy cabs but the yellow ones, too, were soon added to the list. As an elderly Jewish relative of mine, taking me aside at yet another family gathering, explained to me:

"Keep in mind, when you enter a taxi, that more and more drivers these days are from third world countries. They'll take one look at you, see that you're from out of town, and essentially rob you. You'll ask them to take you from A to B, and they'll take you to Z first, to jack up the fare. For example, if you asked the driver to take you from La Guardia Airport to Columbia University, what would you think if you suddenly found yourself on the Verrazano Bridge? Exactly. You'd think nothing. That's the problem. The Verrazano Bridge is fifteen miles, and about a hundred dollars round-trip, out of your way. So what I suggest is that you carry a map with you at all times, so that you have some basis for knowing whether they're taking you in the most efficient direction. Another useful strategy is to make up a story, at the outset of the trip, about having a cousin who works for the Taxi Commission, saying something like 'Do you happen to know my cousin Howard Stein? He works for the Taxi Commission. That's where you're taking me right now. To his apartment. He told me he'll be waiting for me on the stoop.' That should scare them into behaving. Unfortunately, if they're driving the cab illegally, it might scare them into dropping you off on the side of the Long Island Expressway. There are other problems with taxis we can discuss another time. The lack of seat belts, for instance. A man I knew was thrown from the backseat into the front windshield during a horrible crash. But that can wait for another discussion."

Rocks falling from the sky. Muggers and murderers lying in wait in the subway. Maniacs roaming through the Ramble, and bodies hurtling through the windshields of taxis. From above, from below, from inside and out.

And none of these perils included the perils I discovered on my own, the smells, noises, toxins, and vermin that no one had bothered to prepare me for, on the grounds, I suppose, that, relative to the other horrors on which it was so important to bring me up to speed, they were too trivial to mention. Were two dozen Glad heavyweight trash bags, lying on the sidewalk for days, reeking of sour milk and rotten fish and pulsing with the life of a thousand rats, trivial? Were huge clouds of bus exhaust, the clouds of a thousand cigarettes, billowing up my nose, and into my eyes, and down my throat, trivial? Lung cancer, as I saw it, was a death no less awful than being stabbed, only more protracted.

You're rolling your eyes. You think I'm overreacting. A *thousand* rats? A *thousand* cigarettes? New York City in the 1970s and '80s was not great, but the picture he's painting here is a figment of his hysteria. Well, had you read *The Victim's Song* less than twelve hours before leaving for New York City, you, too, would have seen a thousand rats when maybe there were only five or six. Do I blame Alice Kamin-sky for turning New York City into a nightmare for me? No. As she explains it in her book, the only sensible options facing her, to end her pain, were either committing suicide or putting her rage on paper. Writing that book was a ra-tional act of catharsis. Reading the book cover to cover in one sitting, mesmerized, without allowing for the distorting effects of a mother's rage, and then closing the book with the certainty that if I stood on a subway platform it was more likely than not that I would be stabbed and pushed to the tracks just like Eric Kaminsky, was, yes, a hysterical act of projection, and no one's fault but my own. Give me a magic lamp, and three wishes to go with it, and one of them would be that Grandpa Sidney had never sent me that book.

Wish number two would be that my friend Jason Bag-dade had not given me, for my birthday, in the summer of 1991, a copy of *Muscle: Confessions of an Unlikely Body-builder*, by Samuel Wilson Fussell, the true story of how a man's hysterical fears of the perils and horrors of New York City caused him to quit his job in publishing and become an obsessive, steroid-using bodybuilder, a story that, like Alice Kaminsky's, I took very much to heart. In the summer of 1991, a year after graduating from college, I was subletting a studio on the Upper East Side and working as a paralegal at a criminal defense firm in midtown Manhattan. I needed to support myself, and it was the only job I could find. With thinning hair, and sunken chest, I went to work every day in slacks, loafers, a dress shirt, and tie. My plan was to even-tually suffer through law school, and then become first a balding lawyer, and then a bald one. I no longer thought much about the perils and horrors of New York City, because the perils and horrors of the rest of my life—LSAT, law school, bar exam, job, marriage, children, pension, Medicare, senility, incontinence, death—seemed horrible enough.

One day, one of the clients at the firm, a man named Jackie the Toad, who was in the textile business, was having a discussion with one of my co-paralegals about where to buy a good suit in town, and whether to buy it off the rack or have it custom made. "If you want a good fit, you've gotta get it custom made," he said. To illustrate the point, which clearly needed no illustration at all, since the point was obvious, he pointed at me, and said: "This kid right here, for instance, wouldn't even fit into a Chinese extra small." What Jackie meant by this is that since Chinese people, as he saw them, tended to have very small bodies, then the smallest size possible of a piece of clothing, of all the sizes in the world you could think of, would be a "Chinese extra small," which, as Jackie saw it, would still be way too big for my skinny and pansy-ass body. Everyone in the room thought this was very funny.

Not long after this conversation, my friend Jason Bagdade, at that time an aspiring manager of orchestral conductors, and today a manager in his own right, in case you are an orchestral conductor and need representation, gave me a copy of *Muscle: Confessions of an Unlikely Bodybuilder,* by Samuel Wilson Fussell. Jason, who knew that I had dabbled in various forms of body modification, thought I would find the story interesting. I found it more than interesting. In the summer of 1983, shortly after earning a graduate degree in English at Oxford, Fussell moved, at the age of twenty-five, to New York City, where he got a job at a publishing house, found a sublet on the Upper East Side, and planned, in a year, to enter the graduate program in American studies at Yale, to which he had already been accepted. He had never lived in New York before. He had grown up in Princeton, New Jersey, the son of two academics (his father, Paul, the famous author of *The Great War and Modern Memory*). According to Fussell, within a month of his arrival in New York he "suddenly and spectacularly" came down with one illness after another, including "pleurisy . . . pneumonia . . . colds, hot flashes, chills," and, we find out later, diarrhea that kept him "toilet-bound." The cause of this incredible series of ailments, he claims, though he doesn't explain how he arrived at this diagnosis, was his fear of the horrors of New York City and the "constant state of terror," of being "under siege," into which this fear had plunged him. "The rapes, the muggings, the assaults, the murders. Those were the majors, but the minors were just as bad. I felt trapped by the teeming populace, dwarfed by skyscrapers, suffocated by the fumes from factories and expressways. . . . No matter where I turned, confidence tricksters hounded my path."*

Where was Samuel Fussell when I needed him most, in 1986? One hysteric was no match for New York, but two hysterics, arms locked, could have had the city at their feet.

* The "minors," as he calls them, his list of potential perils putting my own to shame, also included "bag ladies"; "deadbeats"; a "snapping bridge cable"; toppling construction cranes; a "skells" ("a man who lives in the tunnels and trains beneath the city"); falling air conditioners (a fear induced by an actual horrible occurrence, an air conditioner that fell from the window of a fourth-story apartment building on First Avenue and hit a woman named Elizabeth Beaugrand in the head, killing her); and "the nightly serenade of gunshots . . . outside [his] bedroom window," which makes one wonder where, exactly, on the Upper East Side he happened to live, since the Upper East Side, when I moved there, in 1990, was as quiet as a morgue.

"[New York] was going to explode at any moment," writes Fussell, "I could feel it, and unless I gained something fast, some uniform, some Velcro, I would catapult into oblivion along with the rest of the shards. Caught in this nightmare, I needed something, anything, to secure my safety."

He finds this "something" in a used bookstore. Fleeing one day from a man who is trying to sell him a stolen taxi medallion, he runs for safety into the Strand, catches sight of Arnold Schwarzenegger's autobiography, *Arnold: The Education of a Bodybuilder,* and understands in a flash what he has to do to survive: like Arnold, he will build himself a suit of body armor. First, Fussell joins a YMCA and works out obsessively in his free time; then he quits his job in publishing so that he can work out obsessively full-time; he then cancels his plan to go to graduate school so that he can work out obsessively for the rest of his life; he then moves to Los Angeles so that he can work out in Gold's Gym in Venice, the only place to be if you are prepared to be the best; he then pumps his body with steroids so that he can transcend his body's natural limits; and, finally, with eighty additional pounds of muscle to his frame, he becomes a professional bodybuilder. It's an incredible story—thrilling, disgusting, hilarious, an endless carnival of bloated freaks—and I implore you to buy it and read it. Everything you've ever wanted to know about the world of bodybuilding, and steroid use, and how to break your parents' hearts by not going to graduate school but instead becoming a gym rat, is in there.

Muscle was intended to be a cautionary tale. The lesson was that Fussell had lost his mind, and that the armor he had built for himself was an illusion. But that was not the lesson I chose to take from it. The lesson I chose to take, still in evidence in the margins of my copy of the book, where I scribbled exclamation points next to his workout routine and diet, was that I, too, like Samuel Wilson Fussell, could build myself a suit of armor. Not so much to protect myself against the perils of New York, the fears of which I had largely overcome by the gradual process, over five years of exposure, of desensitization, but to distract people from looking at my balding head. On a bodybuilder, the head is completely irrelevant. Because the head, like the hands and feet and fingers and elbows, you cannot build. Everything else you can build. So it is *below* the head of a bodybuilder that one's gaze is naturally drawn. Those of you who did not begin to go bald in your early twenties, as I did, cannot appreciate how crucial it was for me, to stave off a chronic depression that kept me in bed every night, and threatened to kill me, to at least give myself the illusion that everyone around me was not constantly staring at my head. "I ran into Jon-Jon at the Film Forum the other day. Have you seen him lately? He's losing his hair!" You know people are saying this, and it kills you. Evidence of my physical decay was not only in my comb every morning, and on my pillowcase, but, in the form of a gap on either side of my widow's peak, on public display. I understand that every one of us, from the day we are born, is on a gradual march toward death, but do you need to stare at it, and talk about it behind my back? Perhaps, I reasoned, if I took a page out of *Muscle,* five pages actually, pages 75 through 79, the pages in which he discusses his weight-lifting routine, and put my body through a process of monstrous transformation, then my balding head would be as nothing, invisible, when measured against the breadth of my chest.

Just when you were trying to gauge precisely how far my hairline had receded since the last time you saw me, as everyone did when they saw me, you would be distracted by the not one, not two, but three separate "heads" of my deltoids (front, rear, and lateral), and by the gulf between the mountains of my pecs.

Through following Fussell's routine, working out up to six days a week, four hours a day, in the gym (which required, to make it to work on time, getting up at 6:00 A.M. and eating up to six meals and two hundred grams of protein a day), I was able, in the course of two years, to put twenty pounds of muscle above my waist. The result was more monstrous than I had intended, and certainly more hideous than the receding hairline I was hoping to obscure. For I now looked exactly like the sort of psychopath who inhabited my wildest nightmares in the mid- to late eighties: bald and bloated, with veins popping out of his skin, coming after me to rip my head off. And just as my friends would later plead with me to stop getting tattoos—"No more! You already have too many! Leave your neck alone!"—so did they now plead with me, to no effect, to stop going to the gym: "No more! You've gotta stop! You've completely lost perspective and have no idea how ridiculous you look!" It would take eight years of my life, at a cost of hundreds of hours of my time spent looking in the mirror, and thousands of dollars spent on gym memberships and protein powders, until I got the point.

While Sam Fussell, in his state of constant terror, spent his days, as he put it, "running wide-eyed in fear down city streets" and his nights "in closeted toilet-bound terror in [his] sublet. [His] doors triple locked, windows nailed shut, the curtains, needless to say, drawn," I tended, as a scrawny undergraduate, to express my anxiety less demonstrably. I would sit on the couch in the common room on the ninth floor of John Jay Hall, watching TV, or lie on my bed, alone in my room, staring at the ceiling. When I had to leave my dorm, for classes, or the occasional outing, I always took care to put a wide-brimmed hat on my head, and to pull it all the way down to the tops of my eyes, which provided me with a shield of sorts behind which to hide, and the illusion, however flimsy, of being walled off from the world. Equally important, it hid the acne on my forehead, which, in the form of a wide swath of little bumps, appeared out of nowhere, clearly due to shock and stress, about four days after I arrived in New York.

September 1, 1986: The author, age eighteen, standing on the quad at Columbia on his first day of college.

Insulating myself from the horrors of New York by means of a wide-brimmed hat was, sadly, no less necessary a precaution within the walls of Columbia University, the twenty-six acres bounded by 120th Street on the north, 114th Street on the south, Broadway on the west, and Amsterdam Avenue on the east, than it was in the city at large. Though the central campus of Columbia was heavily protected, with security guards posted at every major entrance and in the lobby of every dorm, and an extensive janitorial network that kept the campus sidewalks and lawns and lobbies clear of rats and rubbish, I still felt vulnerable to the students, a fair number of whom had never seen a boy in a skirt before, and a small number of whom—always men, always white, always big—couldn't hold themselves back from expressing their disgust. A rare day went by that a big white boy in blue jeans or sweatpants, with flat eyes and pasty skin, wearing a sweatshirt with Greek letters on it, did not call me, either under his breath, loud enough for me to hear it, or, if he was with friends, loud enough for them to hear it, a "faggot" or "freak" or, the more creative among them, a "butt smacker" or "AIDSmobile."

If this seems implausible to you, that a student at an Ivy League college could be unenlightened enough to call another student a "butt smacker," for no other reason than to make that student feel bad, and to assure his friends that his own masculinity and heterosexuality were not open to question, then you were not wearing a skirt at Columbia College in 1986, an environment sufficiently lacking in civility that there was a bona fide *racial brawl* on campus— a group of drunk white football players versus a black graduate student and his friends, the football players shouting "niggers" while they swung their fists—two months into my freshman year.

When friends from La Jolla, or from colleges in the Northeast, came to town to visit me, using me as an excuse to finally make that big trip to New York City they had been putting off for so long, seeing me as a crucial link to every weird and dangerous and freaky exciting thing going on in the cracks beneath the surface, they were soon disappointed. I had a list of about fifteen to twenty activities, informally compiled in my head, of Benign Things to Do in the City When People Come to Visit. High on the list was the Circle Line cruise around the perimeter of Manhattan, which was useful for covering huge amounts of territory without moving my body from the deck of the boat. After a number of these cruises, I became quite accomplished at pointing out major landmarks along the shore. "Over there, roughly"—pointing toward Weehawken—"is where Burr shot Hamilton. And over there is the entrance to the Lincoln Tunnel." No one could claim, after one of these guided tours, that I hadn't taken them out and shown them the sights.

For my lady friends, a stroll down Madison Avenue, to look at the fancy boutiques, was always followed by a trip to Serendipity, an ice cream parlor on the East Side, popular with teenagers and tourists, known for its frozen hot chocolate, and then, on the way home, Fiorucci for makeup and funky stockings. For my male friends, Crazy Eddie, the stereo store, was always a hit. What my friends never realized was that the "Incredible Blow-out Sale: Prices Slashed to Rock Bottom," which, as luck would have it, always happened to occur on exactly the day they had come to visit, occurred every single day for fourteen straight years, until, one blowout sale too many, Crazy Eddie finally went out of business.

When my best friend from home, Danny Berman, who was a freshman at Yale, just an hour and a half away by train, called me and asked if he could come visit, of course I said yes. I had a richly satisfying itinerary in store for us. Our first stop would be Zabar's, for a knish. (Knishes were hard to come by in La Jolla.) After Zabar's, I would show him the Mitzvah Tank—a van full of highly excited Hasidic Jews, proselytizing, blaring music, and asking people if they were Jewish and, if so, if they would like to come inside the tank and discover what it really means to be Jewish—that was always parked somewhere on upper Broadway, often directly in front of Columbia. There were no Mitzvah Tanks in La Jolla. All we had in La Jolla, by way of the public demonstration of religious observance, besides a handful of churches and one or two discreetly placed synagogues, was a giant "Easter cross" on the very top of Mount Soledad, the highest point in town.

After the Mitzvah Tank, I would take Danny to the Museum of Natural History. After a good look at the dinosaurs, and the cases full of insects and butterflies, we would wend our way over to the dioramas, which have always been a special treat for me, and I knew that Danny, as susceptible to the charms of taxidermy as every other boy I've ever known, couldn't fail to appreciate the incredible skill and artistry that went into their design.

For dinner, Chinese food at Dynasty, on the northeast corner of Broadway and 110th Street, which, despite having the best Chinese eggplant in the city, closed in the late 1990s.

And after *all that,* having whetted Danny's appetite for some real action, I would take him, for the pièce de résistance, to the revolving bar at the Marriott Marquis hotel. I had never been there but had been told, by people in the know, that it continually went around in circles, like a carousel, slowly enough not to give you vertigo, but quickly enough to give you a powerful sense that you had arrived in a city where anything, even a show full of dancing drag queens having sex onstage, was possible.

———

So here I am, at what is now 12:10 A.M., in late October 1986, on Avenue C and Ninth Street, in front of the Limbo Lounge, the show full of dancing drag queens having sex onstage sold out, and facing imminent assault by either Danny, who is continuing to fume and mutter, or these boys on bikes, who are continuing to have the time of their lives by calling me, in a ludicrous imitation of a lisping homosexual, a "poor lethbian."

Finally, rather than shoving me to the ground and kicking me, Danny starts jogging toward the nearest intersection. Walking unsteadily on my high heels, I follow him. In back of me, in front of me, to the sides of me, I hear the whirring of wheels, the bumping of rubber against concrete. "Awwww, look at the lethbian boy try to walk!"

Just as I reach his side, Danny, a man possessed, his eyes on the prize of a warm bed in a safe home, and facing a dead end in front of him, nothing but weeds and dumpsters and haunted-looking buildings, wheels around and starts jogging back in the other direction. As I try to trot behind him, the distance between us gradually widening, it is now unmistakably clear to these boys on bikes, in case it had not been sufficiently clear already, that we have no idea where we are, and no idea where we are going.

The next eleven minutes are something of a blur. Somehow, presumably by moving in a straight line, we eventually make it to Avenue A, though Danny makes it there about eight minutes before I do, and if he manages to hail a cab in time, I have no doubt that he will definitely go back to Columbia without me and wait for me at my dorm. He is so angry at me right now that he can't trust himself to suffer my presence in a twenty-minute taxi ride without risk of pummeling me. In the meantime, as the runt of the litter stumbles his way forward, the boys on bikes, sniffing at my heels, continue to surround me. Every time one of them rides up behind me, I prepare myself to get hit in the back of the head with a baseball bat or metal pipe. Not once, however, do I put my hand up behind my head to protect myself from the blow, or turn around to duck, because to do that, I tell myself, will show that you are scared, and that might be all it takes to push them over the edge. They can sniff at your feet, but don't let them smell blood. When they ride up behind you, *do not flinch.*

And just like that, when the lights and commotion of Avenue A come into view, they take off. That was it! They just took off. Not even with a final, farewell "lethbian boy." No metal pipe. No baseball bat. No pinch in the ass. By all indications, they had no other intention, from the moment they saw me pull on the door handle of the theater in vain, than to make us feel uncomfortable.

That was it? For that, not even a paper wad in the back of my head, my friendship with Danny is almost over?

By the time I arrive at Avenue A, Danny is still trying to hail a cab. Finally, we flag one down, and ride back to Columbia in silence, I in the front seat, he in the back, the back of my head protected by Plexiglas, in case he has an urge to smack me.

The next morning, before I wake up, Danny leaves and catches a train back to New Haven. For weeks on end, for *months,* he won't return my calls. When he finally calls me back, he apologizes and says that he was "incredibly sick," that he was "overloaded with work," that he was "doing a lot of volunteer work at a local shelter," that he was on vacation with his family in Bermuda, and so on, a grab bag of excuses, most of which I can't remember. None of it is true. Many years later, in the mid-nineties, he will confess to me that he was so angry with me that night, for having put him in such a vulnerable position, and for causing him, because of my negligence, to actually fear for his life, that he vowed never to talk to me again, a vow he managed to keep for four months, which was three and a half months longer than we had ever gone without speaking before.

CHAPTER 6

The Vegetable Monster

T IS THE SPRING OF 1990. I am twenty-one years old, naked, hiding under my covers in my dorm room at Barnard College, the school for women, and only women, located directly across the street from Columbia.

Stevie, a senior at Barnard with dark bangs, pale skin, unshaved underarms, and a chest as flat as a boy's, the large, dark nipples showing through the white mesh of her tank top the only evidence that she is not actually a beautiful man, is pleading with me to let her "break [me] in sexually," my having had sex only once in my life, during orientation week at Columbia, almost four years earlier, making me, in her eyes, still, in essence, a virgin.

"The first time doesn't count," she tells me. "You were drunk! You had your shoes on! You had to force yourself to come!"

She's exaggerating. I was not drunk.

"What you had was not sex."

Not by her definition, maybe, but it certainly impressed Danny Berman when I called to tell him about it immediately afterward.

"Your friend at Yale? Who was a virgin too? What did *he* know?"

Once again, she has painted me into a corner. Her logic is indomitable. My Grandpa Sidney would have been proud of her.

For the twentieth time in thirty minutes, she reminds me that I am only two months away from graduating from college, and that "numerous studies have shown" that if you graduate from college still a virgin the chances of staying a virgin for the rest of your life "go up exponentially." It's definitely her strongest argument. When I ask her where these studies were published, so that I can check to see if they were peer-reviewed, she draws a blank, which, under normal circumstances, would make me suspicious, but here, naked, under my covers, wanting badly to be broken in sexually, and desperate for the courage to push through my fears, I let it go.

"Other than wearing ten condoms," I say, "which won't be much fun for me, I don't know what else I can do. My fears are too crippling. Let's just forget it. It's hopeless."

Stevie, brooding and mulling, and playing with my nipples in an effort to arouse me, refuses to give up. Bringing in a second woman, to distract me from the various sources of crippling anxiety that will make it impossible for me to get an erection, is the only half-decent solution she's come up with so far. But it won't work. After a few minutes of distraction, imagining how much fun it would be to tell Danny that my second time in the sack was a ménage à trois, the certainty that I am simply doubling my exposure to potentially harmful fluids would undermine everything.

Stevie's eyes, so dark and pensive, suddenly explode with the force of a new idea. Her lips quiver with the beginning of a smile. She giggles and claps her hands. The Christmas tree at Rockefeller Plaza, three seasons too early, has lit up inside her head, and she's about to share the light.

"Role play!" she says, loudly enough for my neighbors to hear through the walls.

What about it?

"It's the perfect solution to your sickness."

She's clearly lost her mind. It's time to turn off the lights, put the tree back in the closet. Role play is the last-ditch effort on the part of a married couple who sleep in separate bedrooms to rejuvenate a sex life that's been comatose for ten years. The solution to my sickness is not role play.

"You're being narrow-minded," she says. "Hear me out."

She then patiently explains to me that if I plunge my entire Self—heart, soul, mind, and body—into the identities of people whose libidos are not compromised by the fear that sexual intercourse, more likely than not, will result in their death, I can use these false identities as prophylactics, psychological shields behind which my fears of contamination can be at least momentarily repressed. When Alfred Kazin said that Sidney Hook was "the most devastating logician the world would ever see," he clearly had not met the brilliant, bisexual, sexually rapacious Stevie "Socrates" Nidini of Barnard College.

Role play? Can it really work? It's worth a try, no? If I don't get over the hump in the next two months, I may never have sex again in my whole life. "Numerous studies" have proven this. For seven straight years a single horrible syllogism—Major Premise: To consume, whether through eating or drinking or breathing, is to potentially pollute your body with lethal substances; Minor Premise: Sex involves a tremendous amount of consumption; Ergo: sex will definitely kill me—has held me back. The time to break through it is either now or never.

Okay, Stevie. I'm game. Take off those pj's and prepare to channel your inner thespian. The Man in the Gray Flannel Skirt is ready to be cured!

The first sign that I would still, in essence, be a virgin when I was twenty-one and a half years old, and only two months shy of graduating from college, occurred in 1973, when I was five years old and taking the first and only IQ test of my life. Starting off with an easy one, to get me warmed up and put me at ease, the man on the other side of the table, who was determining, for the rest of my life, whether I was Dumb, Smart, or a Genius, asked me, "Which part of the egg is thrown out?" and to show him that I was already warmed up, had already had my shoulders massaged by my mother, who was waiting for me in the other room, I fired back the answer without pausing: "The yolk!" Had the man misheard me? No! "The yolk!" The shell, at least, had calcium. But the yolk, packed with 215 milligrams of cholesterol, was Evil in its purest form. My reasoning, hammered into my head with the same force that the Lord's Prayer is hammered into the head of a little Catholic boy, was simple: To consume egg yolk, which clogs the arteries, is to hasten your death. Death is bad. Ergo . . .

Ergo, the eggs that I ate as a child were not the same eggs that my friends ate, or that the children in books and movies and television commercials ate. Their eggs were yellow, and tasted like eggs. My eggs were white, and tasted like viscous water with salt and pepper on it. The source of these eggs, located an hour and a half drive east of La Jolla, a drive my father and I made once or twice a year, as if we were on our way to Mecca, was a place called Olson Farms. I assumed, from the name, that it was a farm, though I never saw any animals. All that I saw, when my father and I pulled up to the loading dock of a warehouse, was a man coming toward us rolling a dolly full of giant green cartons, about sixteen of them. In each one of these cartons was a gallon of liquid egg white. Olson Farms had gone to the trouble to separate the yolks from the whites of thousands and thousands of eggs. The yolks were sold to bakeries, for creams and puddings and custards and frostings. The whites were also sold to bakeries, for the meringue that went on top of those delicious lemon meringue pies. Olson Farms had no customers in mind, other than bakeries in Southern California, when it separated these yolks from the whites and put them both in the freezer. But once or twice a year, to the surprise of the man who happened to be working on the loading dock that day, a hematologist from La Jolla, California, wearing Birkenstocks and bifocals, would show up in a station wagon, lift open the back, and say:

"May I please have sixteen cartons of liquid egg whites?"

"Just the whites?"

"Yes, please."

"That's a helluva lot of meringue."

Actually, it was no meringue at all. It was a helluva lot of egg white omelets, the cratered surfaces of which looked uncannily like the surface of the moon, and the bottoms of which, when you cooked them without oil in a Teflon pan, as we always did, turned into a hard, brown, rubbery rind, so rubbery that it took one of our sharp and fancy Henckels knives to cut through it. Occasionally, to liven things up, something called "non-fat, dry-curd cottage cheese," which came in little plastic bags, and which my father bought at a health-food store called the New Seed, was added to the mix. I seem to remember this dry-curd cottage cheese tasting slightly sour, as if it was just on the verge, or just past the point, of spoiling.

That was an average breakfast. For lunch, we might have plain corn tortillas with nonfat mozzarella on them, or low-fat chicken franks or turkey franks on pieces of whole wheat bread. For dinner, we might have desiccated chicken breast, the skin, and all trace sources of fat, having first been hunted down, dissected, and removed, and then the chicken breasts baked in the oven until they were so stringy that you could not slice through them without a Henckels knife, or "meat loaf," which was made not out of meat but out of something called Texturized Vegetable Protein, otherwise known as TVP. TVP came in the form of hard, dense, rubbery pellets, the kind of thing you might see in the feeding compartment of a rabbit cage. The chief problem with TVP, at least the kind they made back in the seventies, was that it was basically unmasticatable. One either swallowed these pellets whole or sucked on them for a few moments before surreptitiously spitting them into one's napkin.

Many accounts of childhood suffer from retrospective self-pity. The author, looking back, says, "Look at what I

had to put up with! You can imagine how much I suffered!"
and yet we all know that he really didn't suffer that much.
Children are resilient. As long as you don't beat them, or
lock them in a closet, they can make do with very little.
They learn to accommodate themselves to whatever life is
throwing their way. When I was served meat loaf with TVP
in it instead of meat, and I chewed and chewed and chewed,
and couldn't break through the little pellets, I swallowed
them, or spit them out, and moved on. So what, I thought,
if they eat sirloin steak across the street? When I was
served, for dessert, instead of the real ice cream they were
served across the street, "nonfat ice milk," a gummy sub-
stance that turned completely to ice within days of being
opened, I ate my little bowl of it, sucking on the ice crystals,
and moved on. When you know that your father loves you,
and that he is motivated not by a desire to deprive you of
delicious food but by the urge to increase the odds of your
living a long and healthy life, then it is impossible to be re-
sentful. I knew that he had a very big heart, and that the
best interests of his three children were its chief concern.
That was not open to question to me. I trusted him implicitly. He was a hematologist. Blood was his trade. When
you're a hematologist, or any physician for that matter, or
any concerned parent for that matter, and you are aware of
the scientific evidence showing a correlation between the
consumption of saturated fat and the hardening of arteries,
and you know that your family, on their father's side, has a
poor history of doing battle with hardened arteries, then to
look the other way while your children eat saturated fat
would be irresponsible. As he explained it to us, the purpose of blood is to *whoosh* through the arteries, not to

trudge. He wanted his children to whoosh their way through life, to eighty, to a hundred, and beyond, not trudge their way to fifty-five and then die of a stroke or heart attack. Whenever I look back at my childhood and wonder if it might have been healthier, for my psychological if not my arterial development, had less attention been paid to every single thing I put in my mouth, I remind myself that my father, as I said, and I'll say it again, *had a very big heart*. "Do not judge him harshly," I say to myself. "For your father, based on the available scientific evidence, did what he thought was best."

Were it not for the two dozen "special occasions" every year, when my brothers and I were allowed to indulge in otherwise forbidden foods, I might not be so forgiving. Nothing but egg white, desiccated chicken, and TVP all year round, and I would have run to a child protective agency for cover. But knowing that a special occasion was always somewhere around the corner, maybe weeks away but still there waiting, kept me chewing and chewing and chewing.

One night every month, on a Friday or Saturday, when my parents went out to a play or movie or dinner party, each boy got a Hungry-Man TV dinner of his choice. What was billed as "beef sirloin," which came with a square of mashed potatoes, a square of buttered green beans, and a square of apple cobbler, was my favorite.

One morning every two to three months, on a Saturday or Sunday, my mother made *matzo brei* (which is pronounced not "bree," like the cheese, but "bry," to rhyme with *dry*). *Matzo brei* is matzo soaked in whole milk and egg, and then fried in butter or, in our case, in safflower oil, the healthy oil of the seventies. There are two camps of *matzo brei* eaters, those who like it savory, and those who like it sweet, with, for example, maple syrup on it. I'm the only person I've ever known who was in both camps. I was so grateful for the real egg and milk in it that I would wolf it down, with equal relish, any way you gave it to me.

Once or twice a year, when my maternal grandparents, both of whom, especially my Grandma Ann, thought that my father's diet was "absurd," "nutty," and "irrationally extreme," were visiting, we were treated to a Sunday brunch at a fancy hotel, either the huge and luxurious Hotel del Coronado (where some of the scenes in *Some Like It Hot* and *The Stunt Man* were filmed), near downtown San Diego, or the old and venerable La Valencia Hotel in La Jolla (which, besides Louis Kahn's Salk Institute, is the only venerable thing in town). The purpose of these brunches, where we were given free rein to gorge on anything we wanted, was to convince my grandparents that we should not be kidnapped and deprogrammed. A Potemkin village comes to mind—"Look at our children's smiling faces! Look at how they eat with gusto!" Bacon, I learned during these brunches, and I still believe this, is almost too delicious to take seriously. Am I dreaming when I eat it? It disappears almost instantly after hitting the tongue, never fills me up, and tastes like a salty strip of gold. I would eat twenty, thirty, forty pieces, and then follow them with a plate of real scrambled eggs, infested with real cheese, with real sausage on the side, and the whole thing cooked in real butter, and then I'd top it off with four real desserts. My father, tending to his oatmeal and cantaloupe, would do his best to pretend to take pleasure in our enjoyment, though it must have been torture for him. Beneath our smiling, gorging faces, all he could see, I'm sure, were the globules of saturated fat, slow and stealthy and murderous, crawling like Vietcong through the tunnels of our arteries. We had covered so much ground in the previous six months, we had cleared out so much enemy territory, and here they were taking it all back!

Birthday parties and holidays, reliable and untouchable, were the days of true reprieve. Only a monster would have come between his children and a chocolate Easter bunny. For Christmas, it was my mother's rum balls. For Hanukkah, chocolate gelt. For my birthday, marzipan. For Halloween, whatever would fit into my little pillowcase. One Halloween night, sometime in the early eighties, I was devouring a package of Twizzlers when my father, peering at me through his bifocals, mentioned offhandedly that eating huge quantities of licorice can cause hypertension. Licorice, he explained, contains a chemical that causes the body to retain sodium, and to dispel potassium, raising the blood pressure. That ruined it for me. I stopped eating. I put the Twizzlers back in my pillowcase. My father felt terrible. Only a monster would have ruined my Halloween by coming between me and my package of Twizzlers. "Don't worry!" he said. "Go ahead and eat. You have nothing to worry about. Twizzlers are *artificially* flavored, silly. They do not contain actual licorice. And even if you ate ten pounds of licorice, the spike in your blood pressure would only be temporary. But keep in mind that if you are drafted, and want to avoid military service by, for example, getting a medical exemption for high blood pressure, gorging on Twizzlers will not do the trick. You will have to eat the *real thing*." My father, who knew that I was terrified of getting drafted, was only kidding, of course. He was trying to put my fears to rest by making light of them.

But I took his advice to heart. In case of war with the Soviet Union, I would eat huge quantities of the real thing.

Just as my father believed that it would be morally negligent of him not to make his children aware of the potential hazards of ingestion, so did I feel it would be morally negligent of me not to pass my knowledge of these potential hazards on to my friends. Atomic Fireballs, gum coated with red dye number 2, which were popular in the 1970s and early '80s, were, as I tried to explain, "potentially carcinogenic." Of course they ignored me and kept chewing. When the FDA finally banned red dye number 2, it was crow that my friends chewed in silence. Sniffing modeling glue, popular among little boys who build model airplanes, was also "potentially carcinogenic," as was inhaling their parents' secondhand cigarette smoke; as was inhaling gasoline fumes; as was eating anything that had been overly charred in the oven or toaster; as were smoked foods, like ham or lox; as were preservatives like sodium nitrites and nitrates; as were any possible sources of radiation, such as the sun, or the dentist. Every time I had my teeth cleaned, my dad called the dentist to tell him, quite firmly: "No more X-rays than *absolutely necessary*," which meant no more than once every two years.

Since everything I ate, and drank, and inhaled, and absorbed through the pores of my skin was potentially perilous, the only reasonable inference on my part, when I went to Black's Beach in La Jolla beginning at the age of eleven, to spy, at close range, on the spread legs of naked women, was that the dense mass of coiled hair, covered with specks of sand and seaweed, and the folds of flesh, glistening with sweat, seawater, and other unknown juices, contained substances that were potentially dangerous. Black's Beach, the first legally sanctioned nude beach in the country, was located at the base of a tall cliff, where an old La Jolla family, by the name of Black, owned property. It was where most La Jolla boys got their first exposure to hordes of naked women. It was amazing what an eleven-year-old boy, curious about the female anatomy, could get away with looking at. On a crowded day at Black's, you could set up your towel within four feet of a naked woman, reading or sleeping or sunbathing, whose knees were up and legs were spread. These women must have been oblivious to me, or indifferent to me, or turned on by me, because when I stared, and kept staring, the legs did not close. Most young boys, when they looked at those spread legs, thought to themselves: *One day, not too far in the future I hope, I will stick my penis somewhere inside that dark clump of hair.* What ran through my mind, when I looked at those same spread legs, was: *potentially carcinogenic.*

The early sexual explorations on the part of my most precocious friends only confirmed me in my suspicions. When Anthony "ate out" Angela, as he gleefully reported it to every single person he knew within twenty-four hours, he said "her pubic hair got caught in my teeth," "she got so wet, I almost gagged," and "her pussy tasted *exactly* like red wine." For most of his listeners, it was an unequivocally positive account. For me, it was a thicket of horrors. In "sex education," a two-hour seminar taught by a visiting lecturer named Merle, while the girls were treated to their own seminar in a different classroom, Anthony followed up on his triumph by asking, when it came time for the no-holds-barred question-and-answer phase:

"Hey, Merle, what are you supposed to do if you're eating a girl out, and her pussy is super hairy?" As the class erupted in hysterical laughter, the kids doubling over and gasping for air, Merle stared blankly at Anthony and tried hard to take the question seriously. After all, he had told us we could ask *anything we wanted,* and Anthony had taken him up on it.

"Well," said Merle, "if it's too hairy, then get the hell out. I don't know what else to tell you."

With a *raging libido* (the cliché is unavoidable; a fourteen-year-old boy's libido does nothing but rage), and nowhere to put it, I began to masturbate at least three times a day, which was probably average, or maybe a tad above average, for a healthy and sex-obsessed boy who wasn't hooking up with girls (or "getting together" with girls, as we called it then; as in "Did you get together with her last night? Really? Did you finger her? Did you eat her out? Did you fuck her?"). Since I had no memories of actual sexual encounters on which to draw for my fantasies, I had to make up scenarios out of nothing. But whenever I made the first move in these fantasies, saying to a girl, "I think you're hot; I want to fuck you," I couldn't maintain an erection. That I would have such confidence, in the face of my various physical deformities, and my fear of contamination, to walk up to a girl and tell her I'd like to fuck her, was too implausible for my dick to stay hard. So, to make these scenarios plausible enough to maintain an erection, a woman in some position of authority in my life—Miss Redd, my seventh-grade English teacher; Carol Levy, a friend's mom who was part of the neighborhood car pool; Jan, one of the lifeguards at La Jolla Shores Beach—would always have to make the first move.

But, as we all know, masturbation goes only so far in

satisfying one's sexual urges. One hungers, occasionally, to know what it's like to have another person's hand around one's cock. I was not the only boy I knew who was shy around girls, and it wasn't long before I found myself, on a Saturday afternoon, my parents out of the house for reasons I don't remember, on the floor of the playroom upstairs getting my dick jacked off by a boy from down the block named Gunnar (who, incidentally, would drown eight years later in a surfing accident in Hawaii; the story I heard was that he fell off his board while riding down a giant wave, and the board, attached to his ankle by a leash, smacked against his head, cracking it open and knocking him out). The playdate had begun innocuously enough. There was some roughhousing in the backyard. We threw Nerf footballs at each other and wrestled on the grass. We then tried to make bows and arrows out of sticks and string. But the bows always broke in half when we pulled the strings back. We then collected snails and put them in an empty Yuban can and poured Tabasco sauce on them and watched them bubble to death. We soon got bored with this and went upstairs to the playroom, which was legendary among my friends because it was big, and full of board games and toys, and there was a giant brown beanbag in it, good for hiding under during games of hide-and-seek, and two chairs that spun round and round, which we treated like mini-carousels. There was also a nice view of the ocean from this room (there still is), and the floor was covered, wall to wall, with a comfy, plush, multicolored carpet—intertwined synthetic fibers of beige, and rust, and orange. (The carpet, which went out of fashion almost as soon as it was installed, was removed years ago.) We put on a Beatles record (second volume of the greatest hits, the double album with the blue vinyl), and lay down on the carpet, exhausted, side by side, and stared at the ceiling. I remember, to this day, that I could smell his sweat. I don't remember being turned on by it, but I do remember not minding it, and I do remember noting that it was something I didn't remember smelling when we were younger. *He has hair in his armpits,* I thought. *That's why I can smell his sweat. Maybe he can smell my sweat, too.* Suddenly, and for the life of me I can't remember why he felt so emboldened, I don't know what signal I gave off that made it clear to him he could get away with this, he reached out, slowly unbuttoned my pants, pulled down my zipper, and slipped his hand beneath my boxers. I remember being relieved that I was wearing boxers, and not briefs, otherwise known as bun-huggers. Getting caught wearing bun-huggers was as bad as getting caught wearing a skimpy Speedo bathing suit to the beach. With his hand resting on my pubic hair, like a starfish on a bed of seaweed, he seemed unsure what to do next. Was he feeling how much pubic hair I had and trying to compare it to how much *he* had? Was he getting cold fingers, and didn't know if he should turn back or keep going? Finally, the starfish livened up and began to crawl forward, and began to fondle me, first my dick, lightly and tentatively, as if to say, "If you're not into this, let me know, and I'll stop, and we can pretend this never happened," and then my balls (only two of them, since the third had sucked back into my body as I lay on the carpet), and then back up to my dick. I remember him squeezing my balls very gently, as only a boy would know to do, since only a boy would know that one's balls are very sensitive. I kept my eyes on the ceiling, wondering if this was really happening. When my dick finally got hard, he responded instantly, moving his grip up and down the shaft of my cock more quickly and aggressively and even frantically, and with special vigor on the downward motion. It was as if he were yanking a giant teat, with the hope, quite reasonable under the circumstances, of producing a spurt or two of milk. After a few minutes of this, a noise somewhere—I don't remember exactly what it was—made me nervous. Perhaps I heard a car drive up the driveway and thought my parents had come home. Whatever it was, we both stood up quickly and, with my hard dick bouncing against my stomach, ran to a large, walk-in linen closet, where we quickly lay down on the carpeted floor and he continued to jack me off as if his life depended on it. His hand was wrapped so tightly around my cock that I was worried, seriously worried, that he was going to cut off its circulation. Anxiety over the possibility of losing my penis forever, of it breaking off at the root, distracted me so much that I began to lose my erection, which only served to make his grip all the tighter, and his jackhammer movements all the more forceful and chafing. This was hurting, and I wanted it to end. Desperate to appease him, I closed my eyes tightly, and by mentally removing myself from the linen closet and putting myself alone in my bed, I managed to force myself to come. It filled his hand and oozed through his fingers. I was instantly exhausted. I was hoping he would go home now. But at his feverish insistence—"C'mon! C'mon! Do it to me, too!"—I reached over and unbuttoned his pants, grabbed his thick cock (yes, it was thicker than mine, though I remember that mine was arguably a smidgen longer), and returned the favor.

"Put spit in your hand," he whispered.

"Why?" I said.

"Just do it," he said. "It feels better that way."

So I did what he asked, spitting into my right hand about three or four times to get enough saliva. With my dick chafed and burning, as if Gunnar had taken a piece of sandpaper to it, I remember wishing that I had had the good sense to ask him to do the same. He came in no time at all, his cum squirting onto my chest like a baby's vomit.

"Eww!" I screamed.

"Sorry," he said. "I didn't know it would go that far."

I ran off to get some rubbing alcohol from my father's medicine cabinet to remove it (first checking, I can only assume, to make sure the coast was clear), and by the time I got back to the playroom, he was dressed.

"Thanks for letting me come over," he said, and then he ran down the stairs and went home.

That night, alone in bed, I thought to myself: *Oh, my God. That was the grossest thing I've ever done in my life. Never, ever again. My own hand was* better *than that.*

But as if to confirm my thesis, I found myself, one Saturday night, about six months later, now fifteen, on the floor of my friend Oliver's bedroom, both of us a little drunk (it was New Year's Eve; we had broken into his parents' stash of Manischewitz wine) and naked, and with me on top of him, going through the motions of fucking him, eventually coming all over his groin. How I ended up on top of him is a bit of a mystery to me. I hazily remember him jacking me off ineffectually, taking awkward stabs at my cock. I suppose I got impatient, and took matters into my own hands. Between his wine breath—I remember *that*!—and the sticky cum, like kiddie glue, melding us together, I was immediately revolted and embarrassed and wanted to get the hell out of his house as quickly as possible, but when I tried to pull myself away from his sticky and sweaty body, he vigorously pulled me back, and in a fit of fantastic randyness, or was it madness, he actually began to lick the cum off my cock and groin, which I found so flabbergasting that, by the time I thought to push his head away, he was already finished with his little meal and had rolled over to go to sleep.

That night, alone in my sleeping bag on the floor of Oliver's bedroom, I thought to myself: *Oh, my fucking God. That was the grossest thing I've ever done in my whole life. Never, ever again. My own hand was better than that.*

As if to broaden the scope of my thesis, I soon found myself in an empty lot near the local mall, sitting on a small boulder, about to get a blow job from a twelve-year-old girl named Zoe, whom I had just met at the ice-skating rink (and whom I've Googled many times, but I can't find her; she would be thirty-eight now). I had been minding my own business, waiting in line at the Orange Julius stand (an Orange Julius was a popular frothy drink of the eighties, commonly found in malls), when a slightly chubby blond girl, waiting in line behind me, in a denim miniskirt, and little pumps on her feet, with breasts the size of the snowy parts of snow cones, said, "Your OPs are cool," my OPs being the corduroy shorts, made by a company called Ocean Pacific, that were de rigueur for the cool kids of La Jolla.

"Thanks," I said. "I bought 'em yesterday."

"Cool," she said.

After a few moments of silence, she said: "Do you want to go to the lot out back with me?"

The *lot out back* was where kids at the mall sometimes went to hook up, but it seemed inconceivable that she was asking me to go there for that purpose. Was it possible that she was not put off by the humongous size of my nose? It was true that, when she first addressed me, from behind, she had yet to *see* my nose, in fact, she had yet to see my *face,* so it was possible that she was so horny she didn't care what I looked like at all. I knew boys could be this undis-criminating. But girls, too? And if she was horny enough not to care what I looked like, then she was possibly horny enough not to care how many testicles I had. This girl seemed sent from Heaven.

"Sure!" I said.

So we left our places in line and walked in silence to the lot out back. We sat down, side by side, on a small boulder. It was dark. She smelled like perfume. For a long time—three, four, five minutes?—no one said anything. Finally, taking the initiative, she broke the silence.

"What's your name?"

"Jon," I said. "What's yours?"

"Zoe."

A few more seconds of silence ensued, the crickets chirping away in the bushes. She piped up again: "Do you want me to give you a BJ?"

That nine-word question—"Do you want me to give you a BJ?"—was, and remains, the most amazing thing anyone's ever said to me. For at least two years I had been fantasizing about the possibility of one day having my dick sucked by a girl, and here, now, in the lot out back, a girl, out of nowhere, and oblivious to the size of my nose, was offering to suck my dick.

"Sure!" I said.

But as Zoe got down on her knees and made a beeline for my crotch, grabbing at the button of my shorts, I suddenly became concerned that she might notice there was an extra passenger along for the ride, and be repulsed by it, so, resourcefulness coming quickly to my rescue, I said, "Wait a sec," and quickly got off the boulder and lay down on the ground on my back, with the hope, of course, that Signor Quasi Testicale, the interloping bastard, would be good enough to go out for the night and leave me alone. As Zoe unbuttoned my shorts, and pulled down my zipper, and then pulled my shorts and underwear down to my knees, and then grabbed my Jon-Jon Thomas and voraciously descended upon it, Signor Quasi, tipping his hat, and wishing me the best of luck, considerately squeezed himself back into my body in time for her not to notice him. And then . . . drumroll . . . I got the first blow job of my life! It would happen to be . . . drumroll . . . the last one I'd get, the last one I'd want to get, for *seven years*. As Zoe sucked and licked and gnawed on my cock like a puppy with a chew toy, I had to fight back the urge to scream. It wasn't clear if I was watching a cartoon or being drawn and quartered. The indignities continued. First, she began to slobber. Then she burped. Then her stomach began to growl. Then a movie nearby got out, and people exiting the theater began to walk in our direction on their way to the parking garage. I propped myself up on my elbows, watching out for Peeping Toms. Eventually, by shutting my eyes and pretending that I was alone in my bed masturbating, I was able to force myself to come.

After wiping off her mouth and chin, Zoe lay back on the ground. She unzipped her miniskirt, lifted her knees toward her chest, pulled first her miniskirt off, and then her underwear off, and then, with her pumps still on, put her legs back on the ground and spread them. She closed her eyes, and waited for me to take action. But what action did she want me to take? Was I obliged, since she had given me a blow job, to reciprocate? If yes, then this raised the further, obvious, terrifying question, which Merle had not adequately addressed: In "eating a girl out," as everyone put it, what sorts of microorganisms, lurking within the folds of a girl's vagina, was one consuming? Girls urinated out of their vaginas. I had seen them do it at the beach. Even assuming they generally wiped themselves afterward, which they never did at the beach, a certain amount had to be left behind. In eating Zoe out, I would be eating, at a minimum, trace quantities, and possibly whole droplets, of her piss. I had no idea what piss consisted of. More specifically, I had no idea what *Zoe's* piss consisted of. These were questions that had to be answered before I went any further. There was also, to be appropriately cautious, Zoe's anus to consider. It was located just a half inch south of her vagina, and microparticles of fecal matter could easily have made their way north. To risk eating so much as *one molecule* of her shit was obviously out of the question!

And even if I *wanted* to eat her out, how would I do it? All I had to rely on were my wits, which were good for nothing; and the foggy memory of a few spreads in *Penthouse, Hustler,* and *Oui;* and my friends' unhelpful stories; and various glimpses, over the years, of various vaginas at Black's Beach; and Merle's ominous instruction that *if it's too hairy, then get the hell out.*

Zoe didn't seem too hairy. In the dark, all I could see,

barely illuminated by a streetlight thirty yards away, was some peach fuzz. But for all its hairlessness, the eating of it didn't seem any less potentially hazardous. Zoe sensed my discomfort. How could she not, since I was frozen in place, staring at her spread legs in silence. Reaching into the pocket of her miniskirt, which was sitting in a lump on the ground next to her, she pulled out something and handed it to me. It was a condom. It was the first condom I had ever held in my life.

"Do you want to fuck me?" she whispered. That six-word question was, and remains, the *second* most amazing thing anyone's ever said to me.

Do I want to fuck you? How can I fuck you when my dick, at the thought of eating you out, has gone limp with fear? How can I fuck you when I have no idea how to put a condom on? Merle had left this out of his lecture. *How can I fuck you when, in the event that I was able to put the condom on correctly in the dark, I wouldn't know how to put my dick inside you?* When I went through the motions of fucking Oliver, there was no hole to worry about. The friction of our two cocks rubbing together was all I needed.

For a long time, I held the condom in my hand and stared at it. Then I handed it back to her, saying nothing. Sitting up, she gathered up her underwear and miniskirt, and put them on. She stood up and brushed the dirt off her legs and shirt. Very softly, not the least bit resentfully, she said, "That's okay. Bye." And then she walked off into the night. I never saw her again.

That night, alone in bed, I thought to myself: *That does it. I mean it this time. Never never never never never again. My own hand was* better *than that.*

After my encounter with Zoe, my sexual curiosity

waned considerably. Masturbation suited me just fine for the time being. When masturbating, alone with my fantasies, I didn't have to worry about how someone might react to my engorged scrotum, or whether my nose might be too big to attract them in the first place, or whether her stomach would growl, or his breath would smell, or she'd chew my cock to pieces. Or, at just the moment when I had to be on the top of my game, I would panic, and freeze, and worry about piss and shit and diseases and death and how to use a condom. Sex involved too many uncontrollable variables. Too many potential perils.

At Andover summer school, which I attended just a few weeks after my nose job, and while my nose was still healing from the surgery, I suddenly found myself on the receiving end of far more attention from girls than I was prepared for. Whether my nose might be too big to attract them in the first place was apparently no longer an issue. Whereas, until just a few weeks earlier, I had regularly drawn comparisons, in La Jolla, California, to Pete Townshend of the Who, Pete Townshend having one of the largest noses in the history of rock music, now, incredibly, three thousand miles away in Andover, Massachusetts, I drew comparisons, by people who had not known me before I got my nose job, to Roger Daltrey of the Who. This was certainly an improvement, but not what I was hoping for, Roger Daltrey having what could be characterized as one of the most average-size noses in the history of rock music, a little thicker and meatier than the ideal I had in mind before going under the knife. (As the post-op swelling in my nose gradually subsided, so did the comparisons with Roger Daltrey, and by the time I left Andover they had ceased entirely.)

With hundreds of fifteen- and sixteen-year-olds from all

over the country gathered together on a tiny campus with nowhere to go and nothing to do at night, and with Roger Daltrey's doppelgänger being in relatively high demand, one had to try very hard to maintain one's vow of celibacy. On the first day, kids were already sneaking out of their rooms at night to have sex. By the second day, kids were already in committed relationships. By the third day, kids were already fighting, crying, breaking up, and then spreading mean rumors about each other. Gwyneth, the hottest girl at Andover that summer, spread a rumor about a boy named Philip that he had a "pin dick." She also sometimes called it a "pencil dick."

Philosophically precocious, I wondered aloud to Gwyneth if the amount of friction during sex, the sole (or at least primary) basis for judging the adequacy of the girth of a boy's penis, was a function not only of the girth of a boy's penis but also of the size of the opening of a girl's vagina, and if, while Gwyneth was lying on her back on the baseball field and getting "fucked," in her mind, by a "pin dick," it was entirely possible that Philip, while on top of her, was "fucking," in his mind, what boys sometimes called a "wet pail," or, less poetically, a "loose pussy." Gwyneth said this was impossible. "I don't have a wet pail. My pussy's tight. It was his problem, not mine."

Half suspecting that I had a pin dick, too—anyone could have one, right? How could one be absolutely sure one way or the other? With John Holmes (and my friend Gunnar) on one side of the spectrum, where did that leave the rest of us?—the chances of me pulling down my pants in front of a girl, which had never been very great to begin with, the fear of her discovering my third testicle outweighing my desire for her to fondle the other two, dropped to zero. I was left, once again, with that wise saying on the poster on my Middle Brother's wall: "When life gives you lemons, make lemonade." By now, almost three years after my various bodily deformities had pushed themselves to the surface, making lemonade was no problem for me. I was a lemon-squeezing dynamo. I already had far more lemonade than I knew what to do with, barrels and barrels of it sitting unused in a warehouse. But if life continued to give me lemons, then it was either squeeze them or let them rot. So, while the other kids at Andover snuck out of their bedrooms at night to go hook up with each other on various fields and quads and commons, I, Master Lemonade Maker, stayed home, all alone, in my little dorm room, my walls covered with pictures cut out from *Surfer* magazine, and consoled myself in the knowledge that the girls I hooked up with in my fantasies were either perfectly satisfied with my performance or polite enough, in the event that they were disappointed, to keep the details of my anatomy to themselves.

Though Gwyneth never made a pass at me, she was clearly curious about my sexuality. She would often mention to me that a particular girl had a crush on me, and then stare at me closely to gauge my reaction. My reaction was always the same: no matter who this girl was, she wasn't quite right for me. Her hair was wrong, or her giggle was annoying, or her ass was misshapen, or she had a nose the size of Pete Townshend's of the Who—whatever it took to convince Gwyneth that this girl wasn't good enough. I became an expert in isolating the physical or psychological flaws of every girl on campus, so that Gwyneth, when she tried to flush me out of my hiding place by telling me that all these girls had crushes on me, would be at least half convinced that my sexual aloofness was a function of pickiness and nothing else. Gwyneth refused to give up. Every weekend she sent word to a group of kids, including me, to meet up late at night on this particular field, or that particular quad, for Truth or Dare, and I never went.

"We missed you last night," she would say to me the next morning.

"Yep," I would say, and then change the subject.

When I pierced my ears on the last day of school, Gwyneth laughed and gave me a kiss on the cheek. A few weeks later, she sent me a letter, saying, in essence: "I knew it all along!"

The students at La Jolla High School, who knew me better than Gwyneth did, who had seen me kiss girls at parties in junior high school, had seen me slow-dance with girls, and seem to enjoy it, at school dances, were less sure than Gwyneth of what to make of my transformation. As my friend Macky always put it, when people asked him what he thought was up with me: "Bowie's weird. Jagger's weird. And those dudes aren't fags. So who knows, man?"

Macky's facts were a little shaky. The heterosexuality of neither Bowie nor Jagger was quite as unequivocal as he assumed. But his logic was sound, and convincing enough. *Who knows, man?* Even Macky himself didn't know. He never confronted me directly, and I never brought it up.

The eventual discovery of my hernia by Dr. Schoenberg, and the solving of the mystery of my phantom third testicle, would, you might assume, have been in some sense liberating. A major hurdle to pulling down my pants had been surmounted. No longer would I have to worry about a girl spreading rumors about the "three-balled freak." Unfortunately, by the time this hurdle had been removed, my friends had filled my head with three years' worth of horror stories, enough to cause a lifetime of sleepless nights, about the disgustingness of sex: stories of yeast infections, and the tube of Vagisil that every girl had in her medicine chest to combat them; stories of the itchiness of crabs, and, a subject of great debate, whether to drown them or shave the pubes; stories of the sores and scabs of herpes, oral or genital, and in both cases a life curse; stories of bloody tampons, broken condoms, abortions, and all the sights and sounds and smells that came with anal intercourse; and, finally, what appeared to be the stake through the heart of there being any possibility of my ever having sex in my entire life, and I have Rusty Beitman to thank for this choice morsel of information, something invented by the Devil solely to torment me called a "vaginal blood fart," which I've never seen or heard in all my life and I hope that never changes. Just the *thought* that a girl defecated made it almost impossible for me to think seriously of her as a sexual object, and you have to tell me about *vaginal blood farts*?

In my disappointment over the typically mammalian tendencies of a woman's body, I was neither alone nor original. Jonathan Swift, I learned later, beat me to it by 250 years, with "The Lady's Dressing Room," a poem about a man named Strephon who sneaks into the bedroom of a woman named Celia and finds out, by sniffing her underwear, looking in her toilet, and examining the dandruff in her hairbrush, that women, behind their makeup and perfume and deodorant, are, like men, animals: "Oh!" he cries, in a fit of existential despair. "Celia, Celia, Celia shits!" His punishment, by the Goddess of Vengeance, for encroaching on Celia's privacy, is that he can never look at a woman again without seeing her "with all her Stinks."

What finally compelled me to overcome my fears and try to hook up with a girl was not the certainty that my own body was beyond reproach, or that I would not contract herpes or warts or crabs. What finally compelled me was the need, after three years of masturbating in a state of almost complete remove from actual sexual experience, for something other than my imagination, and the few tidbits I'd managed to cull from that one hookup with Zoe two years earlier, on which to draw for my fantasies. What did sex smell like, taste like, sound like, *feel* like? Potentially disgusting or not, potentially lethal or not, I needed to know. My penis, fighting to stay hard as I hacked away at it, was beginning to tire of cooperating. To stave off what I feared would soon become a permanent state of impotence, the ratio of abstraction to concreteness in my fantasies needed to be reduced.

Deirdre, an adorable fourteen-year-old girl who lived a mile away from me and who, from the hard stares she gave me every time she passed me in the hallway at school, was clearly one of the few girls for whom my effeminacy was a turn-on, seemed like a sure thing. Her family had just moved to La Jolla a few months earlier, from what I would find out later was a famous cult in Northern California. She knew nobody in town. She had no friends. She was a loner. If I embarrassed myself, which was inevitable, it would stay on the block. So I found out her name, called up information to get her family's number, and gave her a ring.

Recently, via Facebook, I got in touch with Deirdre for the first time in twenty-four years, and asked her what she remembered about the forty-five minutes we spent together. She wrote back to me almost immediately: "You came over to my house. My parents were out. We ordered pizza. We started making-out, and then you suddenly pulled away and bolted. You went home and never talked to me again."

That one, fortunately, stayed on the block.

The next and final one, with a girl named Edie, a bout of mild groping and sucking on a grass lawn at UCSD, did not stay on the block but, rather, was observed by a group of college freshmen who were hiding behind the bushes. What I learned that afternoon is that you should always assume, when hooking up in a public space, no matter how well concealed you think you are, by that blanket, or that car, or that tall brick wall, that you are being watched.

Edie had a boyfriend named Eric. Edie and Eric were always breaking up and, during those brief intervals of opportunity, would hook up with as many other people as possible to make each other jealous. That's where I came in. The hookup occurred in the shade of a small tree, behind what I thought was a thick and impenetrable hedge. It was a warm day. We were sleepy. We had been lying on a blanket all afternoon reading magazines. She was wearing a bikini top and jeans. For fifteen minutes she painted her toenails, then lay back on the blanket and let them dry. Soon, she fell asleep. I stared at her sleeping body, making mental notes for future use. At one point, she shifted her body, and the hint of a happy trail, just above the waist of her jeans, came into view. Instinctively, I reached over and touched it. Edie's eyes opened. Her hand, speeding things along, reached over and grabbed my crotch. With Edie now wide awake, and her hand grabbing at me through my thin cotton pants, the question of whether or not I would take her happy trail to the point of its terminus, which, after all, is the point of a trail, now presented itself.

But this was a public space, in broad daylight, and the possibility of getting caught by a cop also presented itself.

I craned my neck in every direction but couldn't see anyone. The coast seemed clear. But just in case, to be safe, my plan was to leave Edie's happy trail and move north, starting at second base, which would only be a misdemeanor, before moving south to third base, which was unquestionably a felony. I pushed her bikini top above her right breast and started playing with her brown nipple, which inflated like a bicycle tire, growing twice as thick, twice as hard, as I rubbed it between my fingers. When I bent closer and began sucking on it, *the first nipple I had ever sucked on in my life,* dozens of Oscar Mayer hot dogs began to fall out of the sky. When I pulled back and looked up, another two dozen hot dogs, all of them cold and wet and uncooked, came arcing high over the hedge, like a storm of V-2 rockets from across the Channel, and showered down upon us. Terrified, I stood up. Someone was pelting us with hot dogs. But why? Then again, from across the hedge, arcing high into the sky, another salvo of fifteen to twenty franks, this time accompanied by giggles and rustling in the bushes and shouts of "Go find a hotel room, kiddies!"

Oh, my God. Of course! PDA! They had been watching and waiting for just the right moment to embarrass me.

How is it possible, in this world of cruelty, and disease, and mammalian excretions, that people manage to develop normal sex lives? You think you've conquered one obstacle, and there's another one around the corner. Or, in my case, there were two dozen flying through the sky. If my masturbatory fantasies were lacking in oomph and color, and fuzzy in the details, so be it. Hooking up with girls was too fraught for me to enhance the picture. I'd have better luck hooking up with a cactus. The only option for me, to avoid further stressful entanglements, was to take myself off the sexual market—not that I had been such a hot item to begin with—for good. Choosing, as my prom date, Courtney Buffington, a girl who had no sexual interest in me and who had a serious boyfriend, was just one of many strategies I adopted, as high school drew to a close, to maintain my virginity. Never getting drunk was another. When my friends were meeting at the AMPM mini market at the intersection of Nautilus and La Jolla Boulevard, to find out, from the stoners and burnouts milling about in the parking lot, where the parties were, I was usually home alone, in my room, under my covers, in the dark, listening to Culture Club or Bananarama. Hooking up on the beach, at a late-night keg party, the sand still warm from the sun, was loads of fun, so I was told, though I never did it. Hooking up in the dugout at a keg party at the Pony field (one of four baseball fields in La Jolla; the others being Pinto, Mustang, and Colt) was less fun, so I was told, because the benches were hard, though I never did that either. And never once, and I'm the only kid I know of who grew up in La Jolla of whom this is true, did I go to Hussong's Cantina, located seventy miles south of the border in Ensenada, Mexico, where beer was served cheaply, and unquestioningly, to anyone who looked over the age of fourteen. Yes, I lived the life of a eunuch. But it was the safe and healthy life of a eunuch. And that's nothing to scoff at.

During orientation week at Columbia College, where the incoming rabbits made the kiddies at Andover look like baby turtles, I should have worn a chastity belt and thrown the key down the drain. Sex in the bushes, sex on the steps, sex in the stacks, sex on the tennis court directly in front of John Jay Hall.* Even the Elephant Man could have gotten lucky that week. Had I not been so distracted by the Perils and Horrors of New York City, I would have been in a better position to realize that my new friend Daphne, a freshman at Columbia from Malibu, had other things on her mind than shopping for skirts and makeup with me. With her blond hair, blue eyes, and tan face, and that pineapple-coconut suntan lotion she always wore, she reminded me of all the girls back home in La Jolla, and I had gravitated toward her instantly because of it. Hanging out with someone equally out of her element was comforting to me, and I found it hard to leave her side. Little did I know that Daphne was using her Southern California vibe as a Trojan horse! She brought down my guard, I let her into my room, and then boom! Out came the Trojan to get me.

What I learned from that early September evening, a lesson I would learn again and again throughout my life, is that certain women in this world, whether because of awful prior experiences with aggressive men or simply out of sheer perversity, are attracted to pansies. *He's so refreshingly delicate. So sensitive. So unthreatening. A car backfires and he cowers in the corner. I can't wait to break him in.* The thrill of not being mounted for once, and doing the mounting themselves, is too much for these girls to resist.

Which explains how I find myself lying flat on my back on my bed, in Room 910 of John Jay Hall, Daphne pinning my shoulders down and bouncing on top of me, my four-

* A tennis court no longer in existence, I recently discovered, in case you're a Columbia student and go looking for it.

inch heels still on my feet, and trying hard to stay fully aroused in the face of an overwhelming number of distractions. The chief distraction is the presence, barely three feet away from me, of my koala bear hand puppet, Mr. Marvel, which I went to the trouble of bringing with me all the way from La Jolla. Ten hours after reading *The Victim's Song*, my mind swimming with a thousand and one horrors, and hastily packing for my new life away from home, I grabbed him for dear life and never let go. He was in my carry-on luggage; he was in my lap during the cab ride from JFK; and now, sitting on the new fan I bought at the Columbia Hardware store on Broadway and 113th Street, just a few feet from the bed on which I am currently being devirginized, he is in my dorm room.

Other distractions making it almost impossible to stay aroused include (1) Is one condom enough? This seems messy enough for five or six. (2) What am I supposed to do with my hands? Since she's no longer pinning my shoulders down, now using her hands to squeeze her own breasts, trying to squeeze them myself would be redundant. (3) Has she come yet? How does one know? I don't recall Merle, or any of my friends for that matter, ever addressing this. (4) Can she possibly be enjoying this as much as her moaning and gasping and near hyperventilating suggest? These convulsions of ecstasy into which she has thrown herself— mouth open, slobber dripping off her lower lip, upper teeth jutting out, like that dying horse in Picasso's *Guernica*—are obviously disproportionate to whatever pleasure I can possibly be providing her. I am clearly a bit player in some larger drama she's concocting in her head. Who is lying beneath her right now in her fantasies? The captain of the football team back home?

"Come, Jon-Jon," she says out of nowhere. "Come for me. I want you to come."

When she says this, I am instantly reminded of a scene in *Petals on the Wind,* the second book in the gothic pentalogy for teenage girls by V. C. Andrews. In *Flowers in the Attic,* the first in this series, a brother and sister are negligently left to the care of a wicked grandmother by a mother who is too busy with her own life to take care of them. The grandmother, resenting the burden, locks her grandchildren in an attic, and then tries to gradually poison them to death by spiking their food with small amounts of arsenic. The siblings, in their early teens, bored and randy, have sex with each other on a dirty mattress. They end up surviving the attempted murder, their mother coming to their rescue at the last moment, but barely. Another few days and they would have died. In *Petals on the Wind,* the sister, now sixteen, has sex for only the second time in her life, with a much older man, who pleads with her, after going at it for an hour, to come. "Come," he says insistently. "Come. Come." Having been holed up in an attic her whole life, not properly educated, the girl has no idea what an orgasm is, and so has no idea what he's talking about. "Come where?" she says in earnest. "Come where?"

Sensing my distraction, Daphne throws herself more forcefully against my body. The sight of her is dizzying. Her long blond hair is in a frenzy. She's a blur of movement. Maybe if I closed my eyes, and removed myself from this ridiculous scene, with Mr. Marvel staring at me from his perch on the fan, and returned myself to the safe abstractions of my fantasies, I could easily come, but then a further distraction presents itself: What am I supposed to do when

I come? In the few porn movies I've seen, the men, all of them bald and fat and hairy, screamed when they came as if they were being disemboweled. I refuse to do that. Saying nothing at all, on the other hand, seems unceremonious. There must be some middle ground, something more demonstrative than silence but quieter than a Comanche war cry, but what is it? Once again, neither Merle nor any of my friends had addressed this.

"Come, Jon-Jon! Come!"

Okay! Give me a moment!

I close my eyes. I concentrate. I eventually come. To herald the event, I make a small peeping noise, like a baby chick.

When Danny Berman and I went east for college, we agreed that whoever got devirginized first would call the other to report. I considered sending him a postcard with a picture of a kosher dill pickle and a bagel on the front of it, the words "I Love New York" across the top, and on the back I would write, "I GOT IT!" a reference to Judy Blume's *Are You There God? It's Me, Margaret,* in which a twelve-year-old girl sends her friend a note saying "I GOT IT!!!" to falsely suggest that she had finally gotten her period. Getting their periods was everything to these girls. It was a crucial rite of passage that couldn't happen soon enough. All of their friends had gotten theirs, and these two girls, lagging far behind, were the odd girls out. Just like Danny and me! The joke was too perfect to resist. The only problem with it was that in my case it made no sense. I had, in fact, gotten it. By sending that postcard, I would be either confusing him, if he knew the reference, or rubbing it in.

So I called him and gave him the full report, sparing myself nothing. I indicted myself for unmanliness and argued my case mercilessly. Danny came to my defense, arguing, with some merit, that my limited sexual experience gave me no grounds for such definitive conclusions, but his efforts to mollify me came to nothing. After hanging up the phone, I was no less mortified than I was before, and I had trouble getting out of bed for days.

On a large, sprawling campus, a place like the University of Texas at Austin, for example, with a student body of thousands, it is not hard, I imagine, to avoid people you have sex with whom you never want to see again for the rest of your life because you are overcome by embarrassment at the memory of what you assume was a pathetic performance. Classrooms are miles apart from each other. Dorm rooms are whole towns apart from each other. You gather up your clothes, do the walk of shame, then change your routine a bit. You start eating in dining hall number 17A, on campus 14B, instead. And you never see the person ever again.

At Columbia College, where the campus was one avenue wide and six blocks long, where there were 750 people in a class, the size of a small public high school, and where the freshmen ate in one dining hall, and one dining hall only, even the Incredible Shrinking Woman, when she has shrunk to the size of the head of a pin, would have had trouble staying out of view.

The Invisible Man, on the other hand, would have had no trouble. By participating in not a single extracurricular activity, not even a single game of Frisbee; attending not a single concert or play or performance of any kind; attending no guest lectures, not even by Václav Havel; joining no clubs or groups or organizations; going out of your way to take classes at odd hours, like 8:40 in the morning, and 8:40 at night; and eating only between one and two quick meals a day, making sure to arrive at the dining hall the second it opens and then scurrying away, tray in hand, no more than fifteen minutes later, it's not hard to avoid being seen. In compulsively keeping myself out of view, I was participating, without realizing it, in a rich New York tradition. Loners and shut-ins and hermits are what keep New York City from imploding. If all the people who never leave their apartments in New York City suddenly left their apartments, the city's infrastructure would crumble. There are not enough stop signs, traffic lights, police officers, restaurants, subway cars, movie theaters, kiosks, hot dog stands, bodegas, or brothels to accommodate these people.

C'mon! you're thinking. You're overreacting! You went to these absurd extremes because of a so-so one-night stand? What happened to you wasn't that bad. So you were distracted during sex. You had trouble keeping it up. You did nothing with your hands, when maybe you should have grabbed her ass. You peeped when you came, when maybe you should have yelped. But these are hardly felonies. Embarrassing sex stories, as we all know, can get much worse than that.

Unfortunately, when something unpleasant happens to you in life, it never does any good to be reminded that someone else has it worse. Just as a case of chicken pox is not made any more bearable by being told that at least you don't have monkeypox (a close relative of smallpox, and just as unpleasant; in 2003, an outbreak of monkeypox in the United States resulted in ninety-three cases, and you should be very grateful you weren't one of them), so is a pathetic performance during a one-night stand, so pathetic that you actually recoiled with embarrassment when she tried to cuddle afterward, not made any more bearable by being told that at least you got it halfway up, a veritable triumph when compared with that other boy, a laughingstock on campus forever after, who couldn't get it up at all.

Chicken pox, while not monkeypox, is still chicken pox. Extreme embarrassment, halfway up or not, is still extreme embarrassment.

So I scurried in and out of the dining hall, and ducked behind lampposts, and hid in the bushes when I thought I saw her coming my way. But still she caught sight of me. Columbia was too small for me. I couldn't hide. In fact, on about three occasions she almost bumped into me. "Hey! What's up?" she would say, with a tinge, if I heard correctly, of guilt in her voice, the guilt that comes from knowing that you have robbed someone of his virginity, corrupting his innocence. "I haven't seen you for*ever*!"

"Not much! But I gotta go! I'm in a rush! I'm late for class!" I'd say, and then, with a tray full of food in my hands, I would go upstairs to my room and not leave it for three days.

In order for me to survive at Columbia, something would have to change. Like the Incredible Shrinking Woman, my sanity was gradually waning to the point of a pin, and about to wash down the drain. What had been a mild case of neurasthenia back in La Jolla was threatening to become a full-blown case of catatonia. Murderers lying in wait for me in the subway; psychopaths with baseball bats lurking on the outskirts of the Ramble; gargoyles falling from the sky; football players calling me "AIDSmobile" and "butt smacker"; and beach bunnies from Malibu taking advantage of my need for comfort, in this horror away from home, by surmounting me and stealing my virginity.

What I needed, clearly, was a better place to hide. The reason it's so hard to find Waldo when you go looking for him is that he's camouflaged against a backdrop of a thousand little men who look almost exactly like him. I needed to take a page out of Waldo's playbook. Just as Waldo blended into the woodwork of other Waldos, I needed to blend so perfectly into the floral wallpaper that, when you saw the high heels, the makeup, the skirt (and the cheeks of my ass through the skirt if I was wearing G-string underwear), you would see nothing but the flowers and move on.

The obvious solution, which I didn't discover until the end of my freshman year, had been staring me directly in the face, directly across the street, all along: Barnard College. A school full of women, only women, nothing but women. And not just women. But women so in touch with their womanliness that only a college *only for women* was good enough for them.

When Columbia College was all-male, an archaic arrangement that had persisted until as recently as 1982, Barnard College was known, invidiously, as its "sister school." The reason you went there, it was assumed, was that they wouldn't let you go to Columbia. But now that Columbia was coed, Barnard was no longer Columbia's little sister but a Proud Women's College in Its Own Right.

So, at the beginning of my sophomore year, I moved across the street. On the central campus of Barnard, in a quadrangle of four dorms full of hundreds of young women, there were about thirty rooms, I discovered, reserved for Columbia students, both men and women. This generosity of spirit is just what you would expect from a Proud Women's College in Its Own Right: we do not hold a grudge against our big brother, who used to look down on us, and still does; we open our doors to him. But the only Columbia students who volunteered to take these rooms were those whose lottery numbers were so bad that the alternative was living on Staten Island. There was no other reason, apparently, why one would want to live on the central campus of a women's college, especially a women's college that, until recently, had been your little sister. When your lottery number improved, as it always did by the following year, you were expected to hightail it back to Columbia.

The number I drew in the housing lottery for my sophomore year wasn't bad. I could have lived in any one of a handful of conveniently located dorms on the Columbia campus. But why live at Columbia, surrounded by men, when I could live, just like Waldo, camouflaged against a backdrop of over a thousand little girls who looked just like me? When they looked my way, they would see a skirt, a long pearl necklace, rhinestone-studded sunglasses, knee-high boots with five-inch heels, a head wrap with peacock feathers attached to it, think nothing of it, and move on. At worst they would flash me a smile of encouragement. At best they would ignore me. That was my hope.

I was often asked by my classmates, and am still asked today by people who find out that I lived at a women's college for three years, if I moved to Barnard because I *felt like a woman,* and had such a strong sense of my womanhood that I needed to be with my fellow kind. The answer is no.

I felt like a neurasthenic man, in a city of horrors, who was homesick for La Jolla. Just as a Jew in Italy during World War II would have gladly sought refuge in the Vatican, not because he was a Catholic but because he didn't want to be carted off to Auschwitz by the Germans, so did I seek refuge at Barnard for no other reason than to hide.

And hide I did. For three straight years, three thousand miles away from the protective embrace of my hometown, I lived in what amounted to an almost perfectly hermetically sealed environment. Everything I needed—mailroom, dining hall, library, café, classrooms—was accessible via a system of corridors and tunnels that ran the length of the Barnard campus, from 116th Street to 120th Street. There was no need to go outdoors. The Perils and Horrors of the city, which, in winter, included bitingly cold wind off the Hudson River, were kept safely at bay. Or so I thought. . . .

At the end of Hitchcock's *The Birds,* there is a horrific scene in which Tippi Hedren, thinking she's safe inside the house, suddenly walks into a room full of birds. For what must have been hours, her boyfriend had been nailing boards against windows and doors, barricading the occupants of the house against the birds outside on the lawn, and, all along, unbeknownst to him, there was a hole in the ceiling of one of the rooms upstairs. They thought they were protected, looking out toward the birds from a position of safety, but the peril was hidden within.

A similar thing happened to me at Barnard. Here I was, in skirt and G-string and heels and halter top, prancing around campus, raising not a single eyebrow on any one of these girls, who took me perfectly in stride, and therefore assuming I was safe from potential predators, when, all along, the peril was hidden within. I wasn't safe at all. And what was this hidden peril? My own sex drive!

After my one-night stand with Daphne a year earlier—correction: one-night *prostration* with Daphne—my libido, scared senseless, had gone into hiding. I even stopped masturbating. It was no longer possible for me to disassociate my sexual fantasies from the Stress and Mess that sex, in real life, I now knew beyond a reasonable doubt, necessarily entailed.

At Barnard, completely unexpectedly, my libido was suddenly liberated. What had awakened it from its dormancy? An emaciated eighteen-year-old woman who, because of the annoying habit she had of hogging the one microwave oven in the Barnard cafeteria, so that she could heat and reheat and reheat yet again the giant mounds of vegetables that she picked at, poked at, nibbled on, and only occasionally swallowed, was known by the horrible nickname the Vegetable Monster.

I thought I would be safe within the four walls of Barnard, but here, in the cafeteria, showing up every single day the second it opened, and not leaving until the second it closed, the Vegetable Monster was lying in wait for me. When I first set eyes on her, the tug in my groin was *instantaneous*. The tug in my heart came a moment later. This woman clearly did not feel at home at Barnard, just as I had not felt at home at Columbia. What, or whom, did she miss? Did she grow up on a farm? Was that why she was hiding behind a fortress of vegetables? To remind herself of the comforts of home? But then why not eat them with greater gusto? Or with any gusto at all? She had surrounded herself with broccoli and cauliflower and carrots in the same way that I had surrounded myself with stuffed animals at home, seemingly as a means of protection, but whereas I hugged my animals, and grabbed hold of them for support, she was picking and poking at these vegetables as if they were worms.

Was this woman not eighteen? Was she sixteen, the same age my brother had been when he went to college? She could easily have been fourteen. Maybe she was a fourteen-year-old genius, and that's why she felt out of place. She looked like a lost little child. She was clearly crying out for help, but no one was offering it. With those dark circles around her eyes, and her gray skin, and her cavernous cheeks, and her bony forearms covered with a thin layer of dark fur, and her dazed, abstracted gaze, she looked freshly liberated from Buchenwald, drastically in need of help, and yet all the other girls were walking by her table as if she didn't exist.

By no objectively reasonable standards would this woman have been considered sexually attractive. No man I've ever known would have wanted her. And yet my lust for her was overpowering. She was the first girl in my life that I could not get out of my mind. Wherever I was—in bed, in the shower, in class—she hovered in my head, staring vacantly and picking at her vegetables. What could possibly have been the basis of my attraction?

And then it dawned on me. You are what you eat! Or, in her case, what you barely eat. One of the main reasons sex was so stressful for me was that I could never be sure what a woman's bodily juices contained. God only knows what most people eat in their spare time or, worse, when you're watching. Zoe, for instance, the twelve-year-old girl I met at the mall, was not chubby for nothing. Hot dogs and pizza and Twinkies and Ding Dongs, all packed with saturated fat, and artificial preservatives and dyes, were coursing through her veins and arteries, and then branching out, setting up stakes, in her skin and inner organs. One bite of Zoe, and before long you're wearing a pacemaker.

But with the Vegetable Monster, there was no mystery whatsoever as to what her body contained. For two hours, setting up my own tray just a table or two away from her, I watched her eat. Unless she was eating hot dogs and Twinkies on the sly, behind my back, which was inconceivable, because there was no place in her body for these substances to take up residence, then her body contained, in addition to tiny bites of vegetables, an occasional egg white, an occasional spoonful of brown rice, and an occasional spoonful of kidney beans.

A woman's sexual history, always a mystery, was another problem for me, because there was always the risk not only of being measured against the performance of other, better experienced men but also of contracting sexually transmitted diseases. Zoe was not aggressive for nothing. That girl, at the age of twelve, probably had more experience than I do now. But with the Vegetable Monster, this would not be a source of concern. Unlike Zoe, who had grown up, I imagine, in a broken home, free to roam like an alley cat through the malls of San Diego, the Vegetable Monster, as I imagined it, had grown up on a secluded farm, an only child perhaps, homeschooled by her loving and protective parents, and was still, I was certain, a virgin. Unscathed by the caresses of other men, she would have no prior experiences against which to judge me, and no venereal diseases with which to destroy me. When I was four years old, I had a friend named Eliza. When we had play-dates, we would go outside, take off our clothes, and hold hands while watching each other pee. And then we would giggle and kiss each other on the cheek. It was the most romantically satisfying relationship I have ever had in my life. With the Vegetable Monster, I can only imagine as I look back at this twisted obsession of mine, I was hoping to recapture the innocence, and playfulness, and cleanliness, of my very first crush.

But hard as I tried to get her attention, so that I could take things to the next step, she wouldn't notice me. Every day I sat no more than eight feet away from her, usually at the adjacent table, well within her line of view, waiting for her to make eye contact with me. My plan was simple. When she caught my eye I would smile. Then, I hoped, she would smile. Then I would hold up a broccoli stalk and say, "Great stomachs think alike!" And she would giggle. A week later we'd be holding hands and watching each other pee.

But I never caught her eye. She was oblivious to me. She picked away at her broccoli, staring vacantly at her plate, too lost in her tortured abstractions to notice even herself.

In the face of her persistent inability—not refusal, mind you; that I could not accept—to acknowledge me, I was finally reduced, in an effort to wrest her attention away from her food, to trying to stimulate her attention by emulating her. With no other options open to me, I followed her example and built myself a fortress of vegetables, surrounding myself with plates and bowls and teacups full of heaping mounds of broccoli, cauliflower, carrots, and asparagus, which I picked at, poked at, and nibbled on, and continually reheated in the microwave. Since I was skinny to begin with, the effect was almost immediate. What had been any-where between 127 and 132 pounds when I got to Colum-bia quickly dropped, in the course of about two weeks, to anywhere from 118 to 122 pounds. My hope was that, by drastically dropping in weight, and becoming, in a sense, less visible than I was before, I would, paradoxically, be-come more noticeable to her, for she couldn't help but rec-ognize me as a fellow member of the tribe. She would be titillated, roused into action by the sight of my increasingly emaciated body, much as a dwarf, shipwrecked on an island of giants, would be turned on by the sudden arrival of an-other dwarf. My reasoning, I felt, was ingenious. Unfortu-nately, my irresistibly anorectic body, or so I thought, was still no match for the cloud of abstraction in which she was irretrievably lost. A few times I thought I caught her eye, and smiled her way, but no. In my desperation I had imag-ined it. I got nothing but the same vacant stares, the same digging of fingernails into stalks of broccoli.

Eventually, she disappeared. At the beginning of the sec-ond semester of my junior year, she didn't come back to school. As rumor had it, she had died of malnutrition, but of course rumor would have had it that way, and there was no way to confirm this. I have no idea what happened to her. I never once met her. I never found out where she came from. I never, as far as I was aware, even caught her eye. I never found out her real name. The Vegetable Monster. That's how I knew her. And that's how she will live on in my memory.

Meanwhile, although the sight of my increasingly ema-ciated body was powerless against the walls of broccoli and cauliflower and asparagus that had surrounded the Vegetable Monster, it was far more powerful than I had intended it to be against the wall of aloofness that had kept the rest of the Barnard women (or, more accurately, one woman in particular) from noticing me. Suddenly, clearly as a result of my brief flirtation with anorexia, whether because it made me attractively taut and bony or attractively pathetic and in need of help, a senior at Barnard named Stevie Nidini, with small breasts and unshaved underarms, and a healthy appetite for both men and women, made it clear to me, through hard stares and smiles, and sitting near me in the cafeteria, and leaving messages on my answering machine, that she wanted me. For Stevie, it is clear to me now, a womanly man was two for one. Which explains how Stevie and I ended up in my room together, with me naked and scared beneath the covers, and her wanting to break me in sexually before I was reduced to a state of permanent and irremediable virginity.

So here I am, two months shy of graduation, role-playing my way to sexual maturity. Our understanding from the outset, since this was her idea, and since she's the only one, of the two of us, with relevant sexual experience on which to draw, is that she should always be the dominant character. Just as she compelled me, through the force of her logic, to submit to this outlandish method of sexual therapy, so shall she compel me, through the force of her dominance, to let her mount me.

For our first scenario, I am a sixteen-year-old boy who is in the hospital about to have a hernia fixed. I am lying on my back, completely naked, on a hospital bed, the sheet pulled up above my nipples. I am lonely, scared, thinking of my warm bed back home, and the stuffed animals who will be waiting for me. Margaret, the only nurse I have ever seen in my life with unshaved underarms, comes to my side to put a soothing hand on my shoulder.

"Don't worry," she says. "Dr. Proukosh will take care of it. You'll be okay, sweetie. You'll be all better in no time."

"I can't help it," I say. "I'm scared."

Margaret is very nice to me. To relieve me of my anxiety, take my mind off my pending surgery, she rips off the bed-sheet, pulls out a condom, slips it on my cock, and climbs on top of me. Thrilled to lose my virginity at such a young age, I come, effortlessly, and Margaret raises her arms in triumph.

In the second scenario, much harder for me to play, I am supposed to be a nerdy computer technician at IBM named Mort, whose wife, for his birthday, has gotten him a gift certificate to Alpine Meadows Massage Parlor. Mort's posture is terrible. He has been hunched up at the computer for ten straight years, and his wife thought a massage might loosen up the kinks. It will be the first massage Mort has ever gotten in his life. It will be the first time Mort has ever been naked with a woman other than his wife. Stevie is Inga, my Swedish masseuse. Within ten minutes, after barely going through the motions of trying to loosen up the kinks in Mort's back, Inga is rubbing the tip of her tongue around the circumference of Mort's anus. Mort doesn't know what to make of this. His wife has never done this for him. Before he has time to process his emotions, Inga flips him over and sits on his face. Struggling to breathe, Mort flaps his arms wildly. Inga, sensing Mort's discomfort, takes out a condom, slips it on Mort's cock, and climbs on top of him. Before he has a chance to be distracted by the knowledge that he is cheating on his wife, Mort, who has never been mounted before, and who is overwhelmed by how much more pleasurable it is to lie still and let someone else do the work, comes, effortlessly, and Inga raises her arms in triumph.

By the twelfth and thirteenth and fourteenth scenarios, played out over the next two weeks, each scenario more absurd than the one preceding it (the last two or three taking place in outer space, with Stevie always playing the voracious alien, and me the hapless astronaut), it becomes increasingly difficult to stay in character without laughing. With my virginity now a distant memory, and with final exams, for which neither of us has studied, coming up in a matter of days, we raise our arms in victory and call it quits.

Stevie and I parted ways after college. She went on to get a master's degree in "sex education," as she put it, at the University of Pennsylvania, and now lives in Northern California, happily married, to a *man,* and with two gorgeous children. I give her enormous credit for doing her best to help me overcome my fears of sex, though I must admit that she was only partially successful. Two weeks of sex with Stevie, my health and self-esteem still intact in the end, convinced me that sex can be survived, at least in the short term, in one piece. But though this knowledge has helped me break through my fears, I've never once been able to have sex without a running commentary in my head, from the voices of caution, extremely distracting to me, as you might imagine, about all the things that could be going wrong. And when the sex is over, the certainty that all the things that could have gone wrong did, in fact, go wrong always sends me running into the arms of celibacy for months, and sometimes years.

Those two weeks of sex with Stevie, which occurred over eighteen years ago, remain, to this day, the most sex I've ever had with anyone in my life.

CHAPTER 7

"This Is Not Romper Room, Sweetie. This Is a Place of Business"

T IS EARLY AUGUST 1998, about a week before my thirtieth birthday. A letter, in a cold white envelope, arrives in the mail from my dad, otherwise known to me, since I was a little boy, as Dada. It's the first letter—the very first letter!—he's ever sent me. Letters between us have never been necessary. Until I was eighteen, we lived in the same house, and spoke to each other every day. From the age of eighteen to right this moment, we've been speaking on the phone every Sunday, my father on one Panasonic cordless phone, my mother on another, running through the major events of the previous week. The conversations are brief, but full of love:

"Dad, I've been eating a lot of oat groats lately."

"Oat groats? Or steel-cut oats?"

"Oat groats."

"Wow. Those take a long time to cook."

"Forty-five minutes."

"That's what I thought. Steel-cut oats take only fifteen."

"But not as much fiber!"

"Good point!"

"I'll cook them for you when I see you for Christmas."

"I can't wait!"

See? He can't wait. I just saw him in Vermont over Columbus Day, where I made him my new quinoa dish, with onions and capers, and now I'm going to see him for Christmas, when I'll cook him oat groats. I will also make him my new bulgur dish, the bulgur lightly sautéed in canola oil before I add the water.

What could be so important, after nearly thirty years of face-to-face and phone-to-phone communication, full of so much love and nutrition, that Dada has to put it in a letter? Is he worried about something? Did someone happen to mention to him that, although I am about to turn thirty, an important milestone for members of the Responsible, Ambitious, and Worthy, a chance to take stock of where you are in life, what you've accomplished and where you are headed, I have nothing at all to take stock of but, rather, am unemployed, curled up in a ball, and living in a curtained-off portion, roughly sixty square feet, of a woman's living room on the Lower East Side, about a hundred yards from where my Grandpa Sidney was born nearly a hundred years ago, the great trajectory of three generations proving to be, thanks to me, not that of an arrow, shooting straight through the bull's-eye of the American dream, but that of a boomerang, bent in the middle, which has finally come to a clanking drop in the gutter from which it started?

Or did no one say anything at all? Perhaps Dada, despite living three thousand miles away from me, could no longer fail to acknowledge the gradually mounting evidence, over the previous fourteen years, ever since I quit soccer at the age of sixteen despite playing it for ten years and playing it so well, that Son Number Three appeared to have hopped on a different ship from that of Sons Numbers One and Two, their ship heading for Ellis Island and mine heading into an iceberg.

I can't open this letter! To lose Dada's moral support would be the end of me!

———

In the spring of 1983, when I was fourteen years old, I raised my family's hopes for me to an all-time high when I wrote a short essay, for my English class, called "My Life at Thirty: How I Got Here." Everyone in the family who read this essay, especially my Granny Shammy, was shocked into a state of near ecstasy by the depth of my ambition, the strength of my confidence, and the clarity of my vision of what the future had in store for me. Nothing, it was generally agreed, could possibly come between the boy who wrote this essay and a life of intellectual, professional, and emotional fulfillment:

My Life at Thirty: How I Got Here

I have been in Africa for eight months. I am with a group of sixty Americans, all of whom are doctors and nurses, including my wife. I met her at Yale, where I spent my first four years out of high school. We were both pre-meds and natives of La Jolla, so it is not surprising that we both attended U.C.S.D. Medical School.

After medical school our internships separated us. I was in orthopedics at Massachusetts General Hospital.

She was in anesthesia at the University of Chicago. When we were again united, we were not sure of our future. We decided to take a year off, but we wanted to do something medically constructive.

It was then that we heard about a government-sponsored caravan that was going to Africa for a year. Paid by the U.S. government, a group of medical specialists would go and travel throughout Africa offering free medical care. We both applied and were accepted. We were ecstatic. The caravan would be a great learning experience and we would get a good look at Africa. We got married before we left.

Life in Africa has been an adventure. We are constantly moving, a group of medical nomads. Camels carry our tents and supplies. Every day I see another exotic animal. Every week is another village. The people stare at us, afraid.

We are told to work on only those who have a chance of living. Many do not. We cannot spend too much time on any one villager for there are many to attend to. Before we leave a village, we teach a few of the people how to perform tasks such as giving shots. We leave medicine with them. Penicillin is enough to save numerous lives. In one village, I met a child to whom I became very attached. His leg had been severely injured. I was forced to amputate it. In what English he knew, he told me that he wanted to become a doctor, and help people that were as unfortunate as he. I took him along with me. I will take him to the U.S. There, I will assign him a special tutor for he must first learn how to read and write.

Every day is another disease, another poverty-

stricken village. During the day, the temperature sometimes gets up to 115 degrees. At night, we all gather in
a large tent. A fire barely protects us from the 30 degree
weather. There are few luxuries, but it is worth it.

Immediately upon reading this essay, in her fifth-floor
walk-up in Bronxville, New York, my Granny Shammy
called me on the phone to congratulate me on what she perceived to be a definitive, airtight, nonrevocable decision to
be a doctor when I grew older.

"I am so proud of you, sweetie pie!" she said to me. "A
doctor in every generation! Your daddy is doctor! Your
uncle is doctor! You, my youngest grandson, the apple of
my eye, will be doctor! To take care of people. To heal
them. To ease the suffering. The world . . . needs . . .
good . . . doctors!"

What my Granny Shammy did not realize, however, and
what I myself did not realize at the time, was that this remarkably detailed plan of mine—from Yale College to
UCSD Medical School to Mass General Hospital to a year
of nomadic altruism in Africa—was driven not by a desire
to take care of *other people* but by a desire to take care of
me. My plan to be a doctor, as we saw in Chapter One, was
nothing but a psychological ploy, as my nose, and legs, and
scrotum simultaneously revolted against me on three separate fronts, to manage my fears of bodily rebellion. In "My
Life at Thirty: How I Got Here," the little African boy "to
whom I became very attached," whose leg was so "severely
injured" that I was "forced to amputate it," and whom I
then adopted and took back with me to America, was, obviously, the crippled little boy in me I was hoping to leave
behind.

But since I was unaware of this at the time, how was I supposed to make this clear to Granny Shammy? When she told me she was proud of me, I said, "Thanks, Granny! Maybe my dad and I will open a practice together. Goulian and Goulian, M.D.s: Hematology; Orthopedic Surgery; Longevity; and Levity." While the patients were fidgeting in the waiting room, nervously awaiting their examinations, I would do for them what no doctor had ever done for me, and has never done for me to this day: put them at ease. I would sing show tunes to them, do magic tricks, tell jokes, juggle, whatever it took to make these people smile. If the patients were feeling peckish, and needed a little something in the mouth to calm their nerves, there would be a broad menu of treats, all of them low in saturated fat, to suck on—TVP on a stick; TVP in a gel; TVP in a shake; TVP in a bowl of pellets. For breakfast: egg white omelets with dry-curd cottage cheese. For dessert: ice milk.

If I had grabbed hold of my future plans with the same tenacity as Granny Shammy had grabbed hold of them, I'd be a doctor today. I'd be helping people, curing them, am-putating their infected limbs, rather than burdening people with concern about where my next meal is coming from.

But my grip, on my sanity no less than on my future, was shaky. "Dizzy from the height . . . everything beneath me in a mist," as I put it in a journal entry at the time, the fear of not living up to my brothers' examples of academic and athletic success making it impossible for me to climb up "the mountain" any further without pain, I could either climb back down the mountain or "bloody my fingers" on the way to the top. In mid-June 1984, less than two years after writing "My Life at Thirty," and less than twenty-four hours after receiving my 650 on the Achievement Test in

Math, I wrote in my journal, with "my brother's 800 still ringing in my head," that "as I grow older, and the concept of school work becomes less hazy to me, I no longer find myself regarding medicine with such a passion." So that was that. So much, apparently, for my life in Africa. That "government-sponsored caravan" would have to find a new orthopedist.

Informing Granny Shammy of my change in plans seemed gratuitous. She was eighty-five years old. Her memory was fading. If it made her happy to believe that there would be a doctor in every generation of her family, then let her believe it. Soon enough she would forget all about my plans for the future, and we could start from scratch.

Meanwhile, on the home front, my parents were treated to one sign after another that a life in medicine was probably out of the question for me. Refusing to take calculus in eleventh grade, and then taking no science or math as a senior—refusing to take even *physics*—was the first strong indication that my plans had changed. My difficulty in keeping a job, because of my squeamishness and delicacy and crippling assortment of anxieties over the Perils and Hazards of the workplace, was the second. Wherever I worked—and I must have held no fewer than twenty-five different jobs between the ages of sixteen and twenty-one, many of them lasting no more than a day—the environment was too highly pressured for me, or too chaotic, or too competitive, or too dirty, or too mean, or too depressing.

A job parking cars at a fancy hotel was impossible for me to keep because, when I fell behind during the chaotic rush of a Friday night happy hour, I panicked and forgot to put a Ferrari into reverse when trying to back out of a tight space. After slamming into the wall in front of me, I hopped out of the car, told my boss that my mom was sick, and started running home in tears.

A job selling cotton candy at a video arcade was impossible to keep because there was only one bathroom on the premises, and, by the time I had covered the toilet seat with three layers of toilet paper, someone was always knocking on the door to use it next, and knowing that someone was going to be using it next always made it impossible for me to go to the bathroom.

A job making fish tacos, at a Mexican restaurant near the beach, was impossible for me to keep because I was convinced customers were staring at the pimples on my chin; a job folding shirts in the men's department at Nordstrom was impossible for me to keep because I kept pricking my fingers with clothing pins; and a job as a salesman at a hip boutique for women was impossible for me to keep because I refused to lie to the customers, as I was told to do by my boss, when they asked me if a particular dress, or skirt, or pair of pants, made their butts look big. Nine times out of ten the butt did look too big, and I always felt obliged to tell them the truth.

When I was seventeen years old, a newspaper in San Diego sponsored an essay contest, the subject of which was "The Worst Job You've Ever Had." Since, by that time, after only a year and a half in the workforce, the awfulness of employment was something I felt especially qualified to pour my heart out over, I entered the contest, and won third place, by describing a job I had held the previous summer, for four weeks, at SeaWorld. Wearing an orange jumpsuit that said SECURITY on the back of it, and riding a blue moped, I was supposed to follow a group of Jehovah's Witnesses who were begging for money in the giant outdoor parking lot. The reason the Jehovah's Witnesses had a right to beg for money in the parking lot was the same reason the Hare Krishnas had a right to beg for money at La Jolla Shores Beach—in both cases the land was public property. Since the city of San Diego was letting SeaWorld use the land without paying rent, the Jehovah's Witnesses said, "We can use it, too." Fine, said SeaWorld. Use it. In the meantime, while we try to convince the city of San Diego to sell it to us, we will make your life miserable by hiring a young boy to follow you. When the Jehovah's Witnesses approached a tourist stepping out of his car, and began to ask him for money, I was supposed to scream the following message through a megaphone that I carried: "Please keep in mind that the views of the Jehovah's Witnesses in no way represent the feelings, thoughts, or philosophies of SeaWorld." You can imagine the look of confusion on a tourist's face when he stepped out of his car to enjoy a nice day at Sea-World with his family and found himself with Jehovah's Witnesses beseeching him from one side and a boy with a bright red face, on a blue moped, screeching at him from the other. The stress of the job was too much for me, and four weeks after being hired, I quit.

If there was any remaining doubt that I was not born to be a doctor, momentarily blacking out at the sight of two dozen cadavers in varying states of dissection put an end to it. The indirect cause of this experience was my discovery, while massaging my upper back, of a small lump in my trapezoid muscle. I was nineteen at the time, and home from college for spring break. My father, who was normally blasé about the bumps and bruises and splotches I showed him, thought enough of this lump to take me to his friend Dr. Nevus at UCSD, a lump specialist of some kind, to take a look. Dr. Nevus told us to meet him outside his anatomy class. When he wasn't there at the appointed time, my father walked inside the classroom to hunt him down, and I followed him. And there they were: two dozen dead bodies, with real faces on them, being preyed upon by medical students, who were so unfazed by the sight of these former people that you would have thought they were tearing apart frogs. I staggered, saw blackness and stars, then felt my father's firm grip on my shoulders.

"You okay?" he said, as he led me outside.

"I think so," I said.

"I should have prepared you for that. I apologize."

"Were those dead bodies?"

"I hope so! If they're alive, then they're in tremendous pain."

"I don't think I want to go back inside that room."

"I'm sorry about that. I wasn't thinking. One is so used to these things that one easily forgets."

Were it not for the discovery of that lump in my upper back, I would still, to this day, have yet to see a dead body, for no other dead body, in any form, dissected, embalmed, or lying in pieces on the side of the road, has ever again come into my view. In one sense I am grateful for the experience. Now, when I find myself, on my deathbed, wondering if I wasted my life, if I should have stuck with this, or stuck with that, if I should have stopped doing this, or stopped doing that, at least one regret I will *not* have, as I think back to the sight of those two dozen dead faces, and the sensation I immediately felt of having all the air sucked out of my body, and then blackness and a thousand stars, is that I did not cave in to my Granny Shammy and become a doctor. As for the nature of that fortuitous lump: when Dr. Nevus finally came out of his battlefield to give it a look, he diagnosed it, in eight seconds, as "nothing to worry about; it's a knot in the muscle," and promptly went back inside.

Continuing to pretend to Granny Shammy that I was prepared to spend a lifetime in the company of blood and guts was now ludicrous. The jig, emphatically, in La Jolla at least, was up. Jonathan the Orthopedic Surgeon, cruising on his camel across the plains of Africa, subjecting himself to the greatest range of exotic diseases, performing on-the-spot amputations, and moving his bowels behind the nearest rock or tree, in easy sight of the sixty-odd members of his "government-sponsored caravan," became a big joke at home. But it was a joke we couldn't bear to tell when Granny Shammy was visiting. The risk of her collapsing in disappointment was too great. Jonathan the Orthopedic Surgeon was not just one of many joists in the foundation of her happiness, easily survivable if it cracked in half from the rot of lies at its core, but a major supporting beam, in fact the *only* beam, besides God, that kept her going at times. My only hope was that eventually, as she pushed her way into her nineties, as her mind became less focused, and her memory more diffuse, she would relinquish her hold over my future and the Great Lie could be put to rest.

Unfortunately, though Granny Shammy's memory, as we had all anticipated, gradually deteriorated as I made my way through college, the most basic facts about her life becoming difficult for her to recall, her certainty that I was going to become an orthopedic surgeon refused to slacken.

In fact, thrown into relief by the fuzziness of most of the rest of her past, her memory of "My Life at Thirty: How I Got Here" only got stronger.

Had we grown apart when I got to college, had my studies, and my sex life, and my partying, and the various clubs and publications and political movements I was involved in, made it impossible for me to keep regularly in touch with her, keeping up the appearance of a doctor in training would have been effortless. It's not hard to claim to your grandmother that you are taking a full load of premedical courses, and that you are gearing up for taking the MCAT, if you spend ten minutes on the phone with her once every six months. "Yes, Granny. Everything's fine. Doctor in training! Of course! I should be an orthopedic surgeon in no time at all! I'll talk to you next year."

But my collegiate life consisted largely of either staring at the ceiling or staring in the mirror. There was no sex life, no partying, no clubs or publications or political movements of any kind, to come between me and the things I would otherwise have been inclined to do. And one of those things I was inclined to do, in fact practically the only thing, was keeping regularly in touch with my Granny Shammy. We were deeply enmeshed, after all, and though our bond transcended the limitations of words and language and phone calls and letters, I still called her at least once every two weeks, and tried to visit her at least once a month, even after she moved, during my freshman year of college, to a retirement home in the town of Hastings-on-Hudson, a forty-five-minute train ride north of the city. That was not a trip I was always eager to make. It took me about six hours round-trip, including a long subway ride from Morningside Heights to Grand Central Terminal; the forty-five-minute train trip on Metro-North; a cab ride to the retirement home; and a good two hours spent in her company. Sometimes, it was a chore. Many of those Sundays I would have rather been sitting in my room doing nothing.

But knowing that my visit would be the highlight of her month, how could I disappoint her? Along with the precise moment I would enter medical school (the fall of 1990, assuming I took my MCATs in the spring of 1989), the precise moment I was coming to visit her every month lodged itself firmly within her consciousness and refused to budge.

As the day of my arrival drew closer and closer, she got more and more revved up, leaving me long, impassioned messages, at least one a day during the final week leading up to my visit, on my answering machine. In her excitement at hearing my voice on the machine, she often got confused and thought that I had actually answered the phone, where-upon she would rush into an entirely one-sided conversation with me, telling me to make sure to eat enough before I left so that I wouldn't get hungry on the train, telling me to go to bed early so I wouldn't miss the train, and promising to give me the food she had saved from the dining hall, pieces of bread and fruit that, she was afraid, would be thrown away if she left them on her plate. Anything of possible use in life that was salvageable, including dirty rubber bands, stray buttons, pieces of string, was salvaged. To pay for something that you could have had for free was absurd. My dad was delivered, on December 31, 1929, by his uncle, a physician, on the kitchen table. Why pay for a doctor when you had one in the family? Four years later, on the same kitchen table, that same uncle removed my father's tonsils, after sedating him, as my father remembers, "by catching me off guard and shoving a chloroform-soaked rag over my face." Granny Shammy made her own yogurt, all her own clothes, and even her own soap. As my father explained it to me when I was a kid, "We'd save the leftover cooking grease. And then add lye to it. That's all you really need for soap. Not the best-smelling soap in the world, but still soap." So I always accepted these rotten pieces of bread and fruit, some of them weeks old, without complaint, even pretending to be grateful, and then I would throw them away at the train station.

How could I break this woman's heart, a woman who had refused herself all indulgences in life, who had worked herself raw so that her children and grandchildren and great-grandchildren could have better lives than she did, by telling her I had long since given up any plans whatsoever of becoming a doctor? She risks her life to come to this country. She works twelve hours a day as a seamstress, putting away every last bit to send her two sons to college and medical school. She makes her own soap! If having a doctor in every generation of her family was her greatest wish in the final years of her life, then, for the sake of her happiness, and for the sake of my not going crazy with guilt, I had to continue lying. So when she introduced me to Elsie, her new next-door neighbor at the retirement home, as "my youngest grandson. Second year at Columbia College. Oldest brother, who went to Yale, is lawyer. Middle one, who went to Harvard, is physicist. This one is going to be doctor just like his daddy," I shook Elsie's hand and accepted her congratulations.

In May 1988, just after my sophomore year of college

had ended and shortly before going home for the summer, I was having dinner with my Uncle Dicran, my dad's brother, at a restaurant called the Balkan Armenian, near the base of the Fifty-ninth Street Bridge, when he casually asked me if I had given any thought to my post-college plans.*

Over dinner, as we showed our support for the only Armenian restaurant in Manhattan, Uncle Dicran said, "So. What's next after college? Any idea?"

It was an innocent question. He wasn't trying to smoke me out. It was an uncle making polite conversation with his nephew.

"I don't know exactly. I'm still mulling it over. Maybe law school. It seems like a safe thing to do for three years."

He nodded and kept eating. I watched him slice his meat. A vein, a piece of gristle, skin, bones; all of it was isolated and removed with a few quick flicks of the wrist. His hands were legendary in my family. They had fixed so many noses, reconfigured so many faces, augmented so many breasts. They had built a harpsichord in his spare time. And a telescope. And a special knife, called the Goulian knife, for performing a difficult cut that no other utensil in his arsenal could quite achieve.

"You could go into practice with your brother," he said, after a few bites.

---

* The Balkan Armenian, incidentally, was, at that time, the only Armenian restaurant in Manhattan. When it closed, in 1998, the number of Armenian restaurants in Manhattan dropped to zero, while the number of Turkish restaurants remained steady at around twenty-five. The disparity is easily explainable. When you kill over a million people, it makes it harder for them to open restaurants. Also, when you open restaurants in places where people don't want to eat, such as the vicinity of the base of the Fifty-ninth Street Bridge, and charge twenty-five dollars an entrée, then people won't eat there.

"Or with my mom."

"Or both!"

"Or neither! I could get the degree, and then go work as a cabana boy at Club Med in Cancún."

"That would be one highly educated cabana boy!"

And with that, the subject of my future was put to rest, and we moved on to other things.

About six weeks later, out of the deepest, darkest blue of the John E. Andrus Memorial retirement home in Hastings-on-Hudson, New York, I got a letter in the mail from my Granny Shammy. This was only the second letter she had ever sent me in her life, the first one, three years earlier, having been enough of a struggle for her. Her English had not gotten *better* in the interim. It had gotten progressively worse. More and more frequently, when on the phone with me, or when walking with me across the beautiful grounds of her retirement home, above the Hudson River, grabbing on to my arm for support, she would stop speaking mid-sentence, at a loss for just the right word, at a loss for any word in English at all, and then, struggling to break through the silence, she would fall back on Armenian to take up the slack. If it was getting late, and I had to get back to Columbia, I would nod politely and say, "I'm sure you're right about that, Granny. We'll take up where we left off today next time we talk on the phone." If I had just arrived, and she was beside herself with excitement at the sight of me, I would be blunt: "Granny, I'm not sure I understood what you were saying. Can we go back to where you started speaking in Armenian?"

It was very difficult for me to believe, as I held the envelope in my hand, appraising it cautiously, too scared to open it, then holding it up to the light, trying to see what was inside it, that she had written it. How had she managed, her English as bad as it was, to struggle through a second letter? More important, what had *compelled her* to struggle through a second letter? What was so important, when there was a perfectly good telephone, with my number, like the numbers of all her grandchildren, written very large on a piece of paper tacked to the wall so that she could not fail to see it, that she had to sit down at her desk and put pen to paper? There was no need for a second letter, and I refused to open it!

And then I opened it. And here it is. Only the second letter Granny Shammy ever sent me in her whole life. I give it to you exactly as she wrote it, the underlinings, the ellipses, the misspellings, all her own. (As for the "favabeans" she refers to in the opening paragraph, these were fava bean seeds that a friend of hers had sent to her from Armenia.)

My Youngest and Dearest Grandson Jonathan Goulian:
How are you dear one. Sorry I could not be with you the summer. but my heart and my prayers are with you . . . favabeans <u>were not exactly</u> like the americans. smaller and climbless. . . .

I heard your dicision for lawyer . . . Dear one. I am your Gramma . . . but your mom and dad are very good . . . did you ask their <u>opinion</u> . . . did you want theirs to hear . . . you are <u>you are</u> too young yet . . . your family has two lawyers. and one doctor . . . very needed profession . . . did you ask to know what is the forcomming generation needs . . . to hear their wisdom. also your grampa [Sidney's] wisdom. to give one more year to <u>decide</u> . . . you are a bright student . . . thank god you are very bright . . . student . . . and have 6

*bright relatives <u>Mom</u>. <u>Dad</u>. <u>Grampa</u> [Sidney] and
Gramma [Ann] <u>and</u> 2 brothers [Oldest] + [Middle].
dont dont you want to hear all their opinions to hear
them all . . . any thing after you hear them all. you . . .
you decide . . . one more year. older . . . to be my choise
too. . . . . . with all my love + prayers with you dear one
your gramma Shamiram. . . . . x x x x x x x*

*P.S. dear one please read it 3 times to understand
this . . .
I miss you [illegible] remember me to your pop +
mom . . .*

I did not have to read this letter three times to understand it. One reading was enough to bring me to tears.
Uncle Dicran had clearly casually mentioned to her that he
saw me for dinner, and that I had mentioned, *offhandedly,*
in response to a question about what I *might* be doing after
college, that I *might* be going to law school, and all that she
heard, of course, was that I was *not going to medical
school.* Lying down to go to sleep that night, she must have
stared at the ceiling for a very long time, wondering where
she had gone wrong with me. Her youngest grandson, "the
apple of my eye," who had promised to go to medical
school, with the intention of eventually becoming an
orthopedic surgeon, ensuring that every generation of the
Goulian family would have a doctor in it, had, incompre-
hensibly, lost his bearings. There was only one thing to do
in response. She would have to set me back on course. But
pulling me back from the brink of darkness would require
something much stronger than a simple phone call. On the
phone she would get excited and have trouble making her-

self heard. Before long she'd be speaking in Armenian. Hearing nothing, I'd keep heading down the path of unenlightenment, soon to fall over the cliff into law school. With a letter, on the other hand, carefully drafted to spear me with every line, I'd be immobilized, brought to my knees in guilt for having disregarded my Granny Shammy's wishes, by the end of it.

What would have been amusing to me were it not so poignant was Granny Shammy's request that I first consult with every member of the family before deciding to go to law school, so that I could give them a chance to dissuade me. This request was based on her belief, of course, that they, too, were still under the impression that I was going to go to medical school, and that they, too, would be crushed by my change of plans. But what Granny Shammy did not realize was that her preference for medicine over every other honorable profession imaginable was hers and hers alone, and that, even if my family had still believed, up until that time, that I was going to go to medical school, the news that I had changed my mind and was now intending to go to law school would not have been greeted with disappointment. A career in law, in the eyes of my parents and brothers and maternal grandparents, was just as respectable as any other profession, and a far more respectable profession than any of them had come to expect from me.

To spare Granny Shammy further suffering, there was only one thing I could do. I had to call her immediately and reassure her that my "dicision for lawyer" had not been cast in stone, and that I had reconsidered.

"Granny, I apologize. I am not going to be a lawyer. I made a mistake. I am going to be a doctor. I promise."

"Doctor is much . . . needed . . . profession."

"I know. And that is why I am going to stick with my premedical studies, and become a doctor."

"The world . . . needs . . . good . . . doctors."

"I am taking the MCATs in the fall, and will apply to medical school in the spring. I promise."

"Your mommy is lawyer. And your brother is lawyer. Two lawyers . . ."

" . . . are enough for one family. And that is why I promise to be a doctor."

"Like your daddy."

"Like my daddy."

One of the few arguments in favor of medicine, and in opposition to law, that Granny Shammy did not make in her letter, was that in order to be a lawyer I would have to buy an entirely new wardrobe, including thousands of dollars' worth of suits, ties, shirts, and shoes, while in order to be a doctor I would have to buy nothing. A long white lab coat, supplied by the hospital, and beneath which I could wear anything I wanted or nothing at all, was all that would be necessary. A stethoscope around the neck, some pens in the pocket, a name tag, and my uniform would be complete.

The force of this argument was hit home to me when, not long after receiving Granny Shammy's letter, I was hired, and then quickly fired, by the owner of a store called Chic Accessories, a jewelry store that catered to teenage girls in a mall in San Diego called Fashion Valley. The job listing, in the classified ads of *The San Diego Union,* said that all that was required was enthusiasm, honesty, punctuality, and a willingness to work hard and promised, to the successful applicant, an employee discount of fifty percent on store jewelry. The job would hardly be perfect for me. The girls would stare at my pimples; there would be one bathroom at most, and possibly shared by both employees and customers; I would get nervous and confused when the line built up at the cash register, and punch in the wrong prices, and give the wrong change; and I was sure that I would be told to tell everyone trying on jewelry that "Oh, my God! It looks fabulous on you!" even when it didn't. But I needed a job, and at ten dollars an hour, not including the store discount, I certainly could do no better elsewhere. So I called the number in the ad and was hired on the phone, sight unseen. The owner said she was desperate and didn't have time to interview me in person. A salesgirl had come down with mononucleosis and someone was needed behind the cash register the next morning. I was told to wear something "nice, but not too formal." The nicest piece of clothing I had that was not too formal was a pair of yellow cotton overalls, with a family of riotous bumble-bees, drinking big mugs of frothy honey, embossed across the breast. I felt unusually respectable when I wore them. They were the kind of thing, I imagined, one might wear to a fancy dinner on a farm in the South. In a store that sold jewelry to teenage girls, anything more formal would be off-putting. At any rate, they would have to do, because in addition to being the nicest piece of clothing I had that was not too formal, they were the most formal piece of clothing I had that was not a gray flannel skirt. And that, I feared, would not be appropriate for my first day on the job.

When I arrived at Chic Accessories early the following morning, forty-five minutes before it opened, as I had been told to do, the owner, who was unlocking the front door of the store, took one look at me and said, "We're not open yet. Can you come back in forty-five minutes?"

"I'm not a customer," I said. "My name is Jonathan Goulian. We spoke on the phone yesterday. You hired me to work for you."

She looked me up and down. She frowned. She seemed confused.

"Did I forget to tell you to wear something appropriate?"

"No, you remembered to tell me."

"Then why are you wearing that?"

"Is this not appropriate?"

"Is this some kind of joke? Cause if it is, it's not very funny."

"I'm not sure I understand."

"What is there to understand? You look ridiculous. I told you to wear something appropriate."

"I'm sorry. I thought this was appropriate. I can go home and change, but I don't know what else I can put on."

"Honey, this is silly. You look cute. But no. No. Not here. Not at Chic Accessories."

"Can I wear these just for today, and then buy something else for tomorrow?"

"No. Please. Go home. This is not Romper Room, sweetie. This is a place of business. I'm sorry it didn't work out."

The implicit claim, by the owner of Chic Accessories, that Romper Room and a place of business were mutually exclusive, that a pair of yellow overalls with a family of riotous bumblebees embossed across the breast was a sufficient basis, in *all places of business,* for being shown the door, was put to the test a few days later, when, wearing the very same overalls, I was interviewed for a job at a place of business called the Oceanside Alzheimer's Hospital. Once again, I was tipped off by a job listing—"Wanted: Entertainment Director/Caregiver"—in the classified ads in *The San Diego Union,* this one seeking someone with patience, compassion, and a knack for coming up with interesting ways to divert patients with Alzheimer's disease from their confusion and misery.

When the hospital director set eyes on me, I knew I had come to the right place. No frowning. No looking me up and down with scorn and skepticism. No "We're not open yet. Can you come back in forty-five years?" Just a smile. A big, fat, warm, inviting smile.

"One look at those adorable overalls," she said, "and the job is yours if you want it."

I wanted it!

"Of course there's no dress code," she said, when I told her about the owner of Chic Accessories folding her arms across her chest and refusing to let me cross the threshold. "We're very relaxed here."

When I asked her if that meant I could wear skirts to work, she continued smiling, thinking it over for a few moments, and then chose her words very carefully: "I would love to see you in a skirt. I'll bet you look fabulous. Maybe one day we'll gather up a group and go dancing. And you can show me. But here, I don't think it would be a good idea. I'm worried it would confuse the patients. The struggle to understand things that *should* be familiar to them— the names of their own children, for instance—is already frustrating enough. If they saw a boy in a skirt, I'm worried it would be doubly frustrating for them, because a boy in a skirt was never within their experience to begin with. Does that make sense? Some of these people were born as early as 1900. A boy in a skirt is as familiar to them as a unicorn. At least when they see their children, they know who their children are. They just can't remember their names. But a boy in a skirt they would not understand on a more fundamental level. They would look at you and might actually think they've gone crazy. When of course they haven't. Their brains are not cooperating, their memories have let them down, but they're not crazy."

Understanding that people with Alzheimer's disease are not crazy is crucial, I soon discovered, to being able to take care of them properly. When they forget how to tie their shoes, as they often did, it's impossible to appreciate how painful this is for them, this awareness of their helplessness, if you think they're crazy. And when they urinate in a trash can, or in a flowerpot, mistaking it for a toilet, as they often did, it's impossible to appreciate how embarrassing this is for them, when you gently explain to them not to do that again, if you think they're too crazy to know right from wrong.

Or, if, as entertainment director, you try to organize a game of Nerf basketball, and they simply walk off the court after you've assembled everyone in their positions, it helps, to not quit the job in frustration, to remember that they're not crazy, and to convince yourself that the reason they disbanded and went back to their rooms, more likely than not, is that a game of Nerf basketball, for people in their seventies and eighties and nineties, is not what they had in mind for their morning exercise. My most successful efforts at diverting them were a post-nap bingo tournament every afternoon and a nightly sing-along, after dinner, to records of songs from the 1940s.

Attending to the emotional needs of the residents at the Oceanside Alzheimer's Hospital came very naturally to me. Very often, thinking they were young again, with the rest of their lives spread out before them, they would take me aside to tell me about their plans for the future. Often mistaking me for an old friend, or a business partner, or even a lover, they would include me in these plans, one man assigning me the role of managing his hotels in Florida. Whenever they got frustrated, or angry, at what they considered to be their incarceration, I managed to calm them down, and when they actually tried to escape from the building, as they often did, sometimes successfully, I always managed to convince them to come back. The most difficult patient was a woman whom I will call Pearl, whose disease was still in its early stages, and so she still had a strong memory, and a strong sense of self. But her behavior had become so unpredictable, and potentially self-destructive, that her elderly husband, wheelchair-bound himself, could no longer manage to care for her safely. She would enter strangers' homes and take off her clothes and climb into their beds, or start cooking a meal in their kitchens. Or she would suddenly decide to take a road trip to the desert and run out of gas along the way, in the middle of nowhere. There were numerous run-ins with the police, and she had been committed once to a mental hospital. The Oceanside Alzheimer's Hospital, which patients couldn't leave without setting off an alarm, was the least horrible of the available options. Her husband had no choice. But the reasons for keeping her there were obviously lost on her, and she was furious. At the end of the summer, a few days before my job ended, but not long after she had arrived, she came up to me and looked me sternly in the eye. "Give me one good reason," she said to me, "if I'm not a prisoner, why the doors are locked, and I can't leave this building at will."

"I'm obviously not the right person to ask," I said. "I didn't bring you here. All I can tell you is that not everything in life always makes sense. If the person who brought you here loves you, and I'm sure that he does, then we have to assume it was for the best. I know why you're crying. I understand. But look on the bright side: the food here is delicious; you have a comfortable private room; the people here are friendly; and I'm willing to play gin rummy with you, even though you've beaten me repeatedly, anytime you want. Does that sound like a prison to you?"

A job like that is not for everyone. The fact that I was able to stick with it for eight whole weeks, until the summer ended and I went back to college, makes me wonder, as I look back at Granny Shammy's epic struggle to hold me to my promise to become a doctor, if she saw something special in me, an uncommonly deep sense of compassion, that convinced her the medical profession would be at a great loss without me.

Many years later, when I went to work, in my early thirties, for a famous editor named Bob Silvers, who presided (and still presides) over a journal of ideas called *The New York Review of Books,* my knack for taking care of people, what we might call my *innate capacity for solicitousness,* was, in some sense, reaffirmed. Bob's mind, unlike those of the patients at the Oceanside Alzheimer's Hospital, was seemingly impervious to erosion, and my job as his assistant was not to divert him from any misery or confusion, as was the case with the Alzheimer's patients, but, quite the opposite, to make sure that he was *not* diverted, in any way at all, from his intellectual priorities. If someone wanted his attention, and didn't deserve it, it was my job to prevent this person from getting it. And if something important, such as a sharpened pencil, or a magnifying glass, or a space heater, was needed to make it easier for Bob to continue editing, then it was my job to get it. By insulating Bob from these distractions, I enabled him, at the age of seventy-two, to edit up to sixteen hours a day and, even more remarkably, to keep track, in his head, at any one time, of over two hundred manuscripts, in varying stages of completion, some of them having been in the works for years. A Mr. X, from whom Bob had not heard in many months, might call to ask about the status of his manuscript on the subject of Y, and Bob, as the call was being sent through to him, would shut his eyes very tightly, quickly riffle through the reams of papers in his head, and come up with what he needed before the sixth and final ring, by which time the call would have gone into voice mail and poor X would have had to call back: "Oh, X! You're obviously calling about your piece on Y. Yes, I have it right here, it's on my desk, and you'll have it within the week." A man who can field a call like that with such composure is a man, you might say, whose head is still full of all of its marbles, and yet that would leave open the possibility, inconceivable to me, that Bob might one day lose a few. That leaves only one alternative: Bob's head contains *one giant marble,* one only, and you will have to behead him to make him give it up.

In case you think this admiring portrait of mine, this tes-

tament to an almost inhuman capacity for mental discipline, is nothing but the lingering idolatry of a former servant, let me tell you a story that will put your doubt to rest:

One reason I went to work for *The New York Review of
Books* was that I needed money, and one of the reasons I
needed money was that I had recently spent twelve hundred
dollars, while in a state of near-catatonic depression, the
certainty that my life was meaningless making it impossible
for me to get out of bed, on stuffed animals. I needed, at
this time in my life, to surround myself with creatures who
were fundamentally nonjudgmental, who would accept me
unquestioningly, who would not hold me to any conventional standards of success, dress, or sexual virility, and
whom I could grab hold of without fear of hurting myself.
I was almost thirty years old. And all I had to show for
eight years of postcollegiate life was a law degree I didn't
want to use. My parents, understandably concerned that
they had wasted so much money to send me to law school,
were calling me, without fail, every Sunday, each parent
manning a different Panasonic cordless phone, my father
upstairs in his study, my mother downstairs in the kitchen,
to find out, as my father always put it, what my "grand
plan for the future" was. Every time I tried to turn the subject of the conversation back to oat groats, or steel-cut oats,
or triticale, or bulgur, my father turned it right back to my
nonexistent grand plan.

Most people I know, when they need to escape from
their lives, or their parents, or both, lose themselves in
drugs or sex. But neither of those options, both of them
messy and dangerous, seemed viable to me. My life may
have been meaningless, but that was no excuse to pollute it.

So, instead, I lost myself in the warm embrace of a six-foot-long caterpillar, which I slept with every night, and four giant frogs, each one of them the size of an orangutan, to mention only a small number of the animals that I brought into my ten-by-six-foot living space on the Lower East Side.

Since my living space could barely accommodate these animals, when I was hired to work at *The New York Review,* I brought some of the bigger ones into the office. Bob and his four assistants all worked together in one room, and my animals, perched near me on ledges and chairs, were easily visible to him if he had cared to look, though hardly encroaching on his personal space. For a whole month Bob made no mention of them, and didn't seem to notice them. As much as I appreciated this, having nowhere else to put these animals other than the sidewalk, I began to wonder whether it was the life of the mind that was keeping Bob from noticing them, or myopia. Overcome by the need to resolve this question, I moved the animals closer to his desk. One frog I placed on the office iMac. One frog I placed on top of the tall stack of *Weekly Standard*s, which had been building up, unread, for as long as anyone could remember. One frog I wedged in the bookcase, above the collected works of Isaiah Berlin. The caterpillar, and a long dragon with a stream of fire coming out of its mouth, I draped over one of the fluorescent lights that was suspended in the air beneath the ceiling. And on top of a pedestal of books on my desk, directly facing Bob from a distance of fifteen feet, I placed a fluorescent green lamp, roughly three feet tall, in the shape of a giant gummy bear.

Two more weeks went by, and still he gave no sign of having seen them. Myopia could no longer explain it.

Obliviousness or indifference were the only possible explanations, blindness having been ruled out on the grounds that the manuscripts to which his eyes were glued were not written in Braille.

Finally, one of the typesetters, who couldn't take the suspense any longer, and who refused to believe that Bob had not noticed them, brought the issue to a head:

"Mr. Silvers," she said bluntly, as she handed him a recently typeset manuscript. "What do you think of the stuffed animals in your office?"

Bob looked up from the manuscript and stared blankly at her.

"I'm not quite sure I know what you mean," he said.

"Surely, Mr. Silvers," said the woman, sweeping her hand about the room, "you've seen the stuffed animals that Jon-Jon brought in to keep him company."

At this point Bob stood up. He looked out at his office and, *clearly seeing the animals for the first time,* stared at each one in turn. He was not in the least bit startled at the sight of them. Nor was he unmoved. He studied each animal very closely, thoughtfully, curiously, looking each one directly in the eye, appraising it, taking it in, sizing up its talents and potential, before moving on to the next one. Patton surveying the field came to mind, and I was happy to be one of the troops.

"Well," he finally said, turning back to the woman with a quick nod of his head. "I'm very glad to have them on board. We need *all the help* we can get!"

And that was that. He sat down in his chair, went back to editing, and never mentioned them again. That is a man, it is safe to say, for whom the life of the mind, and a rather focused one at that, is everything. (One person who noticed the animals immediately, incidentally, was a gorgeous French journalist named Alexandra Laignel-Lavastine, who was so taken with the giant green gummy bear that she managed to carve out a cameo for him, *"un nounours vert fluo géant,"* in a profile of Bob that appeared in *Le Monde*.)

One problem, I soon discovered, when the life of the mind is everything, is that it doesn't leave you very much time to buy food. If you are editing late into the night, and all the restaurants in the neighborhood are closed, you are then forced to rely on whatever is at hand, and the only things at hand at *The New York Review* were the small packages of junk in the vending machine in the kitchen. Though Bob's diet was generally impeccable, every once in a while, after six straight hours of editing, suddenly remembering that his body had not been fed since lunch and was burning up the last remaining reserves of glucose, he would leap up from his chair in a fit of desperation, run down the hall to the vending machine in the kitchen, buy pretzels and chips and granola bars, and then quickly return to his desk, where he would continue to edit for another three hours, munching distractedly. I couldn't bear the sight of it. I had been hired to remove distractions from his life, and eating poison, by slowly killing him, would eventually distract him forever. There are times in life, if you are a truly caring person, if your *innate capacity for solicitousness* is deep and effeminately broad, when you must step forward and help someone even though your job does not require it. So I watched him closely, and whenever he put down his pencil and *leaned back in his chair and sighed,* the clear signal that hunger was about to propel him out of his seat, I would rush to his rescue with a paper plate covered with little mounds of healthy treats, like raw almonds and raw sunflower seeds and carrot sticks and dried organic wild blueberries, and maybe a Brazil nut or two for selenium, and perhaps a Dixie cup full of raw, unsalted soy nuts. He was always receptive initially, gobbling them up frantically and editing all the while. But sometimes, usually much later in the evening, he would look up from his manuscript and tentatively catch my eye:

"Oh, Jon-Jon, about that food you gave me earlier."

"Yes, Bob?"

"I fear I might have been *rash* in eating so much of it, and so quickly. Not that I don't trust you implicitly, of course, but—"

"Bob, what I gave you is what you need. Unlike the pretzels and potato chips you eat from the vending machine in the kitchen, full of salt and saturated fat and which cause nothing but a sudden and dangerous increase in your blood sugar, not to mention, in my case at least, bloat, and unlike the granola bars you eat from the vending machine, full of corn syrup and other obscenities, what I gave you is full of good fat, and vitamins, and fiber, and protein. I promise you it will make you stronger, and live longer, and let you edit until you're 102."

"*Stronger* and *longer*!" he shouted, pounding his fist on the desk. "Until I'm 102! That's *just* what I want to hear!"

That's just what we *all* want to hear. And that is why Granny Shammy was so insistent about the need for good doctors. A good lawyer can help you draft a will, perhaps, and put your estate in order, but a good doctor, stripping your diet of all that badness and filth, will make sure that you live so long that you have nothing left, other than the clothes on your back, a closet full of walking sticks, and the example of a life well led, to bequeath.

When Granny Shammy died, at the age of ninety-three, about a month before I took the LSAT, I felt, along with the obvious sadness at her departure from my life, an overpowering sense of relief in the knowledge that she would never discover I had let her down. Though Granny Shammy had left open the option, in her letter of July 12, 1988, that I could decide for myself what I wanted to do with my life when I was at least one year older than I was at the time of the receipt of the letter, that option, which I had failed to exercise, and which was instantly negated when I called her immediately and retracted my "dicision for lawyer," was unrenewable. Therefore, when I graduated from college, and started working as a paralegal at a criminal defense firm, with the intention of taking the LSAT and going to law school, I felt morally obliged, to keep her heart from breaking, to tell Granny Shammy that I had done so well on my MCATs, and gotten such good grades on my premedical course work, that, like my father and uncle before me, I had been admitted to Columbia Medical School, and to accept her friend Elsie's congratulations, followed by a warm hug, at the news. Like Renato in *La Cage aux Folles,* teaching himself how to play it straight so that his son's in-laws would not be outraged, I had taken this ruse, with the most loving intentions, to ludicrous proportions. Role playing had never been a problem for me. I played the Tin Man at the age of eleven. At the age of seventeen, in a high school production of Shakespeare's *Twelfth Night,* I played Sir Andrew Aguecheek. At the Oceanside Alzheimer's Hospital, I played a variety of roles every day, whenever the patients needed me, for the sake of their fantasies, to fill in for an old friend or business partner. With Stevie, I played fourteen different roles in two weeks. But in all those cases, from the Tin Man through Mort the IBM technician, the role playing was brief, anywhere from twenty minutes to three hours. With Granny Shammy, my role as an aspiring orthopedic surgeon had been going on for *eight years*. Had she lived a few years longer, I would have had to don a white lab coat and stethoscope, and diagnose her various aches and pains when visiting her.

It was not long before my other role, as an aspiring lawyer, never played with much conviction to begin with, was, if not blown, at least called seriously into question when I went to work, during the summer following my second year of law school, not for a law firm or judge, as one is generally expected to do, but as an unpaid intern, relying on my savings to support me, in the Washington office of U.S. senator Daniel Patrick Moynihan, where I spent most of the summer trying to write a speech for the senator on the Flag Desecration Amendment, which the Republican leadership intended to introduce for the third time in less than six years, and to which Moynihan was unalterably opposed. Trying to write a speech on the Flag Desecration Amendment, with the hope of one day being hired as a speechwriter on Capitol Hill, is not a dishonorable way to spend one's summer. But it's a curious way to spend one's summer if one has any intention of one day taking the bar exam and putting one's legal degree to good, practical use. Just as my "dicision for law," when my Granny Shammy became aware of it, was so unsettling for her, and was interpreted simply, and correctly, as a *decision not for medicine,* so was my decision to work as an intern in Moynihan's office, when my parents became aware of it, so unsettling for them, and was interpreted simply, and correctly, as an early sign that I had no intention of being a lawyer.

There was nothing wrong, they assured me, with not wanting to be a lawyer. Practicing law, and hating it, and continually trying to find a way out of it, was, they acknowledged, a noble American tradition. But it was a tradition founded on *actual experience*—namely, the practice of law, and the dissatisfaction with it—whereas in my case I had yet to officially embark on a career in law and already I was trying to jump ship. This was not an attitude, they felt, that any parent who is paying for a child's legal education could be expected to tolerate. I had one of two options, as they were presented to me rather starkly: either drop out, and save us a year of tuition, or give a career in law a serious shot.

This ultimatum was unassailably reasonable. And my response to it was unassailably cowardly. Since dropping out, as I was inclined to do, would have put me back in the same position I was in when I had graduated from college—terrified of the future, and with a crippling lack of purpose in life—I decided to stay put and promise to give law a serious shot.

You often hear it said that "there are two types of people in this world, people who X, and people who don't X," and you can put just about anything you want in place of X: people who *like to travel*, people who *like parades*, people who *write thank-you notes*, people who *keep kosher*, people who *change their Brita filters*, people who *wear deodorant*, et cetera. The possibilities are endless, but for most people I know there is one particular way of categorizing people that resonates more strongly than any other. For my friend Jane, for instance, who works as a waitress, there are people who *tip more than fifteen percent* and people who don't.

If I had to divide people into two categories, I would say that there are people who know exactly what they want to do with their lives, and always have—like my Middle Brother, for instance, who was obsessed with science from the age of eight; or my Grandpa Sidney, who fell in love with philosophy at the age of sixteen; or my father, who wanted to be a doctor from the age of seventeen—and those who don't know exactly what they want to do with their lives, and never really have, but who finally pick something to avoid doing nothing.

The reason law school is such a popular *something* for those who are trying to avoid doing *nothing* is that it is considered intellectually challenging and socially respectable, and that it holds out the promise of almost guaranteed employment, at a decent salary, when you are finished, and, most important, that your parents, for the preceding reasons, are more likely to cover the phenomenally high expenses of tuition, room, and board for the three years required to graduate, assuming they can afford it, than they would be for, say, film school or fashion school, both of which I considered upon graduating from college but quickly abandoned out of the certainty that I would have to take out loans to pay for them, and likely have no job waiting for me at the end. Learning how to design, and market, my own line of skirts for men appealed to me immensely, but having to sell them on the sidewalk on St. Mark's Place, rather than in Barneys, did not.

When, at the age of seventeen, I applied to Columbia College, I was asked, on my application, what I planned to do with my life after college, and I replied: "I am going to be a rock singer/playwright, with a degree in law, so that if I ever have any financial difficulties I will have something to fall back on." Eight years later, my career as a playwright and rock singer as undeveloped as my career as a doctor, I was falling back, as I had said I would, on a degree in law.

True to my promise to my parents that I would stick with the law long enough *to give it a real shot,* thereby justifying the expense of their having supported me for a third year of law school, I got a job as a law clerk for a year for a U.S. district judge in the Eastern District of North Carolina but soon discovered, with the help of the marvelously perceptive judge for whom I clerked, that a career in law was out of the question for me and that, therefore, it would not be necessary for me to take the bar exam when the clerkship was over. The problem was not that I couldn't do the work, which a monkey, with enough training, could do, but that I couldn't wear the clothes. Apparently, without my being aware of it, and one could only guess how many years this had been going on, since I had first started wearing men's clothing after college, I had a habit of continually picking and scratching and poking at my body as if I were addicted to amphetamines, and the cause of these tics, it was immediately clear to the judge, was that I felt bound and shackled, straitjacketed if you will, in my suit and tie and Florsheim shoes.

After the judge brought my spastic fidgeting to my attention, I spent a long time looking at myself in a wall-size mirror, studying my reflection from top to bottom, and was finally able to diagnose the underlying cause of the feeling of imprisonment that had set this fantastic assortment of tics into motion—I looked, and clearly had instinctively felt, and clearly had suppressed all conscious knowledge of it, *ugly*. In men's clothing, I looked like the short, bald, big-nosed, beady-eyed, bowlegged man that I had feared I would become so many years earlier. My worst prophecy, that my body would continue to rebel against me, gradually turning me into an ogre, had come to pass, and it was the result, in no small part, of these horrible clothes. In my panic over my future, desperate for financial security, I had chosen a career in law without considering, and without allowing myself to become consciously aware of, the sartorial implications.

Let's begin with my head. My head, my whole life, had been small, though relatively proportionate to the size of the rest of my body. When I began to lose my hair, in my early twenties, forcing me eventually to shave it off entirely in an attempt to mask the recession of my hairline, the size of my head was reduced by about a fourth. I was now faced with two unpleasant alternatives: a shaved head that was arguably too small for my body or a balding head that was relatively proportionate. My hair was hideous. It looked like a field of dying wheat, months into a drought that would never let up, the stalks growing brittle, then breaking, then disappearing, leaving bare ground in their wake. Not wanting anyone, not even myself, to see this mess, I opted to raze it.

What I now realized, unfortunately, is that when you crop a small head at the neck with a tie, the smallness of the head becomes grotesquely exaggerated, because the head is thrown into greater relief. In other words, with no hair, and no open neck, with which to divert the viewer's gaze, the viewer's gaze, as I now so clearly understood while looking at my reflection in the mirror, was drawn inexorably to my pin-size head, and to various features on my face—my still misshapen nose, despite two nose jobs; my pointy, mouse-like ears; my beady eyes—that, I felt, did not bear close scrutiny. In a tank top cropped above my belly button, on the other hand, I would be able to draw the viewer's gaze away from my head and to my choicest spots—my broad shoulders, my slender neck, my slim and muscular arms, and my tight little tummy.

As for my legs, the problem, as I now saw so clearly, was twofold: men's pants are not cut to conceal bowed legs, and men's shoes are not designed to lengthen them. When I wore long skirts, and sarongs, and women's bell-bottom pants, which flare below the knee, the bow in my legs was concealed, and when I wore high heels, anywhere from four to six inches, I looked not like a tree stump, as I did now, but like Baryshnikov.

The reason I had forgotten these lessons—that certain clothes conceal one's bodily defects better than others—is that I had never really *learned them* to begin with. Biting on my turtlenecks to conceal the pimples on my chin, wearing a hat every day at college to conceal the pimples on my forehead, and wearing long skirts and bell-bottom pants to conceal my bowlegs came instinctively to me. When I grad-uated from college, and became panicked about my future, and realized that, in order to get a respectable, well-paying job, I would have to wear normal, respectable, men's cloth-ing, I did not say to myself, "Well, now I'm going to be ugly, because I can no longer hide the flaws in my body." In my lack of self-awareness, I simply said, "Well, now I have to wear men's clothes."

The reason girls don't have to resort to these strategies of concealment *instinctively,* as I was forced to do, is that they are taught these strategies, by their mothers, as early as elementary school. The purpose of clothing, as every girl has always known, is not just to make us look good but to make us look *less bad.* By distorting our bodies, turning stubby legs into long ones, bowed legs into straight ones, hairy arms into covered arms, sagging breasts into perky ones, big butts into invisible butts, and the list of possible distortions is endless, we manipulate the viewer into believing that we are something we are not. To accept your body's flaws resignedly, without doing all you can to take arms against them, is considered unfeminine. But for a boy to take arms against his bodily flaws, by wearing high heels, and a long skirt, and a midriff-baring tank top, and an occasional bit of makeup to brighten those tired eyes, is to be an unmanly faggot. Why men are supposed to take their bodily flaws in stride and women to surmount them has never been clear to me.

Since neither law firms nor courtrooms, where the bulk of legal work takes place, are Romper Rooms, but places of serious business, I would not be able to wear, as a lawyer, the clothing that masked my ugliness and put me in my best light, and since I hated my body, had hated it since I was thirteen, had tried so hard, for so long, to prevent it from getting the better of me, there was no sense in pursuing a career that would rob me of my best defense. Between financial insecurity and ugliness, the choice was clear.

When I informed my parents that I would not be taking

the bar exam, I didn't feel they would fully understand if I told them the truth, that I was giving up the law in large part because it would make my head look too small, and my legs too bowed, and my height too short. So I copped out and told them only the other part of the story, the part of the story that had always been true, which was that "a career in law just isn't right for me; the work is mind-numbing; I feel hemmed in by legal jargon, and legal precedents, and legal reasoning." As Jeremy Bentham once said, "Law sharpens the mind by narrowing it." He might have added, apropos of the obligation to wear a tie, "Law shrinks the head by cropping it."

Had I run away to India at this point, and joined an ashram, and sent my parents a postcard every six months to assure them I was still alive and well, my giving up the law without first giving it a proper chance would have had little direct bearing on my relationship with them. Conflicts between parents and children do not occur when parents and children are estranged. But my parents and I were not estranged. We spoke, without fail, every Sunday, and my life soon became reduced to seven-day blocks of time, seven days in which to try, always unsuccessfully, to come up with a viable plan for the future. By tacit consent, they took different approaches with me, tacking at me from different angles. My mother tended to look backward in time, at my childhood, in an effort to get at the root causes of my torpidity, while my father tended to look forward in time, at my future, in an effort to figure out the steps I was taking, or should have been taking, to put my torpidity behind me.

As for the deficiencies in my childhood, my mother's best guess was that I had been oversaturated with diversions as a young boy, and as a result developed an unrealistic sense of the possibilities in life, a short attention span, and a poor sense of commitment:

"Do you think we exposed you to too many activities as a child? Did we spread you so thin—the painting, the acting classes, the cello lessons, and all the rest—that you lost focus and never regained it? Maybe you were led to believe that, since you could always choose any one of a number of things to do, you never had to stick with any one thing, and do that one thing well."

"But I chose one thing—soccer! at the age of six!—and stuck with it."

"But you didn't stick with it. You abruptly quit at the age of sixteen, a year before applying to college."

"But I played for ten whole years before quitting!"

"That was exactly what we found so troubling. You played it for ten years, and played it so well, and then, just like that, with no explanation, you came back from Andover and refused to play anymore. We never understood that."

As for the measures I was taking to put my torpidity behind me, my father was aware of the absurd, somewhat old-fashioned role he was playing—Dad Presses Son on Future—so he would put on a voice of mock seriousness, which I appreciated, to take the edge off:

"So, Mr. Youngest Son, any ideas about the next step? Any epiphanies come your way?"

Nope. No epiphanies. But I would keep him posted.

"Okay. Forget epiphanies. Any thoughts, large or small or medium? I will even take microscopic thoughts, if you have them."

Nope. No thoughts. But something would come to me

soon enough. When, and from where, I wasn't sure. But I knew it would come.

"Okay. Forget thoughts. Have you taken any *concrete steps,* since we last spoke, toward getting a permanent and satisfying job?"

Concrete *steps?* No. A concrete *step?* Yes. I had taken one concrete step. I had sent my speech on the Flag Desecration Amendment to numerous members of Congress, wondering if they had any openings for the position of speechwriter, and offering my services if they did. Speechwriting seemed like a good fit for me. It seemed like the kind of job one could do out of one's home. None of the Perils and Hazards of the workplace—no messy public bathrooms, no high-pressure environment, no office gossip about my mysteriously nonexistent love life, no backstabbing employees against whom to compete for advancement, no customers staring at my pimples—would come between me and my happiness. I could write the speeches at my own desk, on my own computer, using my own bathroom, cooking at my own stove, and wearing whatever I wanted or nothing at all.

But no one hired me. In fact, very few people responded to me. And for the people who responded to me, never the senators themselves, of course, always staff members, the following four paragraphs of my ten-page speech always seemed to be the sticking point:

The issue here is not whether the burning of the flag is *offensive.* No respectable American disputes that it is. The important question is whether flag desecration, or any form of political expression, is so *uniquely offen-*

sive that we should *amend the Constitution to prohibit it*. When a young, spoiled college freshman, who has had every advantage society can offer, stands up on a podium and shouts, "Down with America!" isn't that just as hideous as the burning of the flag? Every one of us in this chamber would like to muzzle that young man. Some of us, I'm sure, would like to give him a good thrashing. But the reason we restrain ourselves is because we recognize that the right to express one's stupidity—as long as you don't wake up your neighbors while doing it, or burn down the whole block—is necessary for a free society.

Why do so many of my colleagues feel unconstrained when the physical desecration of the flag is at issue? I challenge any one of you to explain to me, without resort to mindless rhetoric about the near-mystical significance of a piece of cloth, why there is a meaningful distinction between the physical desecration of the flag and countless other manifestations of anti-American sentiment, including, to give you just one more example, the grabbing of one's crotch while singing "The Star-Spangled Banner," to which we were treated, not long ago, on national television, and *perfectly legally*, by Roseanne Barr.

I challenge any of you to convince me that when Patrick Henry shouted, "Give me liberty, or give me death," implicit in his demand for freedom was the recognition that certain forms of anti-American expression, such as the physical desecration of the flag, and *only the physical desecration of the flag*, would be exempted from protection.

I respectfully challenge the two senators from New Hampshire, both of whom support the proposed amendment, to convince me that their state motto, "Live Free or Die," really means to say, "Live Free or Die, *but Jail Me If I Dis the Flag.*"

As one chief of staff put it to me, rather curtly, in one of the few replies I received: "You can't be serious. No senator in his right mind would ever read this on the floor of the United States Senate. We have no openings for speechwriters at this time."

I was, in fact, serious, though this man's response did explain to me why Senator Moynihan had never read my speech on the floor of the United States Senate.

My "grand plan for the future," when I was pressed by my father to come up with one, was this: if I reached the age of forty and had yet to figure out a way to support myself that did not require that I subject myself, for most of the rest of my life, to the Perils and Hazards of the workplace, I would be forced to move to Israel and join a kibbutz. The plan was hardly ideal. The sun would beat down on me ferociously as I worked in the fields. And there was always the risk of warfare. But there would be no competition to worry about. No endless striving for advancement, honors, and awards. No dress code. And no lack of fresh vegetables.

"That's your grand plan? A kibbutz?"

"I wouldn't call it grand. But it's a plan. And it's a viable one. As long as you show up, and are willing to put in your six hours on the farm, they'll take you."

"But it's not a fulfilling job. You would not be making use of your intelligence."

"But it's a *way of life*. Not everyone was put on this planet to make use of his intelligence. Some people were put here to milk cows."

———

So here I am, a week before my thirtieth birthday, in the late summer of 1998, in a curtained-off portion of a woman's living room on the Lower East Side, surrounded by twelve hundred dollars' worth of stuffed animals and holding, in my hand, too afraid to open it, the first letter my father has ever sent me.

What could be so important that Dada would have to put pen to paper, and waste a perfectly good envelope and stamp, when we can speak face-to-face all we want at the family's annual Labor Day gathering in Vermont, or at the family's annual Columbus Day gathering in Vermont, or at Thanksgiving, or Christmas, or any one of the dozens of other annual excuses—not excuses, *welcome opportunities*— to get together? What have I done to drive him to this extreme?

Finally, after holding the letter up to the light repeatedly, trying to get a sneak peek at what I have in store for me, deluding myself into believing that there might be a check for ten thousand dollars inside, with the instruction to "go find yourself; seek enlightenment; be at peace," I rip it open.

After unfolding the letter, I find myself facing a great mass of white space, the body of my father's letter occupying what appears to be only the top one inch of the page. The message he is sending seems clear from the outset: *Trying to come to terms with the manner in which you have chosen to live your life leaves me almost speechless.*

And then this, the body of the letter, in four quick sentences:

Jon: I need you to help explain to me what it is you are doing, and how you plan to spend your life. On a number of occasions, I thought that I saw direction and meaning in what you were saying and doing, but that is not the way it has turned out. I remain confused and concerned. Can you help?

Can I help? Dada, I would love to help. But how can I? I, too, am confused and concerned. Whatever direction and meaning you have ever seen in what I have been saying and doing is an illusion. The only way I can think of to respond to this letter is to talk to you on Sunday, at our appointed time, and, in the few days remaining to me until that call, try to come up with another grand plan. In the meantime, I offer you the following consoling thought: Considering that two of your three sons are heading toward the Promised Land, which, rounding up, is a batting average of .667, it doesn't seem to matter very much that one of them (well equipped, as it happens, with twelve hundred dollars' worth of life support) is heading toward an iceberg. Ty Cobb, with the highest lifetime batting average in history, only hit .366. Ted Williams, coming in a distant seventh place, hit .344. Babe Ruth? .342. At .667, Dada, you are in a league of your own!

CHAPTER 8

Most Likely to Be Remembered

T IS LATE JULY 1997. In two weeks I will turn twenty-nine years old, an important milestone, as I see it, for it is the precise midpoint, eleven years from either end, between the arrival of Manhood (eighteen) and Middle Age (forty). I've become an expert, in my Early Manhood, at discovering these important milestones, these opportunities for taking stock of my failure in life, and for measuring the distance between my accomplishments, on the one hand, and the expectations various people in my life, without my asking for them, have thrust upon me, on the other.

The distance, as of today, is great. Though at first glance you would not know it. "You are a law clerk to a federal judge!" you would tell me. "Other than being a resident at Mass General Hospital, Jewish and Armenian parents can ask for little better!" This is true. But this also assumes that my clerkship is a *stepping-stone,* just one of many stepping-stones on a long path of stepping-stones, with the next stepping-stone clearly visible and accessible. Unfortunately, my clerkship will end in three weeks, and my future, stretching out endlessly before me, is completely free of stepping-stones, and appears to me as the deserts and plains and mountains of Africa must have first appeared to Livingstone and Stanley: dark, a tad forbidding, and much in need of a good map. A career in law, of course, would provide me with all the maps I need. But the bar exam is in a week, and, as I decided long ago, but have been keeping to myself, I'm not taking it. The question is how to spring this news on my parents. When I quit soccer at the age of sixteen, I broke the news to them over the phone, from Andover summer school, so I wouldn't have to deal with their upset and bafflement in person. But this time I don't even have the courage to break it to them over the phone. What I'll have to do is call them when I know they're not home, leave a message, and then bolt to Vermont and let them try to track me down.

My best friend from high school, Macky, called me yesterday for the first time in years. We lost touch in the early nineties, but he suddenly needed to get in touch with me to find out: (a) why I didn't go to our ten-year reunion last year, and (b) whether I knew Andrew Cunanan, currently America's most famous psychopath, when we were in high school. Macky must be the twentieth person to have called me up in the last few days to find out if I knew Andrew Cunanan when I was in high school and, if so, *how well*. What has prompted these calls is the recent murder of Gianni Versace, the world-famous fashion designer, who was shot dead a few days ago in front of his home in Miami, bringing to six the number of people whom Andrew Cunanan, graduate of the Bishop's School in La Jolla, California, class of 1987, is suspected of murdering, one of whom he tortured first by stabbing with a claw-shaped tool that he took from the man's garage. The prevailing theory for why Cunanan, who had shown no tendency toward psychopathy before this, has suddenly gone crazy is that he recently found out he was HIV positive, and is now wreaking vengeance on anyone who might have infected him. The only support for this theory is that Cunanan is gay. Whether or not he tested positive for HIV, and whether or not he was romantically involved with his victims, is a complete mystery, though what seems indisputable is that he was not romantically involved with victim number five, a gravedigger in New Jersey whom Cunanan killed in order to steal his car, suggesting that Cunanan's cross-country rampage is driven by something more complicated than mere vengeance. It's one thing to set out to kill former lovers. It's another thing to kill a complete stranger in order to save the cost of a train ticket to Florida.

"Did you know this freak?" asks Macky. "I don't remember seeing him at any parties."

Or, as my mother put it: "Were you at all aware of this so-called gay subculture in La Jolla that this man Andrew Cunanan was supposedly a part of? I knew nothing about it. Did you know anyone who was a part of it? Did you know anyone who knew Andrew Cunanan? Did *you* know him?"

The reason so many people are wondering if I knew Andrew Cunanan is that there appear to be some striking similarities between us. Just as I dabbled in androgyny at La Jolla High School, so did Cunanan dabble in androgyny at the Bishop's School, three miles down the road. Just as I was voted Most Likely to Be Remembered, Class of 1986, so he was voted Most Likely to Be Remembered, Class of 1987. Just as I ran cross-country, before giving it up to dabble in androgyny, so did he. And just as my heterosexuality, in high school, seemed open to question, so, though far more emphatically, did his.

There is one more thing Andrew Cunanan and I have in common that most of my friends, and definitely my mother, don't know about. Both of us own guns. In my case I have been using them, three of them, exclusively to protect myself, while staying at my family's summerhouse in Vermont, from potential assailants. When you live on a dead-end dirt road, a quarter mile between each house, and fifteen minutes from the nearest sheriff's office, it's not hard to mistake every creak in the attic, and every rustle in the bushes, especially late at night, for someone who has come to murder you. "Be not afraid of any man, no matter what his size; when danger threatens, call on me, and I will equalize." That was the motto inscribed on various Colt revolvers back in the nineteenth century, and that is why I own three guns. One for each hand, and an extra one in case one of them jams.

In Cunanan's case, he has been using his guns this summer not to protect himself from potential assailants but to kill people. That is what you call a *misuse*. As far as anyone is aware, danger has not been threatening Cunanan, so there has been no need for him to call on his weapons. So why is he doing this? What has caused him to snap? I have a theory. It is, I will admit, as lacking in evidentiary basis as every other theory proposed over the past few weeks, and it does not explain the killing of the sexton in New Jersey, but since that has not stopped other people from proposing theories, why should it stop me?

My theory is this: Cunanan's realization that he has amounted to nothing in life, when his high school classmates had expected so much, a realization that had been gradually building up for years, and that finally reached critical proportions with the imminent arrival of his ten-year reunion, caused an enormous rupture in the levee of his sanity, whereby a colossal rage toward everyone who had ever wronged him came rushing through. I know, firsthand, how demoralizing it is to face a ten-year high school reunion, that most important of important milestones, when you were voted Most Likely to Be Remembered by your high school classmates but have nothing to show for yourself that could possibly justify that honor. It destroys you. At seventeen they anointed you, telling you what incredible promise you had, sending you off into the world to make a splash. And what do you do? You don't even make a ripple. What, after all, did Andrew Cunanan have to show for himself? Ten years ago he was hooking up with guys, and he's still doing it. Ten years ago he was wearing eyeliner and funny clothes, and he's still doing it. What else? Financial debt, perhaps. Maybe ten extra pounds in his midriff. Some unwanted tufts of hair on his back and toes and shoulders. Otherwise, nothing. Hardly grounds for rolling out the red carpet when you see him pull up his rented limousine for the ten-year bash. A cross-country murder spree, on the other hand, climaxing in the killing of a world-famous and much-loved fashion designer, would put him on the map forever.

I'm not making fun of him. I'm commiserating with him.

The fear that I would not live up to the expectations of my high school classmates began to plague me as early as 1994, during law school, two whole years before my reunion. I had gotten a notice in the mail from the Committee Overseeing the Reunion of the Class of 1986, "Save the date! It's coming up!"

My God, I thought. *Am I ready for this? Am I ready to face them?* What have you done, in the last eight years, to show for yourself? You are a balding aspiring lawyer with a misshapen nose who has trouble sustaining a romantic relationship for longer than forty-five minutes. Will that be enough for them? Did they have more in mind for you when they told you that they would never forget you? You were supposed to go off into the world and make a splash, but here you are, eight years later, still too scared to jump off the diving board.

Robin Wright, three years ahead of me at La Jolla High School, had jumped off the diving board. First she went on to star on the soap opera *Santa Barbara.* Then she was the princess in *The Princess Bride.* Then she was Forrest Gump's wife. Then she married Sean Penn. Splash, splash, splash, splash.

Gore Verbinski, four years ahead of me at La Jolla High School, had jumped off the diving board. First, he directed those Budweiser commercials with the three giant frogs who say, in croaky froggy voices, "Bud," "Wei," "Ser." A huge splash in my book. Then, a few years later, that splash retreating to a ripple, he directed *The Mexican,* with Julia Roberts and Brad Pitt. (*The Mexican?* The only worse title I can think of for a movie would be *The Armenian.*) But then, quickly redeeming himself, he directed *The Ring.* Another big splash. And then, that splash exploding into a cannonball, two cannonballs, three cannonballs, he directed *Pirates of the Caribbean,* part one, part two, part three, and, I hope, four to come.

Warren DeMartini, five years ahead of me at La Jolla High School, had jumped off the diving board. As the lead guitarist of Ratt, one of the most successful glam metal bands of the mid-eighties, he was, and remains, the closest thing to a rock star La Jolla has ever produced. Four platinum albums in a row. A fixture on MTV. Featured on the cover of *Guitar Player* magazine. And spotted in a Ferrari in downtown La Jolla. Splash, splash, splash, splash.

Raquel Welch, twenty-eight years ahead of me at La Jolla High School, known back then as Jo Raquel Tejada, had jumped off the highest diving board of them all. First, while working as a cocktail waitress in Dallas, she got a nose job. Not a splash, but worth noting. Then, as a rather buxom cavewoman, with a beautiful nose, in *One Million Years B.C.,* the weight of her breasts displacing half the water in the swimming pool, she caused a tidal wave, drowning every single boy from the Class of '58 who hadn't had the guts to ask her out.

As of 1994, that was my chief competition. If I could somehow break into that pantheon in the two years left to me before the reunion, I would attend it. Otherwise, not a chance. And at the rate I was going, and that rate certainly had not accelerated by the time the reunion rolled around, in the summer of 1996, they wouldn't even let me into the pantheon to clean the toilets.

What did Andrew Cunanan and I do to deserve this curse? I never asked to be voted Most Likely to Be Remembered. And I don't think he did either. It's an ambiguous honor, when you think about it. Best-Looking, Sexiest, Best-Dressed, Best Personality—those are all unequivocally positive. But to be voted *Most Likely to Be Remembered* requires nothing more than that you did something highly memorable, and not all things that are highly memorable are necessarily good. Immortality, as often as not, is achieved in ways better left forgotten.

What I'd like to know is what *I* did, ignoble or not, to deserve this questionable honor. What did I do that was so unforgettable, so out of the ordinary, that I had to be cursed, forever, with expectations I will never live up to?

———

The answer? Nothing! Nothing worth celebrating, at least.

"You went to Andover a jock, and a surfer, and a relatively normal kid," said Mr. Carey, when I asked him to write me a college recommendation, "and came back I-don't-know-what. You've got to come up with an explanation for that transformation I can work with. Columbia will want to know what happened. Your CV makes no sense. They'll see soccer for all these years. And then they'll see nothing. And then they'll interview you and see the getup. And then, like everyone else in your life, they'll scratch their heads."

My CV *made no sense.* That's the answer. Inducing people to scratch their heads, as if I were a giant louse, was all it took, in a place like La Jolla, California, to burn a place for myself in the memories of my classmates forever. He went to Andover one thing, and came back no-one-knew-what. Scratch. Scratch. Scratch.

There was nothing in the water in central Massachusetts, of course, to explain why my transformation occurred at Andover. The timing alone explained it. My 650 on the Achievement Test in Math was one crisis too many for me. It destroyed me. And then, a week later, as had long been planned, I went back east for six weeks. Had I gone to Maine, or Marseilles, or Madagascar, or Mars, I would have still quit soccer, and informed my parents, by phone, of my decision, and I would have still found myself facing the same problem two weeks before returning to La Jolla: How can I go home again, and subject myself to all those expectations (sexual, academic, and athletic) I know I can't live up to, unless I have some sort of shield with which to defend myself?

And why, exactly, did I think that earrings, some lip gloss, and a depilated body would be an effective shield? Well, my reasoning, to the extent that one can reason subconsciously, and to the extent that a reliable interpretation of one's subconscious motivations in life can be arrived at after only a year and a half of self-analysis, was this: if I threw people off my scent with a "getup" too sexually ambiguous to decipher, then people would have no way to judge me. If I was *uncategorizable*, so my reasoning went, I would be *uncriticizable*, because there would be no obvious standards of behavior to which I was supposed to conform. From a *man* we expect a healthy sexual appetite, and a willingness to be aggressive enough to satisfy it. From a *sexually neutered androgyne*, wearing earrings and skirts and makeup and pearls and God only knows what else, we expect nothing. From a *man* we expect a healthy embrace of danger—surfing, playing soccer, skateboarding down steep hills without a helmet. From a *sexually neutered an-*

drogyne we expect nothing. From a *man* we expect the strength and composure to compete academically and athletically and professionally, not only against his peers but also against his two older brothers, Model Grandsons Numbers One and Two. From a *sexually neutered androgyne,* so I hoped, and boy was I wrong, we would expect nothing. And, finally: while from a *man* we expect an indifference to the flaws in his body, and an ability to take his pimples and big nose and bowlegs in stride, from a *sexually neutered androgyne* we would expect an effort to overcome them. Androgyny, to my fragile and desperate state of mind, was a ready-made, off-the-rack (all I needed was some lip gloss, a razor, and a pair of earrings; one trip to the drugstore and I was good to go!), four-in-one solution to my problems.

Is he a, or b, or c, or d? Or all of the above? My mother didn't know the answer. And neither did my classmates. Wow, they thought, scratching their heads. Look at Goulian. While we were stuck in La Jolla for the summer, doing the same old nothing, he went back east and clearly had some sort of epiphany. He's way ahead of us now. He must be grappling with important issues of identity, facing life head-on and pushing through it, and we don't even know who we are yet. That guy definitely gets my vote for Most Likely to Be Remembered.

But they had it all wrong! What they were witnessing, in my transformation from Jock + Scholar to Sexually Neutered Androgyne was not an act of heightened *self-awareness,* worthy of their respect, but an act of *regression,* worthy of their contempt. *They* were the ones who were brave. Not I. They were the ones who were grappling with Life, real life, with all its perils and dangers and harmful fluids, facing it head-on and pushing through it, while I was fleeing in the other direction.

Mr. Carey, on the other hand, misinterpreted nothing. When he told me that he needed an explanation for my transformation, since the story of my life made no sense, he was obviously right. I couldn't say to Columbia that I played soccer for ten years, and played it well, then quit for reasons unclear to me, and then, for reasons equally unclear to me, I opted to spend the rest of my high school years staring at my reflection in the mirror and exploring androgyny. That is not a narrative that opens doors for you in life.

Unfortunately, as I admitted to Mr. Carey, I didn't have an explanation. I was just doing what seemed right to me, and couldn't account for it rationally.

"Then make something up," he said. "Anything. You had a vision. A dream. Voices spoke to you and told you to turn yourself into a monster. I don't care what it is. But I need an explanation. Your CV *makes no sense.*"

"Can't I just say that I didn't feel like playing soccer anymore?"

"Look. Don't be stupid. Getting into college, like everything else, is a game. Play it!"

So, having no alternative, since I was floating through life rather mechanically, about as self-aware as a jellyfish, I made something up. I invented a story that I knew was untrue but that explained everything perfectly. In a one-page overview of my extracurricular vitae, which I gave to Mr. Carey, and which he sent along with his recommendation, both still on file at Columbia College, I wrote that "a hernia and torn back muscles prevented me from participating in sports, so I pursued singing (I had been taking private voice lessons since ninth grade)," but I "will possibly try out for the soccer team" during my senior year.

This little story, false in every respect, containing five lies in thirty-four words, explained both my decision to quit sports and my new ensemble. As for quitting sports—I had no choice! I was injured. It was beyond my control. And I have every intention of trying to play again. As for the ensemble—I'm a singer now! I'm in touch with my artsy, faggy, effeminate side, so that's why I dress like a *faygeleh*.

What's most amazing to me about this explanation I came up with is that it eerily parallels what Alice Kaminsky wrote about her son, Eric, in *The Victim's Song*, which I did not read until *ten months later*. According to Ms. Kaminsky, the reason Eric gave up running cross-country, his most serious extracurricular pursuit, and took up the piano instead was that he had difficulty recovering from a hernia surgery. We have no idea if this is true or not. Maybe he got tired of running cross-country, and needed to find an excuse for himself to give it up. Regardless, the similarity between our two stories is uncanny: both of us claimed that a hernia (in his case the surgery for it, in my case the hernia itself) forced us to quit sports early in high school, as a result of which we both filled the gaps in our schedules by pursuing something musical, and despite which we both continued to wear T-shirts saying, PROPERTY OF UCLA *ATHLETIC* DEPT, which he is wearing in the picture of him in the book, and which was hanging in my closet as I read the book. No wonder I took the story of his murder so much to heart, and arrived in New York City fearing that I, too, would be murdered.

Most Likely to Be Remembered? Please. Most Likely to Crumble to Pieces Because of an Inability to Put Up with the Pressures of Being a Normal Boy was the only honor I deserved.

———

So here I am, in the summer of 1997, about to finish my clerkship with a federal judge, and devoting my spare energy not to studying for the bar exam, which I will never take, but to obsessing about whether I, like Andrew Cunanan, will one day live up to my youthful promise of unforgettableness.

They've tracked Cunanan to a houseboat. They storm it. He's dead. He shot himself in the head a day or two earlier. A TV is on. By all indications he spent the last week of his life eating sunflower seeds while watching news reports of the efforts to hunt him down.

Well, that's all well and good for Cunanan. Blowing his head off was icing on the cake. Now we'll never know what this was all about. If he had given himself up, and then wasted away in prison, we'd forget about him. But no. He has the genius to add mystery to his mayhem, so that the memory of his crimes, the motive forever unknown, will nag at us forever.

Meanwhile, as Cunanan has been busy blowing his way into the pantheon of La Jolla notables, I'm still out in the cold. If, by my fifty-year reunion, in 2036, I have yet to make a splash, then someone better take my guns away from me.

Oh, and to those of my friends and family who wondered whether I knew Andrew Cunanan when I was in high school and, if so, *how well* I knew him and, if very well, then in what sense, ahem, did I know him very well, the answer is no, I did not know him, never saw him, never heard of him. If there was a secret gay subculture in La Jolla, I knew nothing about it!

CHAPTER 9

The Farewell Party

T IS SOMETIME IN THE MID-1970S. I am eight, maybe nine, maybe ten years old. I'm at a huge party, at La Jolla Shores Beach, for Dave May, my very first soccer coach. He's lying on a lounge chair, hands behind his head, staring at the sea. Or maybe he's sleeping. It's impossible to tell, because he's wearing his favorite dark sunglasses. The dark sunglasses, the bushy mustache, the chubby thighs, the fat belly, the polyester pants. They're all right there. Dave May's got one look, and he knows how to work it.

The name of my first soccer team was the Panthers. We were terrible. But though we lost just about every game during that first season, the season of 1974–75, and came in last place, I fell in love with soccer thanks to Dave's insistence that, because of my great speed and ball control, I had the makings of a brilliant player. Had it not been for his continual encouragement, cheering me on from the sidelines, taking me aside after games to tell me all the skillful things I had done without even knowing it, I could have easily lost interest in the sport and taken up any one of the dozen or so other activities I was privileged enough to be exposed to as a child. Instead of devoting myself more seriously to baseball, or swimming, or singing, for example, all of which I was quite gifted at, I resolved to stick primarily with soccer, and to become a professional soccer player when I grew up.

Fall 1974: The author is second from the right in the front row; Dave May, standing, is on the left.

And for the next ten years, soccer will be everything to me. For one year, to copy my friend Teddy Janowsky, I will play the cello, and torture the ears of everyone in the family, but otherwise soccer will be the only serious extracurricular pursuit of my entire childhood. All of my friends, all of them Jews whose parents were either doctors or scientists or lawyers or academics, were academically gifted, and were expected to go to good colleges, preferably back east. In that sense we were identical. But to the extent that we were all defined by that *one other thing,* besides doing well in school, that would be our ticket to a first-tier college, for me it was soccer. And why? Because of Dave May! It's difficult to think of another person who had, even remotely, as much influence over the course of my life.

This gathering here at La Jolla Shores Beach, full of dozens of kids playing an unruly game of Nerf football, while their parents sit quietly and try to make small talk, is a going-away party for Dave. He's about to take a very long trip. In my sadness at his departure, I don't want to say goodbye. I don't even want to say hello. Though he's no longer my coach, though I've moved on to bigger and better teams than the Panthers, I still want Dave to be there on the sidelines, cheering me on as I prove to him that the promise he saw in me was not an illusion. Dave May no longer on the sidelines? It's all too sad for me to bear. So I just keep playing Nerf football with the other boys, and whenever the ball is thrown to me, and I happen to catch it not far from where Dave is sitting, I always make sure to keep running by his chair. *Don't stop running,* I tell myself. *If you don't stop running, you won't have to say goodbye.*

———

When my Grandpa Sidney died, in July 1989, there were three memorial services for him—one in Palo Alto, one in Vermont, and one in New York—each one catering to a different group of friends, colleagues, and admirers. The planning of these memorial services was, as it always is, chaotic. With one half of your brain you're trying to process someone's death, and with the other half you're trying to find a suitably secular building in which to commemorate it, since the deceased was a die-hard atheist. Then there's the headache of making sure that all the people who should be there are there and, before inviting them, making sure they know he's dead. There's the issue of who wants to speak, and for how long, an issue that becomes more pressing if certain members of the family, after opening their mouths, have trouble closing them. There are flowers to order, ushers to hire, and food to buy for the post-service reception. If you are worried, as my grandmother was, about the possibility that someone reading a notice about the upcoming memorial service in a newspaper will act on this information by breaking into the home of the widow while the service is under way, then you also have to hire a security guard, in our case a six-foot, seven-inch rugby player at Stanford, to guard the house. All the while there are condolence calls, from all over the world, to answer, and condolence letters, from all over the world, to put in two different boxes, one of them marked "Letters to Respond To" and the other marked "Someone Find Out Who These People Are."

If you thought that in the midst of all this chaos there would not be room left over, in one's weary brain, to worry about what young Jonathan, Grandson Number Three, would be wearing to these various memorial services, then you would be incorrect. The last time anyone in the family had seen me in a coat and tie was four years earlier, in the spring of 1985, at the White House, when my Grandpa Sidney had received the Presidential Medal of Freedom from Ronald Reagan, other recipients including such famous "fighters for freedom" as Jimmy Stewart, Frank Sinatra,

Count Basie, and underwater explorer Jacques Cousteau (in honor, of course, of his long service as a fighter for the freedom of scuba divers). To commemorate the event, not of my grandfather receiving the Presidential Medal of Freedom but of me wearing a coat and tie, so that she would never forget it, and would always be sure she had not imagined it, my grandmother framed a photo of me shaking Ronald Reagan's hand, courtesy of the White House photographer, and hung it on her wall.

Grabbing the photo off the wall and holding it up for everyone to see, and stabbing her heavily arthritic forefinger at the head of the nice young boy in the coat and tie, she pleaded with the family to bring him back to her:

"Look at this! Do you remember him? Go find him and bring him back. Go! Please! Someone take him to Marshalls and buy him a tie! For one afternoon, bring him back to me!"

Instead of wasting money at Marshalls—since, as my Uncle Ben put it, "Why waste money at Marshalls if he's never going to wear these clothes again?"—all the men in the family rummaged through their wardrobes, and, piece by mismatched piece, we managed to put something together that would sufficiently camouflage me for long enough not to distract the other mourners from the focus of the occasion. I may have looked like a ragamuffin, but for two hours at least I blended in.

A week before memorial service number two, in Vermont, over Labor Day weekend of 1989, I showed up, by myself, at my grandmother's request, to help her clean up Sidney's study and, most important, to keep her company. By the end of the week, by my count, she had observed twenty-seven different things about me that, in her opinion, were worthy of criticism, and as a means of catharsis I made a list of these criticisms and read them out loud to the family, my grandmother correcting my diction as I read, and telling me to read more slowly.

"Not so fast!" she said. "I'm enjoying this."

The list was titled "An Enumeration of the Faults, Vices, and Idiotic Tendencies of Jon-Jon Goulian, as Determined by His Grandmother, Ann 'Infallible' Hook, During a One-Week Period in Which Grandson and Grandmother Were Imprisoned Together in a Filthy Old House in Southern Vermont." The list included the following: "(2) I am 'embarrassingly delicate,' for I cower and holler at the sight of five-inch moths, hornets, and other 'innocuous' members of the insect world. . . . (5) My fanatical abstinence from, and fear of, saturated fats and cholesterol, is 'idiotic,' 'irrational,' and 'absurd.' . . . (7) My nickname, Jon-Jon, is 'childish' and 'extremely affected.' . . . (9) I am too self-absorbed, narcissistic, and vain. (10) No epithet in the English language can adequately describe the absurdity of my clothing. (11) I spend too much time with my toiletries. (12) My sleeping habits are too erratic. (13) I don't eat often enough. (14) I don't eat at the right times. (15) When I do eat, I spend too much time doing it. (16) I go to the bathroom too much, as a result of numbers 13–15; the theory behind this has yet to be explained. (17) My posture is 'atrocious.' . . . (19) I'm too thin. . . . (21) 'It's scary how indifferent [I am] to the world about [me],' an observation prompted by my inability to remember where the Wardsboro General Store was in relation to the Wardsboro Post Office. (22) I'm getting 'nuttier' as I get older. (23) My hair looks awful. (24) It's 'scary' how much I need attention. . . . (26) I shouldn't dip my bread in my soup. (27) All of the above could have been augured long ago, for I was a 'pathological hypochondriac as a young child.'"

Calling your attention to item 27, I feel obliged to defend my grandmother's use of the phrase *pathological hypochondriac,* which, to many readers, will seem redundant, since hypochondria is already a pathology. For my grandmother, however, hypochondria was such a common malady that two separate categories of hypochondriacs were needed to take account of all of them: the *garden-variety* hypochondriacs, on the one hand, to account for most of them, and the *pathological* ones, to account for me.

As for the cause of my hypochondria, my grandmother usually proposed one of two theories or, covering her bases, both.

Her first theory was that it was my *mother's* fault, for

being too focused on her various careers and, as a result, being insufficiently attentive to me as a child. Deprived of the emotional security of a mother's unwavering love, so the theory went, I felt insecure, vulnerable, precarious, and, by extension, overly sensitive to the potential Perils and Hazards of the world, as well as drastically in need of attention.

This theory, to shine the light back toward the person proposing it, was arguably generated by my grandmother's self-consciousness about having been a stay-at-home mother most of her life. Whether or not to pursue a career, and, if so, which one, plagued my grandmother in her twenties and thirties. Unsure of what to do with her life, she got a master's degree in philosophy at NYU, and it was there, in a philosophy class taught by my Grandpa Sidney, that she first met him. He gave her a C. So much for a career as a philosopher. As she put it later, "I wasn't such a *good* student," but "I was an enthusiastic student," so enthusiastic, in fact, that she eventually married the teacher. In addition to being active in a number of leftist causes, rallying support for striking miners, et cetera, she eventually considered medical school, going so far as to take a few premed courses, but gave up that idea when my mother was born. Taking care of her children, and cooking and cleaning, and being a loving and supportive and nagging wife, and enjoying herself—through mushrooming, gardening, traveling, doing the *Times* crossword puzzle, playing Scrabble, reading mysteries and literature, and putting her youngest grandson to work like a packhorse—was, she finally convinced herself, enough of a purpose in life to keep her happy. Why, I wonder, did it take her so long to be convinced? What a fun life she had! Whenever I meet women my age who haven't been able to find a fulfilling job, and who therefore have guiltily resigned themselves to being stay-at-home mothers, but who are still on the lookout for that one miraculous job about which they will be so passionate that commuting even an hour and a half to get there, and working sixty hours a week, would be tolerable, I tell them: Stay home! Don't feel guilty! Stay in your pajamas and be grateful for it.

My mother, like most women of her generation, had other ideas for herself. When I was born, in August 1968, my mother was in graduate school in biology at the University of Chicago, where my father was a professor of medicine. When we moved to La Jolla, in 1970, my mother, having earned her master's degree, continued to pursue her Ph.D. at UCSD, often leaving me in the care of a live-in Mexican maid, whom I will call Rosa, who doubled as my part-time nanny. Live-in Mexican maids, many of them in the country illegally, were common in La Jolla, even in the homes of families who were not, as mine was not, relatively rich. Room and board were a big part of their compensation, and the salary one paid them in addition was cheaper than hiring a nanny.

My mother, like me, never knew exactly what she wanted to do with her life, but she eventually figured out that it was not biology. So she gave it up in 1973 and worked as a real estate agent for a while instead. But she didn't like that either. A few years later, in 1978, at the age of forty, she decided to give up selling real estate and go to law school. I was ten years old at the time, and my brothers were thirteen and fifteen. My grandparents were appalled. You have three kids, they said, not one of them old enough to drive yet, and you're going to subject yourself, at this late age, to the rigors of law school? And not because of any urgent financial need? They felt it was irrational, irresponsible, and unmotherly. It was especially unmotherly in the case of Jonathan, who was only ten, and therefore less emotionally developed, and less emotionally independent, than the others. His piercing his ears at sixteen, and all that nonsense with the makeup and women's clothing, was obviously a cry for help that had been pent up in that wounded little breast of his for years, a delayed plea for attention in reaction to the deprivation of his mother's love. If he looks like a girl, so he thought, maybe he'll finally get noticed. Otherwise, with two older brothers having beat him to his mother's love, he's redundant. Or so went the theory.

Many years later, when I attended law school myself, at the age of twenty-five, with no children or spouse to divert me from my studies, and only three years out of college, so that my study habits, such as they were, were certainly less rusty than my mother's were by the time she went to law school, at the age of forty, and despite all of which I could barely pull myself through without dropping out from the stress, I looked back at my mother's decision to attend law school with awe. I don't know how she did it. I remember, on countless occasions, at the end of a cello lesson or a soccer practice, or coming back from a field trip with the YMCA, seeing her sitting in the car waiting to pick me up, studying for class. Always a casebook in her lap, with a yellow or pink highlighter in her right hand and a coffee cup, half raised toward her lips, in her left. Just those two words—*casebook* and *highlighter*—make me shudder at the memory of the horrors of law school. I'll say it again: *I don't know how she did it.* I just turned forty a month ago, and I barely have the energy to make coffee in the morning. She made it through in three years, passed the bar, and went on to practice law for twenty years, only recently giving it up. I'm not convinced that law was the perfect career for her, and I don't think she is either. She first tried working as a prosecutor in the city attorney's office, then tried working in a corporate firm for a few months, and then she tried family law, but found none of these jobs fulfilling. She finally settled on juvenile law, primarily representing children whose parents were accused of abusing them. The stress of preparing for these trials took a lot out of her. But she stuck with it, and helped a lot of people in the process. Irrational? Irresponsible? Unmotherly? I don't know what planet my grandparents were living on, but, on the planet I'm from, what my mother did was heroic.

Whenever I assured my grandmother that I had no memory of my mother being insufficiently attentive to my emotional needs, or not being present enough in my life, my grandmother would accuse me of being in denial.

"Of course you have no memory of it," she would say. "You're suppressing it."

Claims about the subconscious—"He's gay, *but doesn't really know it*"; "He suffers from delayed separation anxiety from his mother, *but doesn't really know it*"—have two great virtues: (1) they're easy to make, requiring no hard evidence; and (2) they're irrefutable. When you say, in your defense, "No, I'm not!" your denial can easily be interpreted, and always is, as nothing but a confirmation of the suppression itself.

In the course of writing this book, I hunted down an old box of childhood papers and found two notes to my mother that I had dictated to my nursery school teacher when I was four years old, both of which, if you were desperate for hard evidence, could be used to support my grandmother's case against my mother. The first one reads: "Dear Mommy: Will you buy me a golf set? When I grow up some more I'm going to fly in an airplane to grandmother's. It was so fun on Halloween. I wish I could go again. When I get five I want you to buy me a two-wheeler bike. Love, Jon-Jon." Had my grandmother read this note, she would have argued that little Jon-Jon, even allowing for the greediness of typical four-year-old boys, seems pathologically needy. *Buy me this; buy me that; I want to go here; I want to go there.* The golf set, the trip to Vermont to see Grandma Ann (no mention of wanting to see Grandpa Sidney, incidentally), the candy-filled night on Halloween, and the two-wheeler bike are intended, as little Jon-Jon so clearly does not understand, to fill the void left by the absence of his mother's love.

The second note reads: "Dear Mommy: I love you. I love you so much that I want to sleep with you every night. Love, Jon-Jon."

"Aha!" my grandmother would have screamed as she waved the note in my face in triumph. "That's an awful lot of affection! Every single night you want to sleep with her? Once or twice a week won't do it? This boy is not just thinking fondly of his mother while he absentmindedly plays with his Tonka trucks; he's putting everything he has into *longing* for her. And why is he longing for her? Because she's not there!"

After I read these notes, a strange, some might even call it horrific, memory popped into my head. One day, while at nursery school, which was called, as you would expect from a town that resembled a Disney theme park on the beach, Del Mar Heights, I had a temper tantrum. It was late in the afternoon. It was hot. For some reason I don't remember, things weren't going my way. So I got down on the floor, lay on my stomach, and began to cry and scream and bang my fists against the carpet. The teacher left me alone to vent my rage. Eventually, the school day ended. The mother of one of my friends came to pick us up, and when she dropped me off at my home, Rosa, my nanny, greeted me at the curb. "How did he do at school today?" she asked, to which the mother dropping me off replied, "He did okay, but he had a bad tantrum just before school got out." Rosa walked me up the steps to the front door of my house, holding my hand, making a good show, in front of my car pool, that she was a responsible and loving guardian. And then, when we got inside the house, and the door was closed behind us, she let go of my hand, grabbed my hair, and used it as a handle by which to lift me off the ground. I remember feeling a jolt of pain in my head and screaming. She did this, as I remember it, both to punish me for having had a temper tantrum and to make sure I didn't have another one later that day.

A few hours later my mother got home. I ran up to her and wrapped my arms around her legs. I remember thinking, *Mommy's home. Now I'm safe. Rosa can no longer hurt me.* My mother hugged and kissed me, and then she went upstairs to her bathroom to remove her makeup. I followed her, and sat on the cold linoleum floor, near her bare feet, as she washed her face. I remember wanting to tell her that Rosa had lifted me up by my hair, but not having the courage to do it. Rosa was a very tall and large woman, taller and larger than both my mother and my father. She lived with us in the spare bedroom downstairs, near the garage. If I told on her, she could easily hurt me, since she was alone with me many hours of the day. She could even hurt me in my sleep. So I kept my mouth shut. I did not tell my mother what Rosa had done to me. Nor did I tell my mother what Rosa continued to do to me, periodically, for the next two or three years, whenever she felt it was necessary to severely punish me: lift me off the ground by my hair!

As I look back on these acts of corporal punishment, I try very hard to see them from Rosa's perspective. Four-year-old boys, as we all know, can be astonishingly obnoxious. The purpose of their existence is to defy you. By the evidence of those two notes I dictated to my nursery school teacher, I was relatively greedy and needy. It's not hard to imagine that I gave Rosa ample cause for getting angry at me, and for punishing me. Furthermore, it's not hard to imagine that Rosa, irrespective of my obnoxiousness, was occasionally in a bad mood. She was in the country illegally, and probably felt insecure as a result. What little money she could save she probably felt obliged to send home to her family in Mexico. Toiling away in one of the wealthiest communities in America, surrounded by unimaginable luxury, she was probably envious, maybe jealous, maybe even angry.

Still, even allowing for all of this, Rosa's behavior seems unjust to me. A four-year-old boy is a four-year-old boy. He cannot help but defy you. It's in his nature to defy you no less than the need to sting is in a scorpion's. I was still sorting out the difference, for God's sake, between what I wanted out of life and what I had a right to expect. My mother's soft breasts, in the not too distant past, had been wrested away from me, a cold plastic bottle left in their wake, and Rosa expected me not to have the occasional tantrum?

This memory of rushing to my mother and wrapping my arms around her legs, of being so grateful for her presence, is less indicative to me of my deep longing for my mother, as my grandmother would have argued, than it is of my pathological fear of Rosa. Here I am, at the mercy of this woman, a surrogate mother of sorts to me, and she's lifting me off the ground by my hair. My *loco parentis* had clearly gone *muy loco,* and there was nowhere for me to escape.

Rosa's continual assault on my head when I was a child might explain why, when I was twenty-two years old, and it first became clear that I was beginning to go bald—the indications of which included dozens of hairs on my pillowcase every morning, and dozens of hairs stuck to the shower drain after every shower, and dozens of hairs stuck to my hairbrush every time I brushed my hair, as well as a little space appearing to the right of my widow's peak, the telltale sign, for all the world to see, of a receding hairline—I actually fell to the floor and curled up in a ball and shut my eyes and cried, *as if I were being attacked.*

I can only assume, as I was periodically dangled in the air by my hair, by the very person who was supposed to make sure that nothing bad happened to me while my parents weren't home, that I was afraid my hair might be pulled out of my head, which would have only exacerbated the fear I already had, independent of Rosa's periodic assaults, of going bald. My Middle Brother, who had been afflicted at an early age with what is known as *alopecia,* had lost all the hair on his body, and I was terrified, from as early an age as I can remember, that it would happen to me, too. Though my mother assured me it wouldn't, on the grounds that *alopecia* is not hereditary and therefore could strike me only by a coincidence too unlikely to take seriously, I didn't believe her. Everything in life seemed hereditary to me. When my Uncle Ben was casually flipping through some drawings made by the art historian Meyer Shapiro, a good friend of my grandfather's, he exclaimed, upon looking at a drawing that Meyer had done of his own son, "Ah! He got his father's philtrum," *philtrum* referring to the vertical depression between the nose and lips. When you grow up in a family where "he got his father's philtrum" is thrown around as casually as "please pass the salt," you can be forgiven for worrying that every problem any member of your family has ever had, including diabetes and arteriosclerosis on one side, and various cancers on the other, might be embedded in your genes. And becoming, in the process, a "pathological hypochondriac as a young child."

As for my fear of getting cancer, we need look no further than a warm summer day in 1977 when, while visiting my grandparents in Vermont, I accidentally caught sight of Grandma Ann bathing in the outdoor shower. I had been walking, with a friend, in the woods behind the house, and when we emerged from the forest there she was, naked. We were about twenty-five feet from her, obscured by some bushes, and she couldn't see us. Nor could she hear us, the sound of the water drowning out our footsteps. We froze, mortified, and then ran back into the forest. Sitting on a log beneath the shade of a tree, we tried to come to terms with what we had seen.

"Why does your grandma only have one boob?" asked my friend.

"I don't know," I said. And this was the truth. No one had ever told me that she had had breast cancer. And since I didn't know that she wore a prosthetic breast in her bra, I had always assumed, until that moment, that she had two of them.

"Was she in a concentration camp?" asked my friend.

"I don't think so," I said. "My mom told me that none of our relatives were in the Holocaust. But maybe she was lying."

When I got home from Vermont, the first thing I asked my mother, when she picked me up at the airport, was "Why does Grandma Ann only have one boob?" As my mother explained to me, once again assuring me that none of our relatives had died in the Holocaust, in the late 1950s, shortly after my grandfather had arrived in Tokyo on a teaching fellowship, my grandmother, still in New York, though intending to join him shortly, was diagnosed with breast cancer. So as not to unduly upset my grandfather, since she knew that he would hop on the first plane home if he heard the news, she went ahead and had a mastectomy, and after it was determined that the cancer had not spread, and *only then,* did she tell my grandfather (by telegram, I assume, since the cost of a phone call to Tokyo would have been considered exorbitant) what had happened. It was a story I would hear again and again from my grandfather, as a testament to her courage. In the last few years that I knew her, in the early nineties, I saw for myself how tough she was. Never once—despite a struggle with lymphoma that eventually killed her, causing her to cough up blood the last month of her life; bloatedness in her gut so bad that she couldn't cut her own toenails; and a dog bite, six months before she died, that left her lower leg black and bloody— did I ever hear her complain. And it was this toughness of hers that explains why she found my delicacy, and near-crippling assortment of anxieties, so exasperating.

· My grandmother's second theory for why I became a "pathological hypochondriac as a young child," was that it was my *father's* fault. When you raise your children to live in mortal fear of saturated fat, and to be on the constant lookout, in the food one eats, and in the air one breathes, for potentially lethal carcinogens, and to never pull anything off the shelf of a supermarket without reading the ingredients at least twice, then your children, naturally, will grow up believing that the world is fraught with peril. You name it, I've run from it—air, food, water, sex, school, soccer, my body, my father, my grandfather, SeaWorld, Nordstrom, the Ramble, tall buildings, suits, ties, Florsheim shoes, and so on. The list is endless. "That nutty diet he put you on explains everything!" she would say, as she fed me eggs and bacon in Vermont and watched with glee as I slurped them up.

But my nutty diet, in itself, cannot explain everything, since neither of my two older brothers, both of whom were subjected to the same diet, is even a *garden-variety* hypochondriac, much less a pathological one, or even a garden-variety neurotic for that matter. Romantically, professionally, sartorially, dietarily—they are normal!

Something else seems needed to explain why I, alone, would have reacted so strongly. The best thing I can come up with, what may be my earliest memory of all, occurred when I was three or four years old, when my mother found me sitting on the floor of her bedroom, a guilty smile on my face and an empty bottle of orange-flavored baby aspirin in my hand. She turned pale, she grabbed my hand, she led me into the bathroom. And there, bending me over the toilet, she stuck her finger down my throat, and up and out into the bowl shot a frothy clump of orange tablets. Imagine how this forcible inducement of vomiting would have been observed, and processed, by a little boy: I ate something; it tasted good; so I ate it all; and then Mommy reached into my stomach and took it all back. The moral implications I could have derived from this sequence of events are obviously boundless. I hesitate to bore you by walking you through them. So I won't. Sufficient for our purposes is how my grandmother would have interpreted it, in that inimitably stark, shrill, and exultant fashion of hers: "First she takes her love away from you by working all day, and not being there for you when you need her, leaving you in the hands of a sadist, and then, when you try to replace her love with orange baby aspirin, or, as you saw it, delicious nourishment, she reaches her hand into your stomach and basically eviscerates you. And they wonder why you pierced your ears!"

Fear of evisceration. Fear of maid. Fear of baldness. Fear of bowleggedness. Fear of saturated fat. Fear of carcinogens. Fear of father. Fear of mother. Longing for mother. Longing for golf set. Fear of grandfather. Fear of failure. Fear of heredity. Fear of sex. Fear of diabetes and arteriosclerosis and cancer. I sift through the silt of my childhood traumas, looking for that one nugget of gold that will explain everything, why I'm so fragile and pathetic and unmanly, and here I've come up with a whole sack.

Though the cause of my "pathological hypochondria" as a young boy may be hard to pin down, that I was afflicted with it is indisputable. What else can explain why, when that egg-size lump appeared in my scrotum at the age of thirteen, I was absolutely convinced I would die, the fear of the confirmation of which prevented me from seeking the diagnosis that, as it happened, would have put my fears to rest. Every other boy I know would have pushed through the fear and sought help rather than coming up with excuses for three years. Every other boy I know who had a doctor for a father would, though equally embarrassed by the prospect of showing his father his penis and testicles, have pushed through the embarrassment and said, "Dad, what's this?" But I couldn't do it. I was absolutely convinced I would die, and I refused to let a doctor look me in the eye and say it.

———

So here I am, at La Jolla Shores Beach, in the mid-1970s, at the farewell party for Dave May, the first soccer coach I ever had, and the person who had more influence over the course of my life than anyone else I can think of. Soccer took up more of my time, and more of my love, than anything else in my whole life, and because of this *one man*. That's how important he was to me. All the kids whom Dave ever coached in his life, dozens and dozens of them, and for many of whom, perhaps, he was no less important than he was for me, are here at the beach, playing Nerf football and trying to pretend to have fun, while our parents sit in lounge chairs, eating chips and salsa and trying to make small talk.

The ball is thrown to me. I catch it. I start running

toward Dave's chair. I try to slow down. I'm supposed to say goodbye to him. That's what a farewell party is for. Or at least a simple hello. But I can't do it. I'm too sad. I'm too scared. One thought, one horrible image, keeps me running and running and running and running: *one bad ball.* Dave May wakes up in the morning a few months ago, he finds a lump in his scrotum, and he does what you're supposed to do. He goes to the doctor. The doctor, Dave naturally believes, will help him. The doctor will first give him a diagnosis, and then a prognosis. First one, and then the other. You have this, and we will cure it by doing that. That's what the doctor is for. To cure. That's why my Granny Shammy will one day become obsessed with my becoming a doctor. So that I can cure people.

In Dave's case, the doctor's diagnosis was that he had testicular cancer. But when it came time for the prognosis + cure, there was a glitch. The prognosis, after the test results came back, was that, since the cancer had already progressed, by the time of Dave's discovery, beyond the point of reparability, there was no cure. The prognosis, therefore, was that *Dave would soon die.*

The endless succession of painful moments, from the time Dave was casually feeling his testicles and found a little lump, maybe while lying in bed in the morning, or while taking a bath, his testicles floating in the water in front of him, waiting, as every boy knows, to be fondled and examined, to the moment that the doctor looked him in the eye and told him he would soon die, was especially vivid for me, because my father had described to me once the difficulty of having to give dire prognoses to patients. "I'm sorry, Dave, but you're going to die." I could hear the doctor saying it. I had been saying it myself, almost rehearsing it in my head, ever since I head the news from my mother that Dave May had testicular cancer and that "the prognosis is not good."

Just like that. That's all it takes, *and he's only twenty-eight years old,* to take away my favorite soccer coach, the first soccer coach I ever had: *one bad ball to kill you.*

Greetings from South Wardsboro

WELL, LITTLE MAN, this book was a much longer response to your postcard than I imagine you expected. If you've gotten this far, then you must be at least nine years old by now. I don't expect you to have understood everything. There were certain things in Chapter Six, for instance, that you will want to read at least three times to properly absorb. My only advice to you is that when you're in the *lot out back,* at the age of fourteen, with Zoe, and she says to you, "Do you want to X me?" do not panic. Say: "Yes, please, but I've never done it before. Will you X me instead?" That is your only hope, I fear, for a healthy sexual development. As for my dalliances with Gunnar and Oliver, just keep your chin up and go through with them. Having been there, and done that, made me a stronger person, I feel, and left me not much worse for the wear.

If this journey through your life was traumatic for you, I

apologize. But try to imagine how traumatic it was for *me*. Here I was trying to find my way back to the magic of my childhood, and what did I discover? That beneath the magic, such as it was, a needy, greedy, pathological hypochondriac was making your life miserable. You could have had the decency to prepare me for that, no? Even a subtle clue, something that Hal the Mailman wouldn't have noticed, would have been appreciated. Though I suppose, in your defense, you will claim that you had no knowledge of any of your problems, that life, on the surface, seemed sunny, and full of hope, and that a seven-year-old boy cannot be expected to have the self-awareness of a forty-year-old. Fair enough. No hard feelings from this end.

One other thing that might confuse you, by the way, besides what went wrong with Zoe in the lot out back, is why I left *The New York Review of Books,* since it seemed like the perfect job for me. A boss for whom the life of the mind is everything, and for whom the presence of twelve hundred dollars' worth of stuffed animals is a boon, and who did not care, *did not notice,* if I wore six-inch heels, a skirt, and a midriff-bearing Tommy Girl tank top to work, is not easy to come by.

To begin with, there was the matter of my ego. Watching a man in his early seventies work three times harder than I did and still have the energy to put on a tuxedo and go to the opera, and then a party after the opera, and then come back to the office after the party, at 2:00 A.M., and keep working until 5:00 A.M., and then come back to the office at 9:30 A.M. to continue working, when I barely had enough energy to drag myself home after an eight-hour shift and get into bed, gradually took its toll on my self-esteem. When Bob was thirty-four years old he was the commander in chief, at the helm of the ship, steering the *The New York Review* to greatness. When I was thirty-four I was sharpening his pencils, and feeding him dried blueberries.

Furthermore, and this factor alone would have been enough to send me packing, I was never fully comfortable working for a man who was born on the exact same day as Dada. That's right. Bob and Dada, I soon discovered, were both born on December 31, 1929. Same day, same year. An amazing, and disturbing, coincidence. In fact, it was as amazing to Bob, who was not easily distracted by things having nothing to do with the life of the mind, as it was to me. He was so struck by the coincidence that he called his best friend G—— immediately to tell her:

"Oh, G——, you're not going to believe this, but I just found out a moment ago that Jon-Jon's father was born on the exact same day— What? I'm talking about my assistant. Jon-Jon Goulian. Yes, *Jonathan*. I know that's his real name, but he insists on Jon-Jon, none of us know why, but it doesn't matter. That's not the reason I'm calling. The reason I'm calling is that I just found out from him that his father, a scientist who lives on the other coast, in La Jolla, California, three thousand miles away, was born on the same day, same year, as I was. Twelve thirty-one twenty-nine. The exact . . . same . . . day!"

In Bob, you can easily imagine, I soon saw Dada, and in Dada I soon saw Bob. Once, during a particularly busy week, when we were going to press, and I had John Updike on one line phoning in corrections from Massachusetts, Norman Mailer on another line calling in corrections from the Chateau Marmont in Los Angeles, and, most important of all, John Bayley, whom we had lost track of three months earlier, calling in corrections on another line from his hideout in the Canary Islands, Bob asked me urgently for a sharpened pencil, and, in my confusion, I shouted back, "Just a moment, Baba! I've got John Bayley on the line!" That was it. When Bob became Baba, I knew it was time to go.

But go where? When you've been stuck on the tarmac for sixteen straight years, the possibility of one day taking off is too remote to take seriously. I had given up all hope of finding my place in the sky. I could either keep idling in place, by finding myself yet another cheap sublet, and yet another part-time job to pay for the cheap sublet, or go back to the terminal and kill myself.

It was just about this time, little man, about three years after leaving *The New York Review,* as I was supporting myself by babysitting, for twelve dollars an hour, a seven-year-old girl named Ruth, which paid me just enough to cover the rent for my new apartment on the Upper West Side, a six-by-eight-foot former maid's room, that Dada sent me only the second letter he's sent me in all my life, which I introduced to you in the Prologue, and which I show you once again to remind you:

> *Dear Jon-Jon: For many years I've wondered what direction your life would take. But for some time now there has been, to me, very little change. You seem to be in a chronic state of indecision. How else to view the multiple relocations and short-term living arrangements, a state of existence I long assumed (or hoped) was temporary, but is seemingly permanent? You've provided clues. My interpretation: That you aspire to some creative pursuit and continue to search and wait for the right path or opportunity. Is this at least partly correct? Can you help me to understand? —da*

There were two fundamental questions facing me when I received this letter: (1) Did I *want* to help him understand? and (2) *Could* I help him understand even if I wanted to?

The answer to the first question, initially, was no. His letter irritated me, and I was in no mood to help. No son, at any time throughout history, beginning with the first son of the first *Homo sapiens* dad in 250,000 B.C., has ever been anything less than pissed off when called to account, by his bewildered father, for his seemingly meaningless and directionless existence. No matter how nicely he framed his letter, I was still *in trouble*. When I showed this letter to many of my friends and asked, "What did I do to deserve this constant harassment?" I expected sympathy. Their reaction, however, was very different from their reaction to the first letter my father had sent me. In the case of the first letter, everyone took my side. They said, "Whoa! That letter is a *bitch*! Your old man is hard-core." But this time, everyone took *his* side. "Dude, chill," they told me. "Your poor dad has no idea what's going on inside your head. If I, one of your best friends, have no idea what's going on inside your head, and worry about you constantly, imagine how stressed out *he* is. You owe him an answer! Answer his letter!"

They had a point. I owed him an answer. I now wanted very much to help him understand the purpose of my existence.

But how could I give him an answer when I didn't know the answer myself? That was the great conundrum that had faced me with his first letter, eight years earlier, and it faced me yet again. How do you account for the purpose of your existence when you don't know the purpose yourself?

To deal with this conundrum, I came up with a two-part strategy. The first part was to distract his attention from the

subject at issue—my wayward existence—by opening the
letter with a question concerning the relative merits of
mono- and polyunsaturated fats, much in the way that my
Granny Shammy had put me at ease by opening her second
letter with a discussion of fava beans. Just as I had turned
to earrings, and lip gloss, and halter tops, and stirrup pants
upon returning from Andover—to, in part, throw women
off my scent—so would I now turn to the subject of lipids
to throw my father off my scent.

The second part of my strategy was to try to answer his
letter. What else could I do?

Here's my answer, sent on Father's Day, in June 2006:

Dear Dadda!
    First, HAPPY FATHER'S DAY!
    Second, remind me which are healthier: polyunsatu-
rated fats, or monounsaturated fats. Grapeseed oil, the
egg-substitute in the ersatz mayonnaise I've been eating
lately, has equal amounts of poly and mono, but if
mono is healthier, then I'll switch to ersatz mayo with
canola oil, in which the ratio of mono to poly is much
higher. Either is fine; they taste the same to me.
    Third, I received your letter, the first letter I've re-
ceived by snail-mail in a long time! Your characteriza-
tion of my seemingly unsettled position in life—that I
"aspire to some creative pursuit and continue to search
and wait for the right path or opportunity"—is not
"partly correct," as you wondered, but perfectly cor-
rect. I couldn't have put it better myself. I always have
something reasonably creative in the works—a short
story, a novel, a screenplay, a personal essay, a collec-
tion of bawdy limericks—and, when the time comes

that I finish something that I feel is suitable to be sold, I'll try to sell it. In the meantime, freelance editing pays the bills and allows me to live wherever I want.

Which brings me to your second point, that the "multiple relocations and short-term living arrangements" suggest a lack of direction and "a chronic state of indecision," with which I disagree. I've spent roughly 17 of the last 20 years, since leaving La Jolla, in New York City. That's hardly indecisive. I am, undeniably, a New Yorker, in heart, in spirit, in sensibility, in just about any way you put it (except for my accent, I suppose, which, arguably, still bears traces of my youthful, beachy drawl).

It is true that on two occasions, first in the fall of 1998, and then again in the fall of 2004, I left New York City for Los Angeles, but this was not because of any wishy-washyness on my part but simply because the prospect of facing another bitingly cold New York City winter was too much to bear. (Unmanly of me, maybe, but not indecisive.) Yes, my stay in Los Angeles, on both occasions, was brief. To you and Mom, "troublingly" brief: "Why did you move to Los Angeles if you were only going to stay four months?" I've been asked again and again. As I've tried to explain, again and again: LA has neither the culture, nor the pizzazz, nor the first-rate pizza (in which, it shames me to admit, I do occasionally indulge) of New York City, and is no place for a non-surfing lover of books to live. Perhaps every six years I'll need to go there to remind myself of this.

As for my periodic, and increasingly regular, stays in South Wardsboro, Vermont, this is easily explained, and, in my opinion, justified, by my deep and lifelong love of Vermont, and of our house in Vermont, and of my books in the house in Vermont. As long as my free-lance lifestyle allows for it, and hopefully for the re-mainder of my life, I'll probably spend as much time as I can in South Wardsboro, excepting, of course, the winter months, when the house is for the most part un-inhabitable, and (depending on my willingness to lather toxic DEET all over my body) several weeks in late May and June, when the black flies and mosquitoes are in full flight and ferocity. Hopefully, that several week period is now over, since a heat wave in New York City may send me up there as soon as tomorrow!

All best, jj

Since the claim that I'm working on a collection of bawdy limericks, in the third paragraph, is obviously ridiculous, my reply comes very close to the brink of flippancy. But it never quite crosses the line. This is a strong and respectful letter. It shows a son who cares enough about his dad to give a well-considered reply. So the flippancy of the limerick remark, I feel, is well camouflaged. But now that I read the letter over again, I notice some deeper, unintended irony. My parents paid a lot of money to send me to law school, and what do I do with my legal training? I treat my dad's well-meaning and casually drafted letter like a mini-indictment, carefully dissecting it, isolating and separating the different charges, and then responding, as if it were a defendant's brief I were drafting, with an absurd degree of literalness and formality, and using his own language—*and going out of my way to quote it,* as if to remind the court that he said it—to my advantage. It took some chutzpah to write this letter, now that I think about it. I should have just called him and said, "Dada! Don't worry! I'm fine! I'll figure it all out eventually."

Well, my letter worked. It proved to my father, by its sheer length if by nothing else, that I was not brain-dead, and that my heart, as free of saturated fat as ever, was in the right place:

> *Thank you, JJ. Both mono- and poly-unsaturated fats have similar desirable effects but when you have a choice I would opt for the monounsaturates (for reasons I can go into if you wish). The best common sources of monounsaturated fats are olive and canola oils. Grape seed is similar to corn oil in composition; OK, but I would suggest olive or canola (if there is that option). —da*

Fall 1999: The author and his father on the Lower East Side.

Acknowledgments

For their patience, advice, and encouragement, I would like to thank:

At Random House: Kate Medina, Jonathan Jao, Frankie Jones Danly, Lindsey Schwoeri, and Beth Pearson.

At the Wylie Agency: Sarah Chalfant, Edward Orloff, Taryn Gilbert, Rebecca Nagel, and, for her warm smile on that very first day, Angelin Adams Borsics.

I would also like to thank Alexandra Grannis, arguably the most wonderful woman in New York City, for giving me, when I needed it most, a sympathetic ear, home-cooked meals, and a room of my own.

ABOUT THE AUTHOR

JON-JON GOULIAN was born in 1968, and grew up in La Jolla, California. After attending Columbia College and NYU Law School, he worked as a law clerk for a federal judge in North Carolina, and then as an assistant to Robert Silvers of *The New York Review of Books*. He now lives, by himself, in South Wardsboro, Vermont, where he spends most of his time gardening. *The Man in the Gray Flannel Skirt* is his first book.

ABOUT THE TYPE

This book was set in Sabon, a typeface designed by the well-known German typographer Jan Tschichold (1902–74). Sabon's design is based upon the original letterforms of Claude Garamond and was created specifically to be used for three sources: foundry type for hand composition, Linotype, and Monotype. Tschichold named his typeface for the famous Frankfurt typefounder Jacques Sabon, who died in 1580.